To
Linda Blair

INTERNATIONAL ORDERS

JOHN A. HALL

Polity Press

First published in 1996 by Polity Press
in association with Blackwell Publishers Ltd.

Editorial office:
Polity Press
65 Bridge Street
Cambridge CB2 1UR, UK

Marketing and production:
Blackwell Publishers Ltd
108 Cowley Road
Oxford OX4 1JF, UK

Published in the USA by
Blackwell Publishers Inc.
238 Main Street
Cambridge, MA 02142, USA

ISBN 0-7456-1014-5
ISBN 0-7456-1770-0 (pbk)

A CIP catalogue record for this book is available from the British Library and
the Library of Congress.

Typeset in 11/13 pt Sabon
by CentraCet Ltd, Cambridge
Printed in Great Britain by T J Press Ltd, Padstow, Cornwall

This book is printed on acid-free paper.

The *right of nations* is by nature founded on the principle that the various nations should do to one another in times of peace the most good possible, and in times of war the least ill possible, without harming their true interests.

Montesquieu

The division of Europe into a number of independent states, connected, however, with each other, by the general resemblance of religion, language, and manners, is productive of the most beneficial consequences to the liberty of mankind.

Gibbon

The aim of the ancients was the sharing of social power among the citizens of the same fatherland: this is what they called liberty. The aim of the moderns is the enjoyment of security in private pleasures; and they call liberty the guarantees accorded by institutions to these pleasures ... through their failure to perceive these differences, otherwise well-intentioned men caused infinite evils ...

Constant

It was no easy task bringing together fellow citizens who had lived for many centuries aloof from, or even hostile to, each other and teaching them to co-operate in the management of their own affairs. It had been far easier to estrange them than it now was to reunite them ...

Tocqueville

War is the locomotive of history.

Trotsky

If you love somebody, set them free.

Sting

To robbery, butchery and rapine, they give the lying name of 'government'; they create a desolation and call it peace.

Tacitus

Contents

Acknowledgements

The author of this book is a sociologist rather than an expert in international relations. This may raise expectations of analysis of societal relations and thus of criticism to be directed at the classical realist paradigm of international relations. Such critical commentary is likely to find a welcome within an attractive and open-minded discipline, always in search of new approaches. Whilst these expectations will be fulfilled to a considerable extent, with comments being offered on transnational and ideological forces quite as much as upon domestic politics, it is as well to warn immediately of a strong attachment to realism. This derives both from admiration for the life and work of Raymond Aron and from years of teaching students in sociology that wars, properly seen by Trotsky as 'the locomotive of history', massively structure social life. It would be a great mistake to abandon an elegant position precipitously for a mass of hugely questionable theories, versions of which did much harm in sociology. Accordingly, I do not seek to destroy realism but rather to explain the enabling conditions that once enabled it to function so that an amended version can guide us in the contemporary world.

This point being made, very great thanks must be given to colleagues in international relations who warmly welcomed my inquiries and intrusion. I owe a special debt to Susan Strange for characteristically muscular encouragement at an early stage, but wish also to thank Michael Doyle, John Ikenberry, Bob Keohane, and Peter Katzenstein. Anatoly Khazanov, Mette Hjort, Charles Lindholm and T. V. Paul proved themselves great friends in giving me substantial comments on an awful early draft, whilst David Held, Michael Smith, Canada's Social Sciences and Humanities Research Council, and the Central European University provided support of another kind. The extent to which my thought has been influenced by and remains in dialogue with the ideas of Ernest Gellner and Michael Mann is obvious from the text. I am generally indebted to the most recent volume of Mann's magnificent *Sources of Social Power*, but draw as well on works by David Laitin, Hedley Bull, Kalevi Holsti, and Jack Snyder. As the argument made here both disagrees with and goes further than those of these authors, more than convention is involved in stressing my own responsibility for the general position advanced.

Preface

If nature abhors a vacuum, it may well be that this condition is particularly dangerous, and thereby prone to short duration, in the arena of state competition. Hence it was scarcely surprising that enormous attention was given to Francis Fukuyama's "The End of History," an intelligent attempt to interpret the contours of the modern world in the light of the final collapse of the Soviet Union.[1] Nonetheless, it was a phrase used by President Bush when confronting Saddam Hussein's invasion of Kuwait that did most to capture the spirit of the moment. He first posited the hope for "a new world order" on September 11, 1990, but made increasing use of the phrase throughout the winter. His attempt to redefine American grand strategy was most thorough when addressing the 45th Session of the United Nations General Assembly on October 1, 1990. Bush began by stressing that the end of the Cold War made it possible for the United Nations to be used as it was intended, that is, as a centre for international collective security. If this was sensible, it was not disinterested: it had been a mere two months since Iraq had invaded Kuwait, and the speech was part of Bush's skillful and successful building of a

---

[1] F. Fukuyama, "The End of History," *The Public Interest*, vol. 16, 1989. Fukuyama's argument (especially when expanded as *The End of History and the Last Man*, Free Press, New York, 1992) led to a huge amount of commentary, the most important of which was that of an essay by Perry Anderson in his *A Zone of Engagement*, Verso, London, 1993.

coalition. But the lyricism of later passages seemed to hold out much more:

> I see a world of open borders, open trade and, most importantly, open minds; a world that celebrates the common heritage that belongs to all the world's people, taking pride not just in hometown or homeland but in humanity itself. I see a world touched by a spirit, that of the Olympics, based not on competition that's driven by fear but sought out of joy and exhilaration and a true quest for excellence. And I see a world where democracy continues to win new friends and convert old foes and where the Americas – North, Central, and South – can provide a model for the future of all humankind: the world's first completely democratic hemisphere. And I see a world building on the emerging new model of European unity, not just Europe but the whole world whole and free.

When the Gulf War was so dramatically won, it began to seem possible that this dream of a new world order, of affluence, security, and liberty, was within humanity's grasp.

This notion of a new world order quickly came to be seen as a sick joke. The most striking reason for this reversal was the use of violence, formal and informal, for the purposes of "ethnic cleansing" in parts of Europe and the former Soviet Union previously considered to be beyond such brutality. Faced again with concentration camps and the mass displacement of peoples, it suddenly seemed sensible to talk of the "delusion of world order," even of "new world disorder."[2] The whole episode seemed to justify the dictum of the Australian historian Geoffrey Blainey that "recurring optimism is a vital prelude to war."[3] This had been true before the First World War, and still more strikingly so in the interwar years. All that seemed different was the speed with which hubris had come to haunt grandiloquent, bloated optimism.

Emotions can tyrannize, with revulsion, however justified, being as capable of blocking genuine thought as are Panglossian views presuming that human affairs are necessarily getting better and better. Violent swings in mood between these two poles will not

---

[2] S. Hoffmann, "Delusions of World Order," *New York Review of Books*, April 9, 1992; B. Anderson, "The New World Disorder," *New Left Review*, no. 193, 1992. Cf. T. Sommer, "A World beyond Order and Control," *Guardian Weekly*, April 28, 1991.
[3] G. Blainey, *The Causes of Wars*, Macmillan, London, 1977, p. 73.

do. One way to avoid volatility is to follow Hedley Bull in concentrating attention on international rather than world order, that is, in replacing an obviously emotive label with one whose relatively aseptic nature makes it suitable for social science.[4] If the present inquiry opens with a restatement of Bull's key concepts, it then turns to the different ideal types of international order that can and have characterized international relations. Whilst it would be possible to continue analysis at an abstract level, the cognitive strategy adopted here, that of examining the international orders of the historical record, is different. If this approach entails comparison of historical reality with the ideal types, its deeper purpose is that of allowing for a better understanding of our own international order. This historical turn to the argument should not be read as implying any belief that societal patterning must be of a single kind: to the contrary, historical sociology is of especial use because it enhances understanding as to why, for example, state-formation in the contemporary period *cannot* repeat the experience of early modern Europe.

As my fundamental claim is that this book advances social theory, at both descriptive and prescriptive levels, the reader may be helped if some notion of my position, dubbed "the realism/ liberalism mix," is given immediately. This view is heretical in seeking to join together positions classically opposed to each other. Liberals have often regarded the workings of states as impediments to social progress, a position which has occasionally led, in the opinion of realists, to strategies that so placed hope above reality as actually to have facilitated war. There is much truth to the realist objection, in my view, with states anyway remaining necessary shells given the absence of world government. Still, it is possible to make this point and to remain a liberal: Raymond Aron certainly managed this, albeit my intention is to begin to spell out a connection to which he devoted curiously little attention.

The analysis of international orders in history will show that realism depends upon certain social conditions for its existence,

---

[4]   H. Bull, *The Anarchical Society*, Macmillan, London, 1977. I have no desire to prejudge anything, and turn in a moment to open discussion of the moral connotations attached to the notion of order.

and that these can be – and in contemporary circumstances should be – provided by liberalism. The social constructivism of this argument does not entail, as is so often the case with that school of thought, endorsement of any facile idealism: to the contrary, analysis focuses on nations, states, regimes, and economies quite as much as upon modern ideologies. That the varied intertwinings of these forces are complex suggests a final characteristic of the argument as a whole. No elegant formal model of international order is possible, let alone any *complete* ethical handbook for the conduct of foreign affairs. What is offered instead is a way of looking at key social forces designed to enhance judgment, thereby to encourage prudence.

1

Groundwork

In order to understand what is happening to contemporary world politics, it is first necessary to establish why President Bush's heralding of a new world order was conceptually mistaken. There is no better guide to the nature of sociability, states, and justice than Hedley Bull's *The Anarchical Society*.[1] Discussion of these key concepts is followed by an exposition of five ideal types of international order; this necessarily goes beyond Bull's position, for all that he was aware that international order came in varied forms, given notable intellectual development since his death. Justification is then offered for giving the inquiry an historical turn. The logic of the realism/liberalism mix is first noted in remarks concluding this chapter.

---

[1] H. Bull, *The Anarchical Society*, Macmillan, London, 1977. Bull's conceptual system has been subjected to analysis in J. D. B. Miller and J. R. Vincent, eds, *Order and Violence*, Oxford University Press, Oxford, 1990. Bull admitted an indebtedness to the thought of one of his colleagues at the London School of Economics in "Martin Wight and the Theory of International Relations," *British Journal of International Studies*, vol. 2, 1976. Despite the suggestiveness of Wight's work, my argument is best advanced by utilizing Bull's greater analytic clarity.

KEY CONCEPTS

Perhaps the most important characteristic of social life is one that is taken for granted, namely the success with which we manage most social encounters. Most of our relations in public are with strangers, yet they proceed on an orderly and regular basis, whether piloting a car through traffic lights or negotiating the pitfalls of cocktail parties.[2] That the very notion of society implies a way of life opposed to random violence lay behind Raymond Aron's criticism of Pierre Bourdieu's use of the term "symbolic violence":

> A curious vocabulary because it no longer enables one to dis-tinguish between different modes of socialization: on the one hand, the inevitable and diffuse *influence* on individuals of the social group which tends to reproduce itself, on the other hand, *constraint* which presupposes resistance, whether conscious or not, on the part of those who feel the pressure of social milieu and authority. Violence only retains a specific meaning when it designates a relationship between men which comprises the use of physical force or the threat to use physical force.[3]

Aron is here rejecting the residues of the thought of Jean-Paul Sartre, so evident in Bourdieu's concept. Socialization is less a permanent threat to authenticity than an enabling condition for humanity; the fact that many do not find that daily life resembles the triangular hell of *No Exit* suggests, moreover, that sociability may be more natural than Sartre's supremely protestant hyper-Hobbesianism allows. The sharing of norms offers the possibility of banishing violence, and thereby of moving towards justice. This mattered enormously to Aron from the early 1930s. How could it have been otherwise? Aron was of Jewish background. Witnessing

---

[2]   The great analyst of these matters was Erving Goffman, notably in *Relations in Public*, Penguin, Harmondsworth, 1972. See also H. Garfinkel's *Studies in Ethnomethodology* (Prentice Hall, Englewood Cliffs, 1967) for an account of experiments which make the point powerfully if negatively, by showing how irritated people become once social order is challenged.
[3]   R. Aron, *Penser la guerre, Clausewitz*, Gallimard, Paris, 1976, vol. 2, p. 255 (my translation).

the Nazi book burnings made him realize that the destruction of all baselines of social reciprocity was on the historical agenda.[4]

Aron's notion of sociability has everything to recommend it, but its acceptance should not close off interesting sociological complexities. Let us move from the Kantian essence of sociability to broader reflection on the nature of society. Consider Susan Watkins's impressive recent demonstration that Western European demographic behavior came to be patterned by nation-states in the period between 1870 and 1960.[5] If this strikingly supports the notion that a society can provide a way of life, it also suggests opening out debate in two ways. On the one hand, nation-states had not been unitary societies beforehand, just as they may not be completely so any longer; indeed, the territorialization of social relations is usually more ambition than achievement. If we are to understand the social world in general and international politics in particular, attention needs to be paid both to the processes that build and undermine unitary societies and to the complexities of social identity that exist in their absence. On the other hand, the fact that unitary societies are not natural, even if sociability is, raises the question as to who benefits from a particular set of rules established within a nation-state. If the violence of the Nazis towards some elements within Germany made their rule a revolt against the very notion of sociability, that is, a triumph of force and arbitrariness over settled expectations, the creation of societal order has never yet been the same as the establishment of social justice.[6] In consequence, radicals and conservatives are always likely to differ in their political judgements. But division need not be absolute: there is no reason why one cannot have a reverent appreciation for the importance of the rule of law in combination with an insistence on extending social justice.[7]

[4]   R. Aron, *De la condition historique du sociologue*, Gallimard, Paris, 1971. Cf. N. Bavarez, *Raymond Aron*, Flammarion, Paris, 1994.
[5]   S. C. Watkins, *From Provinces into Nations*, Princeton University Press, Princeton, 1991.
[6]   For a brilliant meditation on social reciprocity, see B. Moore, *Injustice*, Macmillan, London, 1978.
[7]   Superb advocacy of this view is offered by E. P. Thompson, *Whigs and Hunters*, Penguin, Harmondsworth, 1977, p. 265. The point in question could have as easily been made by reference to the work of Barrington Moore, an equally great radical.

Whatever the exact nature of the relations between sociability and society, there can be no doubt but that they are qualitatively different from relations between states. Hobbes makes the point with characteristic brutality:

> But though there had never been any time, wherein particular men were in a condition of war one against another; yet in all times, kings, and persons of sovereign authority, because of their independency, are in continual jealousies, and in the state and posture of gladiators; having their weapons pointing, and their eyes fixed on one another; that is, their forts, garrisons, and guns upon the frontiers of their kingdoms; and continual spies upon their neighbours; which is a posture of war. But because they uphold thereby, the industry of their subjects; there does not follow from it, that misery, which accompanies the liberty of particular men.
>
> To this war of every man, against every man, this also is consequent; that nothing can be unjust.[8]

Sartre's position was deemed "hyper-Hobbesian" a moment ago because he thinks that the war of all against all permanently characterizes "being-in-itself." That is not Hobbes's view. Life is "solitary, poor, nasty, brutish, and short" only in the absence of government.[9] As there is no Leviathan to rule over the conflict between states, violence is natural. This is not to say that no international order can ever be achieved. But such order is likely to be the product of artifice rather than of socialization. Insofar as there are contacts between states, it is possible to talk of a system of states: still, the essence of that system remains anarchic. It was almost inevitable that this position, which can be dubbed that of brute realism, would be theorized so as to stress that states, in a world bereft of justice, seek nothing but power – or, more precisely, the maximization of their "national interest."[10]

This picture needs as much qualification as did that of sociability. Just as there are elements of power within the nation-states to

[8]   T. Hobbes, *Leviathan*, Blackwell, Oxford, 1957, p. 83.
[9]   Hobbes, *Leviathan*, p. 82.
[10]   A prime example of this position is H. Morgenthau, *Politics among Nations*, Alfred Knopf, New York, 1948. In fairness, it should be noted that Morgenthau's later assessments of American involvement in Vietnam introduced a subtlety and moderation largely lacking in his great treatise.

which we are accustomed, so too can there be sociability in the relations between states. International order is likely to be strengthened by the extensive sharing of norms and practices, that is, from the presence of international society. That we live, to some extent and for some of the time, in a society of states was Hedley Bull's central analytic point. The morality appropriate to such circumstances was noted by Montesquieu: "The *right of nations* is by nature founded on the principle that the various nations should do to one another in times of peace the most good possible, and in times of war the least ill possible, without harming their true interests."[11] Aron so loved this prudential maxim that he used it to introduce his great treatise on peace and war.[12]

The nature of international society can be highlighted by returning to demographic patterns. Watkins's study pays most attention to the ways in which nation-states have replaced provinces: Bretons came to behave, for example, as did the rest of France, thereby making Breton identity essentially supernumerary, an option rather than a condition. But as important as this has been the attempt to cage relations which exist outside states within their territorial boundaries.[13] Ambivalent attitudes exist towards such caging. On the one hand, the control of feudalism's violence, that is, the ability of states not just to claim the monopoly of violence but actually to achieve it, has received a good press.[14] On the other hand, understanding between states, each jealous of their sovereignty, is likely to be enhanced by shared by understandings of foreign policy makers.[15] The solidarity of eighteenth-century Europe's cosmopolitan, French-speaking upper class helped ensure the smooth workings of international

[11] C. L. S. de Montesquieu, *The Spirit of the Laws*, Cambridge University Press, Cambridge, 1989, p. 7.
[12] R. Aron, *Peace and War*, Weidenfeld and Nicolson, London, 1966. Bull followed Wright in placing Grotius rather than Montesquieu as the founder of this more complex position: on this see H. Bull, B. Kingsbury, and A. Roberts, eds, *Hugo Grotius and International Relations*, Oxford University Press, Oxford, 1990.
[13] The notion of caging is derived from M. Mann, *Sources of Social Power*, Cambridge University Press, Cambridge, 2 vols, 1986–1993, vol. 1, ch. 1 and vol. 2, chs 20–1.
[14] On this see the argument of ch. 2.
[15] On this see the argument of ch. 3.

order, for example, quite as much as did calculations of power
and advantage in the abstract. In this spirit, the creation, maintenance, and increasing social reach of international norms is often
seen to be nothing less than part of the process of civilization.
This can be accepted as long as the norms in question are universal
and not just widespread, that is, as long as their content includes
the recognition of the rights of other societies and of humane
conduct when at war with them – in contrast, that is, to the
extensive "norms" of fascism and Bolshevism, as well as those
endemic to the racism of the European powers at the height of
imperialism.[16] No attempt to strike a balance between what
should and what should not be contained within states has yet
been successful. Much of this book concerns the changing balance
between the two.

No international order has yet created a world order, that is,
an arena of justice in which human beings would be welcome as
universal strangers anywhere at any time, entitled to the treatment
habitually given to a social group within territorial boundaries.
The concept of international order is not then purely aseptic; to
the contrary, it has a troubled relationship to morality. An
international order may systematically favor the interests of some
states rather than of all states. It is worth recalling in this context
the comment made by the British general Calgacus on the *Pax
Romana*: "To robbery, butchery and rapine, they give the lying
name of 'government'; they create a desolation and call it
peace."[17] Equally, the world restored by the Congress system was
directed against revolution, whilst America's ordering of capitalism gave few favors to the developing world, despite the extension
to it of the norm of sovereignty and non-intervention;[18] more
generally, the long peace established by the freezing of social

---

[16]   This critical point is directed at an important volume edited by Bull and Adam
Roberts on *The Growth of International Society* (Oxford University Press, Oxford, 1984)
which conflates the extensive reach of norms with their having liberal content. "Norms" is
placed in quotation marks to underline the difference, that is, to accentuate that the
regimes in question habitually replaced social reciprocity with force and arbitrariness.
[17]   Tacitus, *The Agricola and the Germania*, Penguin, Harmondsworth, 1970.
[18]   J. G. Ruggie, "International Regimes, Transactions and Change," *International
Organisation*, vol. 36, 1982; S. Krasner, *Structural Conflict*, University of California Press,
Berkeley, 1985.

relations in the postwar era meant very different experiences for those living in the East from those familiar to us in the West. As was the case with social order, opinion is likely to be split between radicals and conservatives as to whether international order is a good *per se*. Again, there is little need to take sides: one can very often (but not necessarily always) favor international order, not least since this now means the absence of nuclear war, whilst wishing to press for an extension of international society so as to allow for greater justice in world politics.

These distinctions allow us to make two points about the heralding of a new world order. Most obviously, a category mistake was being made. A new international order was in question rather than the creation of world order. A second reason for scepticism was the absence of any positive specification of what a new world order would comprise. The presumption was that the removal of evil would allow truth, peace, justice, and all good things to flourish automatically. Such *carte blanche* laxity, taking to be natural what needs to be justified, is very much the intellectual fashion of the age.[19] As the nature of the good is deeply contested, this style of argument is useless.

If the distinction drawn by Bull between international order and world order retains validity, this does not for a moment mean that we can sit back in idleness. To the contrary, very great intellectual labors are desperately needed. Is the contemporary world polity ordered? If so, how should we characterize this order, and how distinguish it from its predecessors? Which social forces in the contemporary world are likely to support and which to undermine international order? Bull's early death necessitates finding our own responses to these questions. Whilst answering these questions, moreover, it is important to bear in mind that Bull's concepts have prescriptive as well as descriptive content – in itself no bad thing, provided that the two are not mingled in any licentious manner. For one thing, Bull himself insisted that international order was a necessary precondition for the development of world order, which is not to say that he felt that every international order made equivalent progress towards justice. For

[19]   E. Gellner, *Legitimation of Belief*, Cambridge University Press, Cambridge, 1974.

another, Bull was critical of the very idea of world government on moral as well as practical grounds, preferring instead a world of states firmly bound by the ties of civilization. This normative position will be maintained in this book, but only with caution and multiple reservations.

IDEAL TYPES OF INTERNATIONAL ORDER

If curiously little empirical work has been done on the incidence of war and peace, the evidence we do have points to a single conclusion.[20] War seems so universal, with peace being scarcely an alternative, given that it was so often used as an arena in which to prepare for further hostilities, as to suggest that the very object of the present inquiry might be mistaken. Closer analysis of empirical findings suggests a more complex view. If war has been ever-present, it is only some wars that have tended towards the absolute. The Thirty Years War caused actual depopulation in Central Europe, whilst the revolutionary and Napoleonic wars brought forth new principles of political rule that threatened all *anciens régimes*. The destruction of the First World War and the rather different horrors of the Second World War require no comment; equally, the foul certainty that the kill-ratio of modern weapons has the capacity to end all human existence has become part of public awareness. In consequence, restraints on the manner of fighting in and limits to the scale of war seem to me all-important, making international orders substantial achievements, despite their biases and their habitual inability to establish peace. But even if this moral gloss is rejected, variation in levels of conflict remains a social fact which demands explanation.

Attention will be given to five theories of international order,

[20]   Q. Wright, *A Study of War*, University of Chicago Press, Chicago, 1965; P. Sorokin, *Social and Cultural Dynamics. Volume Three: Fluctuation of Social Relationships, War, and Revolution*, Badminster, New York, 1962; J. S. Levy, *War in the Modern Great Power System, 1495–1975*, University of Kentucky Press, Lexington, 1983; N. Choucri and R. C. North, *Nations in Conflict*, Freeman, San Francisco, 1975; M. Small and J. D. Singer, *Resort to Arms*, Sage, Beverly Hills, 1982; K. J. Holsti, *Peace and War*, Cambridge University Press, Cambridge, 1990; Mann, *Sources of Social Power*.

each of which offers plans for limiting war (and sometimes for establishing peace) as well as diagnoses as to why wars take place in the first place. Implicit in this comment is the fact that each one of these theories has descriptive and normative components: these are grand theories which need to be judged in practical as well as theoretical terms. In addition, the theories are in mutual contact; indeed they have sometimes been spawned as much by each other as by historical events. It should be noted immediately that not every theory of international order, either extant or conceivable, is included in this typology; a prejudgement is accordingly being made that these five theories are more important than others. One further option does in fact receive detailed attention in the next chapter: nonetheless, imperial order does not gain central billing since it is unlikely to characterize the modern world polity as a whole.[21] The same is true of other principles, including those of international law, Marxism, technological determinism, and dependency theory, all of which accordingly receive short shrift.

The most elegant and powerful theory of peace and war is that of realism. This position received powerful rendition in antiquity from Thucydides, in the early modern period from Machiavelli, Hobbes, Montesquieu, and Rousseau, and most recently from Aron and Waltz. The central tenet of realism is that states live in an asocial society, in which the recourse to violence is normal. The fact that some states have disappeared makes it entirely understandable that the main task of states is that of the search for their own security. A central presupposition of this approach is that states can be treated as entities: leaders of different political persuasions end up behaving in a similar manner because of the force of external circumstances.

The hope for international order that results from realism is that of the balance of power. Whilst there can be various mechanisms involved in balancing, all versions of realist theory stress that states will ally together in order to protect themselves against the hegemonic pretensions of an overmighty neighbor (or

---

[21] I am here differing from W. H. McNeill's insistence in *The Pursuit of Power* (Blackwell, Oxford, 1983, ch. 10 and conclusion) that the presence of nuclear weapons *demands* world government.

any allied set of neighbors).[22] This tends to involve what many, especially in the United States at all times and quite generally elsewhere in the inter-war period, came to see as a measure of immorality. It is necessary, in order for a balance to be real, for powers to shift from one side to another; no permanent set of allegiances can be allowed, for to admit them would be to rigidify the system, and so to cause disaster. The extent to which this behavior has sometimes been accepted is striking: Frederick the Great chopped and changed, but there was no condemnation of him for so doing. Modern scholars imbued with the spirit of realism sometimes argue that it was a mistake to ban Bolshevik Russia from the international community, for it thereby became much harder to balance Hitler's Germany.

Beyond this point, there is a measure of disagreement, allusion to which has already been made when noting Bull's criticism of brute realism. At the core of divergence lies the desire of brute realism to become absolutely parsimonious. States are presumed by this view to be essentially similar, rational, calculative, and coherent, concerned above all to maximize their power in a situation of anarchy. In one famous interpretation of this sort states were compared to firms: not surprisingly, this move opens the door to the high-powered but abstract logic of rational choice theory which so dominates economics.[23] It can be said immediately that the power that parsimony can bring has a high price tag attached to it here, as can be seen by analysis based on an unhappily but necessarily imperfect division between descriptive and prescriptive levels of the theory.

Descriptively, the difficulty is that brute realism has a tendency to become circular. On the one hand, its tenets are held to be in

---

[22]   E. Haas, "The Balance of Power," World Politics, vol. 5, 1953; D. Zinnes, "An Analytical Study of Balance of Power Theories," Journal of Peace Research, vol. 3, 1967; M. Wright, "The Balance of Power and International Order," in A. James, ed., The Bases of International Order, Oxford University Press, Oxford, 1973. I am indebted to a lecture by M. Doyle, "The Classical Balance of Power Theory," given at McGill University in 1992; some of Doyle's ideas on the subject can now be found in "Politics and Grand Strategy," in R. Rosecrance and A. Stein, eds, The Domestic Bases of Grand Strategy, Cornell University Press, Ithaca, 1993.
[23]   K. Waltz, Theory of International Politics, Addison Wesley, Reading, PA, 1979. Cf. R. Keohane, ed., Neorealism and Its Critics, Columbia University Press, New York, 1986.

operation when the balance of power is operating smoothly, when all the actors in a system are seeking to measure the power of their rivals so as change allegiances in order to establish equilibrium in the system. On the other hand, the same tenets are held to accurately describe the alternative position, in which a state first seeks to establish hegemony but is then destroyed by the alliances that are built against it. A theory which gains support from two such different sets of data, and which can thus explain everything, is essentially non-falsifiable and of little scientific validity.

The key point to be made at the level of policy is that states do not always seek the same goals. Some can be modest and appeasing, others desperate for glory. It is accordingly an immense mistake to imagine that state behavior can be subject to the simplifying analyses of any uniform economistic logic. This point was made with unrivaled force by Aron when analyzing the way in which American strategic thought conceptualized involvement in Vietnam.[24] Formal reasoning led to a view that North Vietnam would accept defeat when a certain level of force had been reached. The fact that Aron might well have welcomed such a defeat, given that he saw the war less in terms of national liberation than as an example of communist imposition, makes his ensuing criticism of American thought all the more impressive.[25] The stakes of the conflict were different for both sides, and the failure of American international relations experts, bound to a monolithic conception of interest, to realize this meant that they misunderstood everything. It was necessary to calculate properly, to understand the mental set of the opponent rather than to live within a theoretical model that seemed powerful but which in fact lacked content. Pseudo-scientific hardness is no replacement for judgement – which is the quality needed if we are to "think" an open system.

Aron underlined this basic point towards the end of his career when assessing the contribution made by the thought of Clausewitz. The Prussian theorist of war was initially deeply attracted to

[24]   R. Aron, "Remarques sur l'évolution de la pensée stratégique (1945–68)," *European Journal of Sociology*, vol. 9, 1968. Aron here is drawing on principles enunciated with great force in *Peace and War*, ch. 3.
[25]   Aron, *Penser la guerre, Clausewitz*, vol. 2, pp. 199–210.

the essential purity of Napoleon's military style, above all, by its ability to so concentrate power that it gained complete success. But the more Clausewitz reflected, the more he came to question his youthful admiration. In the last months of his life, he produced a final trinitarian definition of war:

> War is more than a true chameleon that slightly adapts its characteristics to the given case. As a total phenomenon its dominant tendency always make war a paradoxical trinity – composed of primordial violence, hatred, and enmity, which are to be regarded as a blind natural force; of the play of chance and probability within which the creative spirit is free to roam; and of its element of subordination, as an instrument of policy, which makes it subject to reason alone.
>
> The first of these aspects mainly concerns the people; the second the commander and his army; the third the government. The passions that are to be kindled in war must already be inherent in the people; the scope which the play of courage and talent will enjoy in the realm of probability and chance depends on the particular character of the commander and the army; but the political aims are the business of government alone.[26]

This view made apparent that Napoleon's escalation to extremes had been a failure. In contrast, the dull pragmatism of Frederick the Great's limited wars had achieved more. It was Aron's own appreciation of this principle that allowed him to assert, on the very day that the Six Day War between Israel and the Arabs ended, that Israel – about whose fate he cared deeply – had won a victory but not *the* victory (which could only have been, in his view, peace).[27]

Perhaps the dictates of pure logic – namely, the realization that excessive ambition may have deleterious consequences in the long run – should force brute realism away from the unbridled struggle to increase national power towards a realization of the virtue of prudence. However, logic is not always life, and the first point made at a descriptive level by what is best dubbed sophisticated

---

[26]   C. von Clausewitz, *On War*, Princeton University Press, Princeton, 1976, p. 89. Cf. R. Aron, "Reason, Passion and Power in the Thought of Clausewitz," *Social Research*, vol. 39, 1972 and *Penser la guerre, Clausewitz*, passim.

[27]   R. Aron, *De Gaulle, Israel and the Jews*, André Deutsch, London, 1969.

realism is that realism is likely to work best, as was noted when discussing Bull's appreciation of this point, when the ties of international society are strong.[28] This sociological condition is most easily seen at work when state leaders share realist values, not least since this makes balancing a conscious activity rather than the mere end result of a mechanical process. However, international homogeneity of this sort can have several bases: if class solidarity within and racism without characterized European history, the power of capitalism and still more acceptance of the norm of sovereignty characterize the contemporary world polity.[29] Of course, the norms of international society can be shared by the people as much as by the elite; the extent to which this will facilitate the workings of any contemporary international order will be of considerable interest later.

Sophisticated realists also stress that states must calculate, especially given that the goals of state behavior vary. This point was made particularly forcefully by Aron when he emphasized the need to *make* states rational calculators of consequences.[30] What Aron meant prescriptively should also be taken sociologically. For some states are so constrained by pressure groups that they cannot properly weigh priorities and calculate national interest; the same situation can result when state capacities are limited, making for erroneous calculations of an opponent's intentions.[31] Of course, to make this sociological point is not to refute Aron. States blessed with the sociological preconditions for rational calculation will make mistakes if they do not learn the prudential logic of realism.[32] Possessing room in which to calculate is not the same thing as – and no guarantee of – skill in calculation. Hereafter, I use the omnibus term of "the intelligent state," taken as social

[28]   The distinction drawn between brute and sophisticated realism may not appeal to everyone. An alternative approach would be to deny the realist label altogether to theories or actors who ignore prudence. But that approach would foreclose matters, whereas my distinction opens up key issues needing analysis.

[29]   The concept of homogeneity is that of Aron, *Peace and War*, ch. 4.

[30]   Aron, *Penser la guerre, Clausewitz*, vol. 2, ch. 6.

[31]   My stress on institutions follows Mann, *Sources of Social Power*, vol 2, ch. 21 and J. Snyder, *Myths of Empire*, Cornell University Press, Ithaca, 1991.

[32]   T. V. Paul, *Asymmetric Conflicts*, Cambridge University Press, Cambridge, 1994 is particularly striking in this context since it provides superb analyses of war initiation by weaker powers.

achievement rather as presupposition, to capture this second condition of realism's existence.

The main policy recommendations of sophisticated realism are closely related to a proper understanding of homogeneity. Martin Ceadel has very powerfully argued that realism is best termed "defencism" on the grounds that the only war that it can countenance is one to preserve the *status quo*, albeit this can involve initial aggression given that attack can be the best or only form of defense.[33] This was certainly the view of Montesquieu when writing about the Europe of his day. But homogeneity is a sociological rather than an ontological condition; this would surely make sophisticated realists chary of the absolute injunction issued by Ceadel. In this spirit, Michael Walzer's important *Just and Unjust Wars* allows intervention to stop absolute brutality as an exception to the defencism that he proposes under the name of legalism.[34] Similarly, Aron mused that a preventive war against Hitler might well not have been immoral.[35] Prudence demands extreme boldness when faced with an absolute enemy, though there remains everything to be said for fighting with as much moderation as possible.

We can discover a second theory of international order by once again considering Clausewitz.[36] Although he came ever more to reject the Napoleonic escalation to extremes, to stress that the political control of war mattered more than obedience to its pure logic, Clausewitz nonetheless remained true to key principles of the revolution. He had realized that citizens fought better than paid mercenaries, and had accordingly been part of the reform group around Scharnhorst, Yorck, and Gneisenau that had played a major role in the abolition of serfdom. The logic of this position led Clausewitz to support the founding of a citizens' militia in

[33] M. Ceadel, *Thinking about Peace and War*, Oxford University Press, Oxford, 1987.

[34] M. Walzer, *Just and Unjust Wars*, Basic Books, New York, 1977. Walzer also accepts Ceadel's point, that aggression can be a form of defense, and further considers wars just if they support self-determination or counter a prior intervention.

[35] This is not to say that Aron recommended this, at the time or later. His emphasis on calculation, on working out the consequences of action, would have required finding means appropriate to an end. Nonetheless, the basic point – that the end was not intuitively ridiculous – stands.

[36] P. Paret, *Clausewitz and the State*, Princeton University Press, Princeton, 1976.

1813. This was rejected by the King, largely because the act of putting arms into the hands of the people was still deemed dangerous. Clausewitz fought against Napoleon for the next years in the service of the Tsar, and his career never fully recovered from this radicalism. But it was the view represented by the King that came to triumph in the next years, and which gives us a second source of international order, namely that of a concert of great powers determined to prevent revolution. The revolutionary principles in question were of course those of equality, liberty, and fraternity, of a career open to the talents – all ideas, as Tocqueville noted, which spread throughout Europe like a new religion.[37] Although it is far from being historically accurate, Henry Kissinger's *A World Restored* captures the feel of one version of this sort of arrangement.[38] The intent of the system designed by Metternich was to meet at frequent intervals so as to help contain revolution. This arrangement was initially directed against France but, as it unfolded, albeit with the eventual absence of Britain, it was used against liberals and nationalists throughout Europe.

Liberalism provides a third theory of international order, most strikingly in Immanuel Kant's 1795 proposal for "Perpetual Peace."[39] The importance of this mock treaty for peace has recently been stressed by Michael Doyle in a superlative essay, whose huge impact comes from its factual claim that no two liberal states have ever fought against each other.[40] This claim is slightly exaggerated because of an unduly severe and restricted definition of liberalism. A more generous and sensible view would allow that there have been some wars between liberal states, most notably, the Anglo-Dutch wars of the seventeenth century, the Anglo-American war of 1812 and the Spanish–American war of 1898. Still, the relative paucity of wars between liberal states

[37]   A. de Tocqueville, *The Old Regime and the French Revolution*, Anchor Books, New York, 1955, part I, ch. 3.
[38]   Houghton Mifflin, Boston, 1973.
[39]   I. Kant, "Perpetual Peace," in *Kant's Political Writings*, ed. H. Reiss, Cambridge University Press, Cambridge, 1970.
[40]   M. Doyle, "Kant, Liberal Legacies and Foreign Affairs," *Philosophy and Public Affairs*, vol. 12, 1983.

remains striking.[41] A warning should be issued at this point, before Kant's position is outlined. Doyle is not naive. A particular merit of his essay, often neglected by his critics, is that it also notes the presence of an unpleasant and unacceptable side of liberalism's attitude to foreign affairs. Despite their pacific record against each other, liberal states have fought both often and with extreme viciousness against non-liberal states. If one can see touches of this mentality in the history of British foreign affairs, it has often affected the conduct of American policy – most obviously, in the crusade directed against communism.

Kant's position derives from insistence that the idea that peace will be achieved by the balance of power is pure illusion, "like Swift's story of the house which the builder had constructed in such perfect harmony with all the laws of equilibrium that it collapsed as soon as a sparrow alighted on it."[42] His alternative proposal rests on three "definitive articles." First, Kant argues that governments must be republican, by which he means not just political processes open to the views of the people but also the separation of executive from legislature – something which will improve modern republics, in his view, when compared to their ancient forebears. Secondly, a union between liberal states is called for with the specific purpose in mind of agreeing never to make war on each other. Finally, liberal states should agree on a right to universal hospitality, one element of which will include economic affairs – and thus the creation of an interdependence based on trade as well as upon the free movement of peoples.

What strikes one most about Kant's proposal is that it is realist in both senses of the word, that is, realistic and based on the continued presence of states. Most obviously, Kant does not rule out war: to the contrary, the eventual extension of the union of liberal states is ensured by the experience of war. The great educator of mankind is human suffering. Equally, Kant does not imagine that states will cease to exist, nor does he desire any

---

[41]   Mann, *Sources of Social Power*, vol. 2, pp. 767, and 766–74. For a consideration of still more cases, see B. Russett, *Grasping the Democratic Peace*, Princeton University Press, Princeton, 1993, pp. 16–23 and passim.
[42]   I. Kant, "On the Common Saying 'This may be True in Theory, but it does not apply in Practice,'", in *Kant's Political Writings*, p. 92.

empire of the earth since "laws progressively lose their impact as the government increases its range, and a soulless despotism, after crushing the germs of goodness, will finally lapse into anarchy."[43] It is worth insisting, finally, that Kant's position is not one which resembles the collective security attempted by the League of Nations in the inter-war period. For the first preliminary article proposed by Kant in his draft treaty insists that no plans be made for any future war.[44] This makes it clear that collective security was in fact a concert of the left, directed against revisionist and nationalist revolution from the radical right.

The sophistication of Kant's position can better be appreciated by contrasting it with a naive version of liberalism whose application to foreign affairs was disastrous. This alternative view had expected that the entry of the people onto the political stage would in and of itself guarantee the reign of peace. According to this populist vision, wars result from the atavistic drives of a warrior class, trained for and able to benefit from conflict.[45] The optimism of this type of liberalism was put into question, and should have been dealt a death-blow, by the sight of the popularity of French revolutionary militarism.[46] In more practical terms, liberals in the inter-war period, prone to imagine that the experience of the trenches had made for an absolute horror of war, went on far too long imagining that everyone was open to sweet reason. This led to the world of illusion in which the Kellogg–Briand pact banned war, absolutely unconscious of the fact that many still found war to be ennobling.[47] The most powerful theorization of this negative view remains that of Tocqueville.[48] If the people can be remorseless and vicious once aroused, Tocqueville insisted that they are habitually slow to become angered in the first place. Both

[43] Kant, "Perpetual Peace," p. 113.
[44] Kant, "Perpetual Peace," p. 93.
[45] M. Howard, *War and the Liberal Conscience*, Oxford University Press, Oxford, 1981.
[46] M. Howard, *War in European History*, Oxford University Press, Oxford, 1976, ch. 5.
[47] Aron, *Peace and War*, ch. 19. This judgement places me at odds with J. Mueller, *Retreat from Doomsday*, Basic Books, New York, 1989.
[48] A. de Tocqueville, *Democracy in America*, Anchor Books, New York, 1969, pp. 645–51. Cf. J. Joffe, "Tocqueville Revisited," *Washington Quarterly*, vol. 11, 1988.

George Kennan and Henry Kissinger have argued that this slowness to anger can impede the effective conduct of foreign affairs.
Thus popular pressures prevented Sir Edward Grey from making
it apparent that an attack on Belgium would lead to war, and
Roosevelt from joining the fight against Hitler early on.[49]

Popular participation does not guarantee peace, nor can it ever
do so if war is seen only as a sinful aberration against the very
nature of humanity. But to admit this is *not* to accept most of
what is implied in the negative case outlined. Most obviously,
popular participation has prevented or curtailed war rather more
than it has occasioned it; accordingly, any final balance sheet of
the costs and benefits of popular participation must be complex,
not least since the statesmen/theorists Kennan and Kissinger are
not above blaming the people for their own mistakes. Elitism is
not necessarily better than populism.

But to leave matters at this point would be very unsatisfactory.
Kant's starting point *was* realism, and his greatest contributions
are made at both institutional and normative levels.[50] Crucially,
liberal institutions increase the intelligence of states. Philosophical
support for this view can be found in Popper's convincing
demonstration that objective knowledge depends upon critical
discussion much more than it does upon finding virtue in our
souls.[51] If liberalism helps to weigh and establish priorities, quite
as important is the fact that its system of checks and balances has
prevented or shortened hapless adventures. I do not wish to deny
that tension results from conducting diplomacy within an open
political system, but will show that domestic pressures in some
authoritarian regimes have curtailed rational calculation much
more – and with disastrous consequences.[52] Of course, rational
and democratic formation of national priorities is often less reality
than ambition. Hence, liberal institutions are likely to work best
when they rest upon prudential norms, that is, hatred of war

[49]   G. Kennan, *American Diplomacy*, Chicago University Press, Chicago, 1951; H. A.
Kissinger, *White House Years*, Little, Brown and Company, Boston, 1982.
[50]   Russett, *Grasping the Democratic Peace.*
[51]   K. R. Popper, *The Open Society and Its Enemies*, Routledge and Kegan Paul, London,
1957.
[52]   R. Putnam, "Diplomacy and Domestic Politics," *International Organization*, vol. 42,
1988.

combined with awareness that the use of force has sometimes been necessary. It is important to stress again that there is no reason to presume the people to be blindly passionate and the elite moderate in this matter, nor indeed to argue the opposite case: what will matter in liberal democracy is a process of dialogue between two parties equally capable of error. Finally, it is worth noting that both norms and institutions can work outside the state, at the level of international society. Aggression is certainly likely to be limited by feelings of solidarity between peoples, whilst international liberal institutions, as will be seen in a moment, can encourage rationality on the part of states.[53]

A fourth type of international order pays more attention to economics than to the nature of a political regime. Auguste Comte's crude position suggested that the coming of industrialism would ensure peace, given that the fundamental cause of war was scarcity.[54] More important has been the insistence that the growth of commerce would make war less feasible. This theory of interdependence is by no means new – not surprisingly, given that capitalism predates the industrial revolution. Perhaps the most striking early formulation is Benjamin Constant's *The Spirit of Conquest and Usurpation*, published in Hanover in 1814. Constant had distanced himself from Napoleon's drive for imperial glory, and used the occasion of his impending downfall to sit in judgement on the very idea of the acquisition of wealth via territorial aggrandizement. In his discussion of "the character of modern nations in relation to war," he asserted bluntly that: "War then comes before commerce. The former is all savage impulse, the latter civilised calculation. It is clear that the more the commercial tendency prevails, the weaker must the tendency to war become."[55] In addition, Constant insists that territorial conquest has now become self-defeating: it leads to a "universal

[53]   The outstanding analysis of international institutions is R. Keohane, *After Hegemony*, Princeton University Press, Princeton, 1984.
[54]   Aron criticized this thesis with characteristic brilliance on two occasions: *War and Industrial Society*, Oxford University Press, Oxford, 1958 and "War and Industrial Society," *Millennium*, vol. 7, 1978/9.
[55]   B. Constant, "The Spirit of Conquest and Usurpation," in *Constant's Political Writings*, ed. B. Fontana, Cambridge University Press, Cambridge, 1988, p. 53.

horror" that defeats the purpose of the enterprise.[56] That this was so delighted Constant: the more powerful the warrior ethic, the less likely was it that constitutionalism, which he admired and endorsed, would be safe, let alone have the capacity to spread.[57] Constant is a powerful thinker who added much to what he learnt in Edinburgh whilst a student of the Scottish moralists, and his hopes were accordingly by no means unqualified. The rational calculation brought by commerce was not, Constant feared, sufficiently strong to overcome the capacity of Parisian life to create excessive ambition; as importantly, the privatization endemic to commercial society might lead a passive populace to gain vicarious pleasure from conquest.

In contrast, few doubts as to the peace-inducing consequences of the spread of commerce were entertained by the Manchester School, perhaps because their experience was of industrial capitalism. The views of this school were marvellously captured by Cobden in his parliamentary speech during the Don Pacifico affair in 1850:

> The progress of freedom depends more upon the maintenance of peace, the spread of commerce, and the diffusion of education, than upon the labours of cabinets and foreign offices ... [There should be] as little intercourse as possible between Governments; as much connection as possible between the nations of the world.[58]

This prescriptive view had turned into a descriptive account of reality by 1909 in Norman Angell's *Europe's Optical Illusion*: the intercourse of capitalists was held to be so extensive that war was impossible.[59] However, other important liberal voices could not accept that a harmony of interests would be brought about

---

[56]   Constant, "The Spirit of Usurpation and Conquest," p. 79.

[57]   S. Holmes, *Benjamin Constant and the Making of Modern Liberalism*, Yale University Press, New Haven, 1984; B. Fontana, *Benjamin Constant and the Post-Revolutionary Mind*, Yale University Press, New Haven, 1991.

[58]   R. Cobden, *Political Writings*, William Ridgeway, London, 1867, vol. 2, p. 377, cited in A. J. P. Taylor, *The Troublemakers*, Panther, London, 1969, p. 50.

[59]   Simpkin, Marshall, Hamilton, Kent and Co., London, 1909. Both Howard, *War and the Liberal Conscience* and Taylor, *The Troublemakers* have excellent accounts of his views; cf. J. Joll, *The Origins of the First World War*, Longman, Harlow, 1984, p. 137 and passim.

naturally and spontaneously. Such thinkers favored social engineering so that basic liberal values and institutions could be put in
place.[60] The market mechanism, upon whose beneficent workings
so much depended, had to be established by an act of will.
Equally, most liberals allowed some room for intervention so as
to help the fight of nations struggling to throw off the oppression
of foreign rulers, although the extent of such intervention was
very much a matter of debate.[61] Similarly, where Cobden was
prepared to leave the abolition of slavery to the workings of the
market, John Stuart Mill insisted that the West African Squadron
of the Royal Navy be kept in place so as to establish basic
workings of civilized society – within which, of course, market
principles might then work. Interestingly, Mill's views on this
point angered his friend Tocqueville, who saw the Navy's actions
in terms of the interests of Britain rather than those of humanity.[62]
This type of reaction proved to be much more general.

Alexander Hamilton made an early contribution to the alternative approach when insisting, in his 1791 "Report on Manufac-
tures," that the young United States needed to protect its infant
industries against Britain's commercial might. An open world
economy was very much in the interest of a nation which had an
established economic lead; it was advisable, in Hamilton's view
for latecomers to reject the terms of the leading power so as to
ensure their own development. The need for special practices to
overcome economic backwardness was articulated still more
clearly by German thinkers, most notably by Fichte's *The Closed
Commercial State* (1808) and by List's *The National System of
Political Economy* (1841); it is generally familiar today in the
form of dependency theory.[63]

---

[60] The basic distinction between a natural and an engineered harmony of interests is
that of E. Halévy, *The Growth of Philosophical Radicalism*, Faber and Gwyer, London,
1928. Cf. S. Collini, J. Burrow, and D. Winch, *That Noble Science of Politics*, Cambridge
University Press, Cambridge, 1983, especially ch. 4 and W. Thomas, *The Philosophical
Radicals*, Oxford University Press, Oxford, 1979.
[61] Howard, *War and the Liberal Conscience*, ch. 2.
[62] B. Semmel, *Liberalism and Naval Strategy*, Allen and Unwin, Winchester, MA, 1986.
[63] A superb discussion of this whole approach, together with the claim that Marxism is
its greatest representative, is provided by R. Szporluk, *Communism and Nationalism*,
Oxford University Press, Oxford, 1988.

The fact that capitalism was divided by states in time led other theorists to a much more pessimistic view. Karl Polanyi remains the most considerable of all the pessimists.[64] His rich and subtle *The Great Transformation* was a sustained reflection on the social origins of the wars that began in Europe and which then engulfed the world. Polanyi argued that capitalism depends upon constant changes, thereby providing a never-ending story of the destruction of settled social and economic practices. This circumstance naturally creates a demand for the protection of society against impersonal forces. The desire to shield society often entailed a search for full economic security only realizable through conquest. The essence of his position then is that the spread of capitalism ensures geopolitical conflict.

The key insight of Polanyi's account has been formalized and developed by modern American thinkers, particularly by those who posit a "theory of hegemonic stability."[65] The most obvious claim of this school (which is my fifth ideal type of international order) is that capitalism works best when a hegemonic power is capable of providing it with certain services or public goods, most notably a top currency, capital for export, absorption of excess world product, and an insistence on establishing generalized free trade. Both Britain in the nineteenth century and the United States after 1945 are held to have served as liberal leaders. Self-congratulation can lead to a picture of such leaders as beneficent norm-givers devoted only to the greater good; but the theory can manage without this moral coloring, indeed should do so given that one of its tenets – that the leading state wishes to export – suggests self-interested reasons for involvement in the world's affairs.

If this first claim tends to tautology, a second claim makes entirely concrete predictions. Problems for international affairs are posed by the uneven development of capitalism: more particularly, there is a complex interaction between the hegemon and its rivals, the former seeking to retain its lead in adverse circum-

[64]   K. Polanyi, *The Great Transformation*, Beacon Press, Boston, 1957.
[65]   The earliest statement was C. Kindleberger, *The World in Depression, 1919–1933*, University of California Press, Berkeley, 1973. The fullest working out of the thesis is R. Gilpin, *War and Change in World Politics*, Cambridge University Press, Cambridge, 1981.

stances, if necessary by establishing protection so as to protect its own tiring industries, and the latter all the more driven to grab at world power in consequence. The justification for this claim is to be found in its rather idiosyncratic interpretation of modern world history. Peace reigned whilst Britain was hegemon but war followed thereafter, both because of Germany's challenge and the United States' unwillingness, during the inter-war years, to take on the mantle of leadership which its actual power would have allowed it to bear. Similarly, peace reigned while the United States was supreme, but the undermining of its position may well, the logic of the theory suggests, lead to a renewal of major war. In all this, it should be noted, stands an ambiguity. The principal proponents of hegemonic stability theory are indebted to realism, and hence are likely to see the actions involved as having been taken by state leaders for reasons of national interest. But the theory is open to more economistic readings. The demand for openness to or protection from international economic forces can be interpreted as being occasioned by special interest groups pressing their points of view upon state leaders.

A final claim, implicit but decidedly present, concerns decline. Virtue does not bring its own reward. The leading power shoulders excessive burdens, it is maintained, when providing services for capitalism as a whole, and this slowly undermines its position. Decline is thus, to adapt Jean-Paul Sartre, due to the selfishness of others. This ethic is widely endorsed in the United States, where it has the capacity to affect behavior. It accordingly makes sense to note immediately that this is not the only notion of decline available in the body of social theory.

The most important point to be made is that much decline within capitalist society is normal. The center of capitalist society has never remained in the same place for long and this, the result of comparative advantage and the advantages of backwardness, that is, the ability to develop using the most up-to-date equipment and methods, suggests that the United States is as likely to lose its dominant role in the long run as were Genoa, the United Provinces and Great Britain. Importantly, there is nothing wrong with the fact that this diffusion of techniques and practices throughout capitalist society inevitably creates relative decline: the growth path of the most advanced state can remain strong and its

economy healthy even as its share of total world product dimin-
ishes. Equally, decline which results from geopolitical exhaustion
can be quite as much a factor beyond national control. But
geopolitical exhaustion can also be, so to speak, self-inflicted:
overextension can be so great as to undermine the economy.
Realization of this point made it possible to predict the impending
collapse of the Soviet Union, something well beyond alternative
social science paradigms.[66] Quite as striking, finally, are the
wounds caused by social sclerosis. The American political scientist
Mancur Olson has interestingly argued that states find it hard
continually to adapt because over time their societies come to
control them; differently put, countries tend to institutionalize
their moments of success.[67] This too is historically normal, but
the fact that the rigidities are self-inflicted at least allows for the
possibility of change – something which entails a conception of
responsibility different from that proposed by hegemonic stability
theory.

BRINGING HISTORY BACK IN

Whilst I hope that some flavor of the different ideal typical
positions has been conveyed, no claim is being made that a
complete theoretical analysis has been offered. One obvious
avenue of inquiry that remains open concerns the ways in which
different positions can form combinations. The originality of
Kant's position derives, as argued, from his working with rather
than against realism. A different combinational logic can be seen
at work in a more modern work, Keohane's *After Hegemony*,
which suggests that co-operation in the world economy is made
possible by the presence of international liberal institutions.[68]
Keohane's emphasis on trade relations suggests at first sight that

---

[66]   R. Collins, *Weberian Sociological Theory*, Cambridge University Press, Cambridge,
1984, ch. 8.
[67]   M. Olson, *The Rise and Decline of Nations*, Yale University Press, New Haven,
1984.
[68]   Keohane, *After Hegemony*.

he seeks, as do so many in the American academy, to marry interdependence to liberalism. But closer analysis reveals a measure of realism: if international liberal institutions force continual meetings, it is states that then learn the rationality of moderating their behavior. This is close to Clausewitz's final position, for all that its language – its insistence that the interaction between states is an iterated game – derives from the cutting edge of rational choice theory. Powerful formal debate continues as to the status and validity of this liberal institutionalist position.[69]

This book advocates its own combination, that of the realism/liberalism mix, but its cognitive strategy is idiosyncratic in choosing immersion in the historical record. The purpose of the next three chapters is to confront the ideal types of international order with the creation and workings of the Westphalian system, with the great escalations that ended in 1815 and 1945 and with the period of restraint sandwiched between them, and with the long postwar peace. Considerable effort will be made to ensure that immersion does not lead to drowning of the intellect: the presentation of historical evidence is systematically linked to the ideal types in the conclusions to these chapters, and much highlighting will be given to the realism/liberalism mix. Still, the fact that the intent of the book is to advance theory should not hide fundamental scepticism about the rather formal modeling, so often based on rational choice theory, that dominates contemporary American political science. This is not for a moment to deny the high-powered achievements of that discipline, nor to suggest that there is any single path to knowledge, not least since my own choice of strategy results in largest part from temperament.[70] Still, two reasons for my cognitive strategy should be noted.

First, formal analysis seems to have a tendency to so generalize contemporary circumstances that they come to be taken as if they were the human condition. Keohane has rightly been taken to task along these lines by a critic who notes a narrowness to his

---

[69]   R. Powell, "Anarchy and International Relations," *International Organization*, vol. 48, 1994.
[70]   The reader will discover in the later chapters that I am hugely indebted to the work of David Laitin, a brilliant political scientist making elegant, innovative, and persuasive use of rational choice theory.

appreciation of the larger social surround that brute realism ignores.[71] Keohane's social bonds are generated by rational choice, rather than by historic forces such as Christianity, class solidarity, racism and anti-communism. This is not for a moment to say that the particular arguments made in his book are wrong: the economistic calculative spirit on which he relies does characterize *our* contemporary social world.

An objection to my characterization of American political science can usefully be considered since it will advance the argument. Is not one of the signal virtues of much recent political science its consideration of historical cases of very varied sorts? To be honest, it is at this point that I have the strongest reservation. History is too often sampled once categories have been deductively established. This seems to me true, for example, of some of the historical assertions made in Gowa's exceptionally intelligent recent analysis of trade and alliances.[72] Most particularly, the application of rational choice theory to history can lead analysts to ignore the fragmented nature of many states, and thereby to construct case studies whose seeming plausibility is gained only at the expense of a fundamental loss of reality. In contrast, any open-minded plunge into the historiography of Wilhelmine Germany, whose historical importance is immense, will soon make one realize that it was ruled by a court more than by a state, amongst whose mechanics were both the Kaiser's personality and the deeply odd sexual politics of the time.[73] Accordingly, I am recommending at least a measure of what is currently taken to be the most disreputable of all methodologies: inductive discoveries can result from immersion in history, thereby allowing reality to influence and inform our categories – a stark contrast with current practice which so tidies definitions in advance as thereby actually to obscure empirical material. Realizing that this is utter heresy, I cite on my behalf similar methodo-

---

[71]   A. Wendt, "Anarchy is What States Make of It," *International Organization*, vol. 46, 1992.

[72]   J. Gowa, *Allies, Adversaries and International Trade*, Princeton University Press, Princeton, 1994.

[73]   I. Hull, *The Entourage of Kaiser Wilhelm II, 1888–1918*, Cambridge University Press, Cambridge, 1983; J. G. Rohl, *The Kaiser and His Court*, Cambridge University Press, Cambridge, 1994. For further development of this point see ch. 3.

logical arguments about the benefits of a sense of historical context made by Edward Thompson in his celebrated assault on structuralist Marxism.[74]

A second argument is less contentious. It concerns structure and agency within international relations. One of Popper's arguments against historicism was an insistence that human consciousness makes a difference to social and historical processes.[75] The world is not an object in itself, about which we theorize as if we were creatures in another planet. To the contrary, our theories can have decisive impacts on social events: if the findings of a model of interest rate behavior, for example, become well known and affect social action, then interest rates may begin to perform in previously unpredicted ways. This sort of view probably derives from the tradition of the *Geisteswissenschaften*, that is, from the intellectual tradition asserting that human studies differ systematically from natural science, and it has become something of a staple in modern thought. Accordingly, it appears in the work of Anthony Giddens as the notion of a double hermeneutic: humans seek to understand structures of society, but that process of understanding produces and recreates the structures themselves.[76]

Whilst there is unquestionable truth to this, much exaggeration nonetheless surrounds the notion – itself often more prescriptive than descriptive – of societies being sites of reflexive self-monitoring. For one thing, scepticism should be directed towards the belief that intellectual findings and theories are widely consumed: there is something to be said for Pareto's view that he had no need to worry about publishing his rather repulsive findings since few would read them. More generally, this position encourages that idealism which so plagues the social sciences, that is, the view that ideas make the world go round – and thereby that we can study ourselves rather than fulfill our proper duty of conducting research into actual structures of society.[77]

[74]   E. P. Thompson, *The Poverty of Theory and Other Essays*, Merlin Press, New York, 1978.
[75]   K. R. Popper, *The Poverty of Historicism*, Routledge and Kegan Paul, 1957.
[76]   A. Giddens, *The Constitution of Society*, Polity Press, Cambridge, 1984.
[77]   J. A. Hall, "Ideas and the Social Sciences," in J. Goldstein and R. Keohane, eds, *Ideas and the Social Sciences*, Cornell University Press, Ithaca, 1993.

These crabby comments are introduced to underscore my acceptance of the undoubted fact that in the international arena human agency does matter enormously. It is not enough to examine social forces such as those of capitalism, states, and regimes. For international orders are often the result of conscious strategy. Wars are often ended by treaties whose purpose is that of designing forms of international order. This was most obviously true at the end of the Thirty Years War, in Vienna, and at Versailles. Although the Second World War was not concluded by a peace treaty we do know a good deal about the extensive plans made in the United States between 1943 and 1947 for the postwar world – plans which stand in great contrast, of course, to the lack of thought and perhaps of interest shown after 1989, a second occasion when the end of a great conflict was not marked by a peace treaty. It is important to stress that this emphasis on agency is, so to speak, absolutely concrete. Actors matter quite as much as structure in these circumstances because they are "macro-actors," differing from most of us in having behind them great structural forces.[78] A part of our data must be the ideas of these key strategists.

All this has recently become obvious due to the publication of Kalevi Holsti's powerful *Peace and War*. Holsti is particularly helpful in providing standards of judgement by means of which the quality of a planned international order can be judged. These standards include a mechanism of governance, a measure of legitimacy, and means of deterrence. But more important than all these is the capacity of an order to be sufficiently flexible and open to encompass change, to allow it to deal with issues that will arise rather than those which have just been resolved.[79] At the heart of this analysis is a deeply felt idea: just as the old quip has it that French generals prepare for the last war, so too do peacemakers. The way in which the war is held to have come about accordingly matters for the designs of new international orders. Most architects of international order have paid a good deal of attention, and have sometimes themselves added a good

[78]   N. Mouzelis, *Back to Sociological Theory*, Macmillan, London, 1991.
[79]   Holsti, *Peace and War*, ch. 13.

deal at the theoretical level, to the injunctions of realism. But all
the ideal types of international order discussed have had their
salient moments. The importance of a concert against revolution
was clearly in the mind of Metternich, whilst the notion of a
beneficent hegemon, keen to encourage economic interdependence
under the wings of its geopolitical protection, comprised much
American self-understanding in the mid 1940s.

A final comment is very much in order at this point. Some of
Holsti's best pages deal with the mind of Woodrow Wilson, a
theorist *par excellence*, and it seems that a complex attraction is
present at this point.[80] Holsti's analysis is at one with Wilson's in
arguing that nationalist demands were a fundamental cause of the
First World War.[81] Nationalism is certainly a vital structuring
force of the modern world: it is a fundamental category in Dur-
kheimian terms, that is, one through which we think rather than
about which social scientists have – at least until recently – thought
enough. But welcoming the attention given by Holsti to this force
should not be equivalent to accepting the Wilsonian interpretation
of the causes of the First World War – although, the rather
different causal account that will be offered here does depend upon
giving nationalism its due. Attention must be given equally to the
consequences of Wilson's belief that national self-determination
would lead to peace. It is as well to note immediately that this view
puts Wilson very much at odds with Kant, whose mock treaty had
insisted that borders should not be changed and that no planning
should take place for any future wars, even were they to be
conducted under the aegis of a League of Nations.

AN ELECTIVE AFFINITY

Whilst it is both a fond hope and a considered belief that the
realism/liberalism mix follows from and gains force as the result
of the analytic history to which attention now turns, clarity may

[80]   Holsti, *Peace and War*, ch. 8.
[81]   Holsti, *Peace and War*, ch. 7.

be enhanced by noting something of the abstract logic of this position before the consideration of evidence. As there is truth to the view that the terms of description are not neutral, immediate openness may anyway make sense since an attentive reader will already have intimations of what is to follow.

Given the sense of Hedley Bull's insistence that international order is likely to be a necessary condition for world order, recognition will later be given to the constructive role sometimes played by concerts and hegemonies, but much less so to the principle of interdependence, for all that it may be having some impact in very recent years. Far more sympathy will be shown, as might be expected, for sophisticated realism. The great merit of this position is that it has an awareness that social homogeneity and intelligent states are conditions upon which its proper functioning depend. Nonetheless, the position to be articulated, in part descriptively and wholly prescriptively, goes beyond sophisticated realism in stressing the possibility and necessity of mutual interpenetration between realism and liberalism. A clear basis for rapprochement exists on each side.

Realism cannot be abandoned as long as the world polity remains asocial: states remain vital for protection, whilst their continuing salience in terms of political economy means that a large part of the identity of most human beings is fixed at this level. Still, realism can be informed by liberalism in two ways. States are likely to be rational only when they have the capacity to think clearly, and liberal institutions, both inside and outside states, have helped and can help further towards this end – both by providing room in which to calculate and by providing checks whose greatest benefit is that of improving policy by preventing adventurism. Of course, rational policy formation in the past has not solely been the result of the presence of liberal institutions. Nonetheless, at a prescriptive level this option has gained importance from the fact that the traditional alternative, that of insulating foreign policy making from all societal influence, is being closed down by our democratic era. The struggle to ensure that an increase in popular control and participation will improve foreign policy making is one of the most vital issues of the age: here my stress on the benefits of liberal institutions should not be read as denying the need for an improvement of norms, best achieved by a continual process of dialogue between elite and people – since both are fallible there is much to be said for learning from the other. Secondly, whilst the homogeneity of the system which helps policy makers understand each other is not necessarily based on liberalism, the Kantian idea of liberal normative integration has some descriptive force and is still more powerful in prescriptive terms. If the first of these two points in effect argues that liberalism alone can provide the sociological base for realism, the second goes a little further. The fact that national calculations are less likely to go wrong when international solidaristic sentiments exist is not just to underwrite realism; it is rather to imagine a world in which the necessary salience of realism would begin to diminish as other countries ceased to be objects of suspicion.

These considerations should not be taken to mean that liberalism is flawless, with all the correction that is needed being a one-way affair. A limitation of liberalism already implied is that it tends at times to forget the importance of state power, although this is not true of the sophisticated position of Kant. Philosophical difficulties abound at a deeper level. Those imagining themselves in possession of the truth can all too easily be disastrous makers of policy. The danger of self-righteousness is that it can lead to ruling others out of existence altogether. But the other side of the coin, that of imagining everyone to be like us, can be as dangerous: there was nothing to be said at any time for the belief that Hitler would be satisfied by appeasement. In a nutshell, liberalism has at times been both insufficiently and excessively tolerant; that this is so suggests a clear *caveat*, namely that we should not be too pleased with our purported accomplishments.

The concept of "elective affinity" gained currency in social science from Max Weber, whose sociology of religion suggests a fit between social circumstance and self-image. Weber derived the notion from Goethe's 1809 novel of that name, a novel in which human relations are seen very much in the light of chemical reactions:

> Those natures which, when they meet, quickly lay hold on and mutually affect one another we call affined. This affinity is sufficiently striking in the case of alkalis and acids which, although

they are mutually antithetical, and perhaps precisely because they are so, must decidedly seek and embrace one another, modify one another, and together form a new substance.[82]

This precisely applies here. Liberalism and realism traditionally have been antithetical, but they can and should embrace so as to form a new substance. That substance should be called neither realist liberalism or liberal realism, but the realism/liberalism mix.

[82]   J. W. Goethe, *Elective Affinities*, Penguin, Harmondsworth, 1971, pp. 52–3.

2

The European System

World history has a particular shape. Max Weber's celebrated identification of the pattern of the past was correct: a rather uniform agrarian era gained distinct civilizations thanks to the emergence of the world religions, with one such civilization endogenously pioneering the modern world. Recognition of Weber's achievement in this regard does not entail accepting his particular explanation for the rise of the West.[1] Nor does acknowledgement of this pattern mean that I am committed to any crass European triumphalism.

The argument to be made can usefully be seen as complementing fundamental work by Immanuel Wallerstein.[2] I agree with Wallerstein that a particular political frame made possible the emergence of capitalism in the West, although it seems strange that he continues to consider himself a Marxist having made this argument. But I differ from Wallerstein on another crucial point. The binary opposition between world empire and capitalist world system upon which the whole Wallersteinian *oeuvre* is based will not do. To the contrary, the European polity developed a particular type of state system after the fall of Rome which had thereafter

[1] For a rather different account of the logics of the classical agrarian civilizations, see J. A. Hall, *Powers and Liberties*, Penguin, Harmondsworth, 1986.
[2] I. Wallerstein, *The Modern World System*, Academic Press, New York, 3 vols, 1974–88.

certain powers over capitalism for all that it provided a good shell for the maintenance of this new economic system. The dynamism unleashed by early modern Europe depended upon the logics of (at least) two different sources of power, namely those of economics and politics. It is worth noting that this pattern initially owed most to political competition, given that the level of economic interchange was small, albeit of great importance for state leaders whose revenues depended upon customs and excise. In this whole area, Wallerstein's more economistic view of early modern Europe illegitimately reads back into the past the economic interdependence of a much later world.

IMPERIAL ORDER

The image to the forefront of our minds when we think of empires is that of great strength. This is largely the result of the mental image created by the monuments and records of arbitrariness such empires have left behind; this image was formalized by Wittfogel, whose view of hydraulic empires stressed their total control over their societies.[3] A moment's reflection must make us doubt all this. It is always dangerous to take written records at face value, and this is especially true in pre-industrial empires where the demands of ideology and myth-making are great. We know that such empires could not have been so strong: economically they were made up of separate segments, unless there was water transport, whilst logistical limitations drastically curtailed their military capacities.[4] That most empires were but puny leviathans is nicely confirmed by the behavior of one Roman emperor. He threatened all administrators who prepared or submitted illegal rescripts, but "he openly admitted his impotence by declaring

[3]   K. A. Wittfogel, *Oriental Despotism*, Yale University Press, New Haven, 1957. The Marxist notion of "an asiatic mode of production" has received definitive treatment in B. O'Leary, *The Asiatic Mode of Production*, Blackwell, Oxford, 1989.

[4]   D. W. Engel, *Alexander the Great and the Logistics of the Macedonian Army*, University of California Press, Berkeley, 1978; P. Crone, *Pre-Industrial Societies*, Blackwell, Oxford, 1989.

invalid in advance any special grants in contravention of the law, even if they bore his own signature."[5] Those who have written about empires have tended to stress one or the other of these factors. But in fact both were present: the paradox of empire is that its great strength – its monuments, its arbitrariness, its scorn for human life – is based upon and reflects social weakness. For there are two faces of power.[6] One view of power has always seen it in terms of command, of the ability to get people to do things against their will. But a different view has stressed that power is an enabling means, created by an agreement as to what is to be accomplished. A central tenet of this chapter is that a contrast can be drawn in terms of this dimension between a capstone state, strong in arbitrary power but weak in its ability to penetrate its society, and a more organic state, weaker despotically but with much greater reach into social relations within its territory. I first consider capstone rule – and so, as noted, characterize an ideal type of international order additional to the five already discussed – by analyzing the Chinese case. This makes particular sense in terms of claims already made. For the Chinese empire was based on a bureaucracy manned by meritocrats trained in a statist creed: if this agrarian empire lacks real strength, it is more than likely that all others did so as well. This leads naturally to discussion of the situation in Europe. Whilst the Roman empire had much in common with the Chinese, the capacity of the latter to renew itself was not matched by that of the former. An explanation will accordingly be given of the way in which the fall of Rome contributed to the creation of a European multipolar system.

The sinews of state power lie in taxation. All pre-industrial regimes had to tax through local notables, and China, despite having an historically large bureaucracy, was not different in this respect. Simple figures show the fantastical nature of Wittfogel's thesis of a state exercising "total power" over its society. The first Ming emperor in 1371 sought to have but 5,488 mandarins, and even at the end of the dynasty there were still only about 20,400

---

[5]   A. H. M. Jones, *The Later Roman Empire*, Blackwell, Oxford, 1973, p. 410.
[6]   M. Mann, "The Autonomous Power of the State," *European Journal of Sociology*, vol. 25, 1984. For a critique of this important piece, see J. A. Hall, "Understanding States," in J. A. Hall, ed., *The State*, Routledge, London, 1993.

in the empire as a whole, although there were perhaps another 50,000 minor officials.[7] As a very large number of these were concentrated in Peking, an official in one of the 1,100 local districts might well have managed 500–1,000 square miles with the aid of only three assistants.[8] Of course, the state sought, as did other empires, to gain such autonomy, and the use of eunuchs – supposedly biologically loyal to the state – is one index of this. Importantly, the mandarinate was always jealous of eunuchs, since it was aware that an increase in central power would be at its own expense. When the state was strong, most usually when it had just been founded, decentralizing tendencies were strongly counteracted. Land was shared out, taxes were collected and abuses corrected; at the accession of the Ming, over 100,000 members of the gentry may have been executed. Moreover, individual members of the gentry always had something to fear from the arbitrary exercise of state power; the making of a fortune in state service was best followed by a discreet withdrawal to the country where profits could be enjoyed in peace. But all this was counterbalanced by an inability of the state to go against the gentry class as a whole. Reformer after reformer tried to establish a decent land registry as the basis for a proper taxation system, but all were defeated by landlords' refusal to co-operate.[9] Chinese society thus witnessed a "power stand-off" between state and society, a situation of stalemate which led to the inability to generate a large total sum of societal energy. Accordingly, most social relations were provided in a self-help manner, through local kinship networks. The state was distinctively not capable of providing as basic a social service as that of justice.

---

[7]   R. Huang, *1587*, Yale University Press, New Haven, ch. 1.

[8]   Cf. M. Weber, *The Religion of China*, Free Press, New York, 1964, p. 134.

[9]   Taxes could be avoided in a number of ways. Underassessment by the landed elite habitually hid much from the state. False registration and collusion with local officials served the same purpose: landlords protected their wealth by "giving" it to officials and former officials, who were exempt from tax – and who accumulated fortunes by charging "management fees" in this manner. On these matters, see F. Liang, "The Ten-Part Tax System of the Ming," in E. Sun and J. de Francis, eds, *Chinese Social History*, Octagon Books, New York, 1966; N. Tsumuri, "Rural Control in the Ming Dynasty," in L. Grove and C. Daniel, eds, *State and Society in China*, Tokyo University Press, Tokyo, 1984; and R. Marks, *Rural Revolution in South China*, University of Wisconsin Press, Madison, 1984.

The mechanism of this power stand-off can be seen at work in the cyclical process whereby disintegration was followed by imperial reconstitution. Naturally, each historical case had its peculiarities, but it is nevertheless possible to detect a pattern. A newly established dynasty sought to create a healthy peasant base for both its tax and military potential. To this end seeds were distributed and some attempt made to promote agricultural development, not least through the printing of agricultural handbooks. Yet even without internal or external pressures, the state tended to lose control of society, most obviously since the power of the local gentry allowed them to increase their estates and to avoid taxation. But pressures were in any case usually present. Internally, prosperity led to an expansion of population, by no means discouraged by the gentry, and this eventually caused land hunger and peasant rebellion. Externally, the nomads on the borders found the empire more and more attractive as its prosperity waxed in front of their eyes. There is some scholarly debate as to whether such nomads invaded of their own will, or whether they were forced into such action by mercantilist policies of the state, keen to keep its riches to itself and loath to treat with nomads for whom trade is virtually a necessity. Whatever the case, nomads did not often, as Hollywood representations might suggest, come into empires intent on loot, rape, and destruction. Invaders wished to possess the benefits of civilization, and proved increasingly capable of getting them. For they were often employed as mercenaries by empires in their later days and, as a result, they learned military techniques which, when allied with their inherent military resource of great mobility, made them a formidable force. In these circumstances, the imperial state was forced to increase taxation rates, and it was at this moment that the power stand-off between state and society proved to be important. Many landlords chose to shelter peasants who refused or were unable to pay such increased taxation, and thereby increased their own local power. The combination of feudal-type disintegration and overpopulation led to a constant decrease in the number of taxpaying peasant smallholders. Rodinski cites as one example of this process the census of 754 which showed that there were only 7.6 million taxpayers out of a population of 52.8

million.[10] In such circumstances the state was forced to tax even more heavily where it could, and this in turn fueled peasant unrest. This situation of breakdown and division could, as noted, last for a long time, but a new dynasty was established in the long run, usually in one of two ways. Nomads succeeded in establishing only two dynasties which united all of China, namely those of the Mongols and the Qing, albeit they ruled various segments of northern China on several occasions. Other dynasties resulted from peasant revolt. As peasants found it hard to link their laterally insulated communities successfully, non-local revolts often depended upon the help of *déclassé* mandarins, members of millenarian groups, or discontented gentry. The leaders of such revolts, when they proved successful, eventually co-operated with the gentry and founded a new dynasty which again began the cycle of Chinese history.

These considerations underline weakness in the empire. But this was not the whole story, as we can see by asking why it was that time and time again the empire was restored. The mandarins always remained true to the imperial ideal, preferring to stay away from a dynasty that did not respect the fundamentals of Confucianism. A famous example of this was that of the Mongols who once contemplated turning north China into pasture for their horses. This phase did not last long. The Mongols wished to enjoy the benefits of the settled world and this meant that they had to adapt to and to adopt the imperial form.[11] Any consideration of the rather small numbers of the elite shows that an enormous confidence trick was played on the gentry. They remained loyal to the state, but the paucity of their numbers is evidence that they did not do all that well from it, especially given the great insecurity attached to office holding. This is not, it must be stressed, to resurrect the notion of totalitarian strength on the part of the state. This did not exist, and in most matters and for most of the

---

[10]   W. Rodinski, *The Walled Kingdom*, Fontana, London, 1984, p. 78.

[11]   The social pliability of the Mongols stands in contrast to the inflexibility of nomads in the Arab world once in possession of their own civilization. On this point, see M. Cook and P. Crone, *Hagarism*, Cambridge University Press, Cambridge, 1977 and A. Khazanov, "Muhammad and Jenghiz Khan Compared," *Comparative Studies in Society and History*, vol. 35, 1993.

time the scholar-gentry class could block imperial initiatives, although individuals amongst its number did suffer in one way or another. Still, the state was strong enough to force class relations into a particular pattern. Of course, this pattern was maintained by the acquisition of solid profits, via state service and by cultural indoctrination stressing imperial loyalty; and the latter was much reinforced by the Chinese ideograph, which increased cohesion amongst the elite by making their monopoly of literacy, as is historically rare, firm and immovable. A further part of the explanation may be found in the nature of Chinese culture. The more cosmopolitan world of the Near and Middle East allowed for different ideological options; the centrality of Confucianism in China meant that alternative ideological options were less available. But whatever the exact explanation for elite loyalty, it largely explains the power of the empire to reconstitute itself.

This raises a question interesting in itself and absolutely vital for later comparative purposes. In what ways, if any, did the empire affect the Chinese economy? It is worth remembering in this context that if greater taxation and control of landlord classes was one way in which empires could have counteracted barbarian invasion, another method would have been to increase state revenue by means of an expanding and improving economy. Was that within the state's power? Or should we rather endorse Max Weber's contention that the bureaucracy of pre-industrial empires killed off capitalist developments within their territories?[12]

It is as well to concentrate our attention on the great economic advance of the tenth or eleventh to the fourteenth century. There are obvious indices of economic progress in this period. A striking revolution in water transport occurred, itself a necessary precondition for greater economic interchange. Business and financial organization were equally subjected to radical change, and the commercial spirit penetrated much of society.[13] The government provided a sound copper currency; as a result, where only 4 per cent of taxes had been paid in money in 750, about 50 per cent

[12]   M. Weber, *The Sociology of Agrarian Civilisations*, New Left Books, London, 1978.
[13]   Y. Shiba, *Commerce and Society in Sung China*, University of Michigan Press, Ann Arbor, 1970.

were so paid in 1065.[14] Furthermore, the production of at least 125,000 tons of iron in 1078 meant that China led the world in the production of a very basic commodity. But, in the end, this fabulous start did not lead to any "take-off," and we must ask why this was so.

The first point to note is that the greatest expansion took place during a period of disunity of the empire. The Northern Sung did, supposedly, rule all of China from 960–1127, but even in that period they were faced with the militant nomadic Jurchen who conquered their capital Kaifeng in 1127. After that, the Southern Sung (1127–1269) were always faced with competitors to the north, first Jurchen and then Mongol. The fact of disunity is exceptionally important. It encouraged the Southern Sung to build a navy in order to man all waterways which stood between them and their northern competitors. This construction produced techniques and skills that proved beneficial to the economy as a whole and, most spectacularly so, to the Chinese voyages of discovery of the fourteenth century. Further action of this sort was forced on the Sung by the presence of real competitors. One of the greatest of sinologists, Etienne Balazs, was wont to argue that the market and cities gained autonomy during periods of disunity in Chinese history, and this finding has received support from later research.[15] Elvin notes that the quality of money improved for the simple reason that traders would not return to or trust governments which manipulated the coinage too much for their own ends.[16] The general principle is clear: "Competition between equals, whether the Southern Sung and the Mongols, or the contestants in the Japanese civil wars, or the states of early modern Europe, is an indispensable condition of progress in military technology."[17] There is something like conclusive proof of this point. Much of the interest shown by the Sung in military matters resulted from their nomadic neighbors in fact having the edge over them. Thus

---

[14]   L. J. C. Ma, *Commercial Development and Urban Change in Sung China*, University of Michigan, Ann Arbor, 1971, p. 17.
[15]   E. Balazs, *Chinese Civilization and Bureaucracy*, Yale University Press, New Haven, 1964.
[16]   M. Elvin, *The Pattern of the Chinese Past*, Stanford University Press, Stanford, 1973, ch. 19.
[17]   Elvin, *The Pattern of the Chinese Past*, p. 97.

Mongol use of gunpowder forced the Sung to adopt it as well. Yet once the empire was firmly reunited under the native Ming it proved possible for many decades to downplay gunpowder. The nomads to the north, even when they continued to use gunpowder, could always be defeated by sheer logistical weight; and it was best that gunpowder was controlled since it would all too easily aid in further disunification of the empire. Only an empire, free of rivals of equal status, could afford this sort of policy; in Europe it would have been suicidal.

But once imperial rule was securely re-established by the Ming, market forces began to be controlled. This can be seen clearly in urban affairs: cities lost their autonomy as they again became centers of government. Very little is known about the cause for the collapse of the iron industry of Sung China, but it is plausible, perhaps likely, that imperial interference in pricing policy with an eye to revenue gains undermined this spectacular success story. However, there is sufficient information available to be fairly definite when discussing the collapse of Sung naval power. The navy retained some strength even under the Mongols, but the foundation of a native dynasty with an improved Grand Canal, no longer necessitating ocean-going transport from south to north, led to a series of edicts that undermined its position. Most obviously, between 1371 and 1567 all foreign trade was banned. This is not to say that trade in fact ceased; instead it was organized by "pirates," often of Japanese origin, in conjunction with local gentry who thereby gained considerable profits. But such a ban must have had a great effect; certainly the ban instituted in 1430 against the construction of further ocean-going ships led eventually to technological amnesia. However, the most spectacular way in which politics could affect the economy concerns the fate of the explorations undertaken by the eunuch admiral Zheng-He in the 1430s. As befitted an empire, these expeditions to both the Pacific and Indian oceans were mounted on a large scale. They were, moreover, entirely successful, and they placed China in a position to reap the benefits that were shortly to fall to the Portuguese, Dutch, and British. But the character of politics in China, in this case largely court politics, determined that none of this was to happen. The mandarins were always extremely jealous of the emergence of sources of power alternative to their own: sudden renewed nomadic pressure on the northern frontiers allowed them to argue that resources had to be spent to meet a more immediate problem – a policy change perhaps eased by the fact that eunuch generals had recently led the army to defeat in Annam. In a centralized system relatively minor conflicts and pressures could thus have major effects.

Let us return to Max Weber's dictum that bureaucracy killed off capitalism in the pre-industrial world. Certain reservations must be made about such a blunt formulation. On the one hand, this view tends to underplay economic advance within empires, in particular agricultural advances to which the state did, so far as its limited resources allowed, sometimes contribute. On the other hand, Weber's formulation occasionally gives the impression that the state was all-powerful, and that bureaucratic interference in pre-industrial and industrial societies is somehow of the same character. In fact, Weber was well aware that bureaucracy in pre-industrial societies was puny, and that a stronger state might have been able to foster economic advance. But ultimately Weber's argument gains support from the Chinese case. It is true that there is one undeniably intangible point. The Ming were unusual compared to other empires in history in, as it were, stepping backward by abandoning coinage, and creating a purely natural economy.[18] Had they continued along the path laid down by the Sung, it is possible that greater tax revenues could have enabled them to provide the greater social infrastructure their society needed for economic take-off. Still, there seem to be plenty of factors at work to suggest that the habitual character of imperial politics was exerting its sway.

Such imperial politics deserve the capstone label that I have pinned upon them. The interest of the mandarinate/state lay in preventing horizontal communication of any sort between the series of laterally insulated areas on the top of which it sat. It sought control rather than efficiency. Thus the mandarins undermined the positions of generals, Buddhist monasteries, eunuchs and capitalists because they felt that their power was dependent

[18]   R. Huang, *Taxation and Governmental Finance in Sixteenth-Century Ming China*, Cambridge University Press, Cambridge, 1974, p. 2 and passim.

upon social passivity rather than upon social mobilization. This can be seen particularly clearly by means of Huang's brilliant analysis of Ming taxation. The main task of the administration of the Ming was that of imperial cohesion. To that end, the Ming sought to have taxation paid mostly in kind, and so chose not to provide a sound copper currency. Probably the fundamental reason for this change was political: the Ming did not wish monetary supplies and surpluses to be located at any single point where they could be seized and thus support rebellion. "The empires's fiscal operations were so fragmented as to make them virtually safe from capture, and the mere knowledge of this fact was sometimes sufficient to discourage potential rebels."[19] It is worth remembering that the empire founded by the Ming, and continued by the Qing, lasted from 1371 to 1911, the longest period of uninterrupted imperial rule in history. The capstone system removed alternative bases of power, and there were no successful internal revolts for half a millennium. The Ming and Qing had learnt how to perfect government.

Chinese capstone government blocked the fully-fledged emergence of intensive capitalist relationships, but this is not to say that the impact of the state upon capitalism must always be negative. On the contrary, a different type of state, the European organic state, proved capable, once capitalist relationships were established, of providing crucial services for this type of economic system. It is very noticeable that Chinese capstone government was incapable of providing equivalent services. The fixing of once-and-for-all equal tax revenues at the beginning of the dynasty proved to be a terrible mistake, especially given that the administration was initially conceived on such a small scale. The administration was underfinanced, and thus too weak to take advantage of such expansion of the population as took place. A strong peasantry could only have been assured had the state been powerful enough to establish decent currency and credit arrangements, instead of allowing the peasantry to be exploited at the will of moneylenders and gentry; the dynastic cycle resulted in part because the state taxed too little rather than too much.

[19]   Huang, *Taxation and Governmental Finance*, p. 321.

Businessmen were not given legal protection, and this together with the attraction of office and land, led to a decrease in business involvement.[20] The weakness of the government is beautifully caught in a dilemma in which they found themselves when administering the salt monopoly. Quotas for salt had initially been set without an eye to expanding consumption, and the government simply had no machinery by means of which it could itself increase production, even though thereby it would have made substantial profits. Merchants did start new production, and they were soon able to undercut government-produced salt. When government revenue fell, the state decided to clamp down on private production, even though this caused widespread hardship.[21]

TRAHISON DES CLERCS

Rome's system of rule had much in common with that of China. Both empires were created by conquest, as their extant great walls indicate, thereby demonstrating that militarism can be productive.[22] More important, the spirit of capstone rule was as present in Rome as in China. A particularly revealing story in this connection concerns a reply sent from Rome to an inquiry from Trajan when governor of Palestine as to whether a local association of firemen could be established. The answer was firmly negative: any independent organization outside official channels could be turned to other uses. It was accordingly better not to mobilize, at the price of sterility, than to risk losing control. Such capstone logic helps explain why the state felt so suspicious of early Christianity: it represented just the sort of non-official, horizontal communication channel which it distrusted.[23] Nonetheless, after much struggle between the state and the Christians led

---

[20]   Huang, *Taxation and Governmental Finance*, pp. 318–19.
[21]   Huang, *Taxation and Governmental Finance*, ch. 5.
[22]   M. Mann, "States, Ancient and Modern," *European Journal of Sociology*, vol. 18, 1977.
[23]   M. Mann, *Sources of Social Power*, Cambridge University Press, Cambridge, vol. 1, 1986, ch. 10.

to stalemate, an attempt was made to join forces. If Rome could not suppress its Christians as China had its Buddhists, might it not at least turn them into the ideologists of the empire? In fact, matters did not turn out like this, and our first task must be that of examining how both sides fared in the new relationship.

The church gained enormously from détente. It became extremely rich. More importantly, its very form of organization, the hierarchy of bishop, deacon, and presbyter, was modeled on that of the Roman state. The church also called upon the state to help it fight its battles. Throughout the fourth century the church pushed the state towards a position increasingly hostile to traditional paganism, even though such paganism was especially strong amongst the traditional landed and Roman aristocracy. Augustine had no compunction whatever in using the secular arm to hunt out those he considered to be heretics; Christian persecution, designed to establish a single church organization, rapidly took the place of the earlier persecution visited on Christians.

But what of the state? How well did it do from the bargain? The surprising and interesting answer to this is that it did very poorly indeed out of the deal, and that it is proper to talk only of an attempted takeover of the church, since that attempt in fact failed. One imagines that Constantine himself might have had some disquiet by the end of his reign. In the course of the two decades after the adoption of Christianity he found himself in a hornets' nest of controversy. Donatism in North Africa asserted that those who had apostatized during the persecutions should not be accepted as leaders of the church. Constantine also found himself deeply involved in the long-running squabble between Arius and Athanasius as to whether Christianity was to be rigidly monotheist or not. But are these matters not theological in another sense entirely, that is, trivial and unimportant to most Christians? Even more important, did not the empire slowly begin to gain loyalty from the church? Certainly Eusebius of Caesarea positively welcomed his role as creator of a sort of Caesaropapist doctrine centered on Constantine, and it seems that some Western bishops were also rallying to the empire. Augustine after all fiercely attacked the Donatists, and did so with some success.[24] Yet we

24   P. Brown, *Saint Augustine*, Faber, London, 1967.

must note the arguments Augustine used against the Donatists. He accused them of lacking imagination in wishing to be a sect, an anti-society. He was quite as puritanical as they were, but insisted that a much greater historical opportunity lay in front of them: the church could become society rather than merely constituting an opposition to it. So if the church integrated people into society, that society was Christian rather than Roman. Still more strikingly, *The City of God*, perhaps the single most important theological work in medieval Christendom, famously argued that God's kingdom could not be associated with the destiny of Rome: God's timetable was his own, and should not be conflated with the destiny of Rome. This was a remarkable, indeed foolhardy, judgement given that at the time the basic infrastructure of the church, namely literacy, was not yet provided by the church but was the general product of Roman civilization.

In the West the church moved from ingratitude to, and scorn of, the state to a realization that it could in fact do without it.[25] It was the church which negotiated with the barbarians at the walls of most cities, and arranged for them to be saved rather than destroyed. Where Chinese intellectuals refused to serve barbarians until they accepted the imperial form, and thus put themselves on the road to assimilation, in Western Christendom exactly the opposite was the case. The elite broke ranks. The intellectuals went out to the barbarians and provided services for them as well as the promise of universal salvation. For the chiefs of tribes, the church, as the bearer of literacy, proved invaluable in allowing legal codification. Thus Gregory the Great's mission to England landed in 597, and by 616 more than 90 laws had been written down. Much the same story could be told of the codification provided for the Lombards and the Franks. But underlying all this is something much simpler. The church wore the mantle of Rome: it was civilization and the hope of a better life.[26] Europe did not revert to localism, but retained unity.

[25]   The East was different, perhaps because the emperor had come to spend so much more time there – which perhaps resulted in the fact that the empire did survive, as Byzantium.
[26]   P. Anderson, *Passages from Antiquity to Feudalism*, New Left Books, London, 1973, pp. 128–44.

So the City of God came to be dissociated from the imperial structure due to the most striking of all betrayals by intellectuals. In China and Rome, a large geographical space was chained together by political/military means. But in Christian Europe cultural identity was more extensive than the political order. Latin Christendom held together an extensive space until approximately 1100. The church served, in Thomas Hobbes's phrase, as "the ghost of the Holy Roman Empire." Ideology at this time did not reflect so much as create society: the church provided norms, and, through the declaration of "Peaces of God," managed to limit violence as well.

Durkheim's most famous notion, that consensus must underlie contract, helps us understand the economic importance of the Christian *ecumene*. The commonplace view of historians of the medieval economy of Europe is that what was once considered a "dark age" in fact witnessed fundamental advance, seen in the widespread use of the heavy plough on clay soils and massive investment in watermills; progress seems to have been possible precisely in those years when Europe was held together culturally but not, in the fullest sense of the word, governmentally.[27] The extensive area of Latin Christendom created a market, and helped the restoration of trade. Further, the egalitarian nature of Christian belief, so much in contrast to classical Hinduism, perhaps proved to be an energizing force. Crucially, the fact that the Christian church was not a full-blooded government meant that property relations were especially secure. Given the absence of chances for social mobility within a state, medieval lords and richer peasants had to look to their land for increased income. This was an acephalous society in which power was not in any single set of hands.

That last statement is slightly incautious. Surely, it might be objected, the church eventually developed a political theory, and did seek to establish a real imperial papacy? By the middle of the eleventh century a reforming spirit originating in Cluny swept the church, and created a drive for power seen most clearly in the

[27]   G. Duby, *The Early Growth of the European Economy*, Weidenfeld and Nicolson, London, 1974; C. Cipolla, *Before the Industrial Revolution*, Methuen, London, 1976; M. M. Postan, *Medieval Economy and Society*, Penguin, Harmondsworth, 1975.

papacy under Gregory VII, Innocent III, and Boniface VIII, that is, between approximately 1050 and 1300. In this period the papacy had, to oversimplify somewhat, certain doubts as to the wisdom of the crowning of Charlemagne as Holy Roman Emperor in 800, and it sought to qualify this. Most dramatically, the papacy humiliated the Emperor Henry IV who famously had to ask penance of the pope at Canossa. The origin of this argument between pope and emperor was over the right to grant clerical appointments. Formally the pope won, and it was such victories which help account for the creation of the papal governmental and juridical machine at this period. The church grew ever richer and more powerful. Yet did it manage to establish a new primacy sufficient to give it something like an imperial status? The answer to this question must be negative. The papacy never possessed its own army, whilst the various kings of Europe very plainly did. Thus it was never able to establish a priestly imperial structure.

But if the drive to an imperial papacy was defeated as much by the presence of diverse states as by anything else, how did those states come into being in the first place? The church did most to make empire impossible. It refused to serve as second fiddle in an empire equivalent to those of China and Byzantium, and thus did not create a Caesaropapist doctrine in which a single emperor was elevated to semi-divine status. Very much to the contrary, the church's habitual playing of power politics encouraged the formation of separate states whose autonomy eventually led to the failure of its own imperial drive. This whole process was symbolized in 1312 when the Emperor Henry VII asked the pope to send Robert of Sicily, the pope's vassal, to the imperial court at Pisa. Clement V issued the bull *Pastoralis Curia* in which he argued that a king owed no duties to the emperor, and was instead master in his own realm. And this was not the only way in which Christianity provided the best shell for the emergence of states. The church provided such numinous aspects of kingship as the coronation and the singing of the *Laudes regiae* which made a king more than one amongst equals. Even more important was its attack on extended kinship systems.[28] In other

[28]   J. Goody, *The development of the family and marriage in Europe*, Cambridge University Press, Cambridge, 1983.

civilizations the lower classes could often rely upon kinship systems as a means of protection and mutual aid – and in Islam as a resource for mobilization against the state. The removal of this weapon made the European peasant that much better fodder for state formation.

MURKY WATERS

The emergence of the European state system has traditionally been seen, especially by international relations experts, in very simplistic terms. Special place is habitually given to the Peace of Westphalia of 1648.[29] The treaties of Osnabrück and Münster, between Protestant and Catholic parties respectively, which comprise that peace are held to have ended the hierarchical and extensive world of the papacy and the Holy Roman Empire and to have introduced a world of competing sovereign states.

History is rarely neat and tidy, and the creation of the European system rests on particularly murky waters. Most obviously, the extensive powers of the church had long been in disarray as the result of the slow emergence of states whose importance, as we have seen, had in fact been encouraged by the Latin Christian church. One way in which the lack of extensive powers of religion is most strikingly demonstrated is by the fact that the Reformation, together with the subsequent century of religious wars, made not a jot of difference to Europe's map. States chose one or the other side, but they were neither created nor destroyed by religion – much in the way that the Ayatollah Khomeini's Iran found that Shi'ism was not a genuinely transnational force capable of hollowing out the Iraqi state. Further, the late fifteenth and early sixteenth centuries clearly witness practices usually held to be

---

[29]   The classical statement is L. Gross, "The Peace of Westphalia, 1648–1948," *American Journal of International Law*, vol. 53, 1959. J. Mayall's fine *Nationalism and International Society* (Cambridge University Press, Cambridge, 1990, ch. 2) is very representative of contemporary international relations in regarding Gross's statement as canonical. For a powerful revisionist critique, see S. Krasner, "Westphalia and All That," in J. Goldstein and R. Keohane, eds, *Ideas and Foreign Policy*, Cornell University Press, Ithaca, 1993.

associated with Westphalia. Thus, diplomacy is first established in northern Italy in the fifteenth century: its practices, notably freedom of worship for diplomatic staff, rapidly spread throughout Europe.[30] More obviously and importantly, Francis I's alliance with the Turks in order to counter the hegemonic thrust of Charles V is the purest example of balance of power politics imaginable. More subtly, it slowly began to become apparent that states based on national territories had the greater chance of increasing power.[31] If the collapse of non-territorial Burgundy in 1477 was a first sign that the future would eventually belong to national states, the inability of the city states of northern Italy after 1492 to continue their practice of purchasing the leading edge of armed might was a still more powerful indicator of fundamental change. Many more ought to have been able to recognize the writing on the wall from 1555, the year in which a first round of inter-state conflict mixing dynastic rivalries with religious loyalties was ended at the Peace of Augsburg. For that peace enshrined the notion of *cuius regio, eius religio*, that is, the notion that a country would adopt the religion chosen by its prince.

Before returning to an assessment of Westphalia something must first be said about the fact that war became slowly but surely more lethal after the fifteenth century. Three particular conditions need to be borne in mind. The first and foremost factor must be the ever-increasing tempo of the European arms race. This mechanism was at work in Europe roughly from 1200 when the multi-state character of Europe began to crystallize. Throughout the middle ages there was a breeding race to provide heavier, more effective cavalry, and other great changes were associated with the rise of bowmen and pikemen. Nonetheless, while many of the most famous wars of the late middle ages had ravaged particular areas, they had in effect been conducted by large bands, as prone to disintegrate as to congregate for battles in an orderly and systematic manner. But the widespread use of gunpowder in the fifteenth century vastly increased the cost of war, both because

[30]   G. Mattingly, *Renaissance Diplomacy*, Dover, New York, 1988.
[31]   H. Spruyt, *The Sovereign State and Its Competitors*, Princeton University Press, Princeton, 1994.

cities required Italian defences and because armies needed to stay much longer in the field in order to conduct successful sieges. Still more important, however, was the military revolution of the late sixteenth and early seventeenth centuries.[32] This entailed greater training of far more troops so that they could perform as serried blocks on battlefields.

Secondly, it is indeed the case that wars were given an edge because of the superimposition of religious upon dynastic conflict. The intensity of the conflict of these years resulted from the breakdown of social homogeneity. The Habsburgs wanted to establish a universal monarchy for the Counter-Reformation, and their opponents in the Thirty Years War understood this. Gustavus Adolphus might have been worried about the security of his Baltic possessions, but there can be no doubt of his genuine Protestant piety.

Thirdly, the level of violence was especially high, in most of the early modern period, because states were so weak – or, in an alternative formulation, because key aristocratic subjects were so powerful.[33] Such aristocrats were still part of a transnational European society. Accordingly, they had no vital loyalty to their particular state, and were prepared to call in outside powers against it. The Guises had no compunction in calling on Spain to protect their Catholicism. Most spectacular of all, in this connection, was the career of Wallenstein. This great military pioneer began by fighting for the Catholic cause but rapidly became an independent agent. In a sense, this move was forced upon him: the failure of the weak state that employed him to serve as a reliable paymaster meant that he learnt to raise supplies from taxing territories which he controlled. Within a very few years, he was contemplating building himself a kingdom in Central Europe – a splendid testimony to which is the Wallenstein Palace and Gardens, still extant in Prague.

The consequence of these conditions was the Thirty Years War. This was a European-wide war, riddled with complexity: France

[32] J. Roberts, "The Military Revolution, 1560–1660," in his *Essays in Swedish History*, Weidenfeld and Nicolson, London, 1969. Cf. G. Parker, *The Military Revolution*, Cambridge University Press, Cambridge, 1988.
[33] D. Kaiser, *Politics and War*, Harvard University Press, Cambridge, MA, 1990, part 1.

fought with Sweden against Habsburg hegemony without having any loyalty to Protestantism, Sweden sought to extend its Baltic possessions, the Electors of the Holy Roman Empire wished to secure their privileges – whilst key military entrepreneurs changed sides on more than one occasion. The war was so extraordinarily brutal that the population of Central Europe may well have been halved, through malnutrition, the deliberate slaughter of civilians, and emigration.[34] Absolute exhaustion eventually made peace talks necessary.

The meetings that led to the Peace of Westphalia had as their principal business the entirely traditional one of rearranging territory in such a way as to make any future Habsburg bid for universal monarchy more difficult.[35] But the two sets of meetings were novel in that a deliberate attempt was being made to deal with horror. This is not to say that the participants were great philosophers with ideas of such cogency that political history thereafter ran along new lines. In fact, their thought can helpfully be seen as looking two ways. They did indeed stress the importance of sovereignty: states were held to rule over particular territories, within whose borders they could do as they wished without occasioning intervention. If this was to codify the pre-existing fact that the hierarchy and extensiveness of papacy and Holy Roman Empire had long gone, to reiterate that religion was a matter internal to states, this should not be interpreted as saying that they conceived of everything in modern terms. The Holy Roman Empire was in effect given a new lease of life. The Imperial Knights, to give a single example, survived, and were only territorialized as the result of Napoleon's later incursions. More generally and importantly, the national state, let alone the nation-state, did not even at this late stage have any sudden and uniform triumph. Eighteenth-century Europe sees several composite monarchies in existence, not least that of George, the Elector of Hanover who was also King of England.[36] There was still a long

---

[34]   G. Parker, *The Thirty Years War*, Routledge and Kegan Paul, London, 1984.
[35]   Holsti, *Peace and War*, ch. 2.
[36]   The notion of composite monarchies is drawn from H. G. Koenigsberger, *Estates and Revolutions*, Cornell University Press, Ithaca, 1971. Cf. J. H. Elliott, "A Europe of Composite Monarchies," *Past and Present*, no. 137, 1992.

way to go before the 500 units of sovereignty extant in Europe in 1500 dropped to the 25 present in 1975.[37]

Nonetheless, Westphalia does mark a watershed. One relevant point to note is that new ideas did emerge as the result of the long crisis of the seventeenth century. There was a certain ideological benefit to stalemate, to the discovery that neither side could dominate the other.[38] In the late seventeenth century a series of thinkers, not least John Locke, began to develop the concept of toleration, thereafter a major, self-conscious element of European civil society. But if new ideas mattered, still more fundamental was a substantial change in state organization which made real the notions of sovereignty within the Westphalian package. The change in question is that growth of state powers which meant that the means of violence could finally be territorially controlled. Wallenstein was the last of his breed. State revenues throughout Europe grew at the end of the seventeenth century, and this allowed for the creation of standing armies – whose existence is the single main characteristic of absolutism, the key political change on the European continent at this time.

The more measured system of inter-state competition that characterised the European scene from 1648 rested upon states finally making real their claim to monopolize violence. This is not to say that there were fewer wars in this period. Plenty of reasons to fight remained, not to mention conflicts occasioned by lack of skill in calculation. Dynastic claims remained a potent source of conflict, and the British certainly felt that Louis XIV's bid for hegemony threatened their religious independence. Moreover, the desire to round out meaningful territorial boundaries was a continuing source of conflict, and there were new struggles over colonial possessions.[39] Nonetheless, war itself was relatively measured, a distinct means, as Clausewitz was soon to put it, for the realization of political goals, rather than a pure end in its own right. Battle deaths dropped, civilities increased. Most important of all, it is in this period that it is possible to detect the balance of

[37]   C. Tilly, *Coercion, Capital and European States*, A.D. *990–1990*, Blackwell, Oxford, 1990.
[38]   E. Gellner, *Conditions of Liberty*, Hamish Hamilton, London, 1994.
[39]   K. J. Holsti, *Peace and War*.

power working in something like its purest form. Balancing had of course gone on beforehand, but habitually in an instinctive form. In this period, balancing became an art and an aim in itself rather than the result of a naturalistic mechanism, the matter of prudential wisdom outlined by Hume in his celebrated 1752 essay on the subject.[40] Perhaps its greatest moment was seen in the diplomatic revolution of 1756: Britain drops its alliance with Austria in favour of Prussia, whilst France abandons Prussia to ally itself with Austria. The beautiful symmetry of this reflects the fact that this takes place within an international society sharing realist norms: no state is blamed for realignments. More importantly, the realignment makes sense in terms of balance of power theory: Prussia ought to have switched alliances because Austria was weakening at the time that the strength and threat of France was increasing.[41] At this moment the combination of rational states and upper-class solidarity gave Europe an international order whose moderation was admired by contemporaries as much as it has been by later realist scholars.

COUNTERING EUROCENTRISM

To leave things at this point, that is, at mere description of the European multipolar polity, would be a mistake. For the points made need to be drawn together so that Europe's fundamental dynamism can be properly highlighted. Here we enter perilous territory, for evaluation and description, perhaps properly, have become utterly conjoined in the discussion of the origins and nature of European power. Consider the very word "dynamism" – or such different formulations as "the rise of the West" and "the European miracle." Such expressions habitually encode a bias in favour of development. But to change may well be less a sign of maturity than of delinquency. The theory of social

---

[40]   D. Hume, "Of the Balance of Power," in *Essays: Moral, Political, and Literary*, Liberty Classics, Indianapolis, 1985.
[41]   M. Doyle, "The Classical Balance of Power Theory," lecture given at McGill University in 1992.

evolution properly understood stresses that normality consists in adapting to circumstances, with change most likely to come from the ill-adapted, so unstable that they occasionally invent something new. This general view should underlie any account of the rise of the West: a failure to adapt, to create a high civilization as patterned and successful as those of the Orient, led to the creation of a new form of society whose power proved to be so great that world history since has consisted in trying either to adopt it or adapt to it.[42] Putting matters in this way allows for the fact of evolution to be retained whilst divesting it of moral connotations. This uncoupling is a precondition for reflection on the much debated question of the moral status of the power achieved by the West. But before comments on that difficult matter are offered it is first necessary to spell out the sociology of European exceptionalism.

To begin with, it is worth reiterating the key argument made, namely that the most obvious fact about a state system is that it leads to a high degree of emulation. This can be seen in European history most spectacularly in the history of art. The invasion of Italy by the French in 1492 spread the styles of the Italian Renaissance around Europe, and thereafter rivalry and status-seeking ensured that what was fashionable in one area had to be copied at home. In fact, this emulation was not at all confined to artistic matters. The fundamental mechanism at work was that of military competition. A revolution in military technology had to be adopted very quickly by neighboring states, on pain of dismemberment – something which notoriously happened to the Polish state at the end of the eighteenth century. Such new technologies had to be paid for, and no state could afford to ignore economic practices which could be translated into military advantage.

These considerations suggest a prior question. Why was capitalism able to triumph in north-west Europe? Bearing in mind the history of China, the importance of European multipolarity becomes obvious. Imagine what European history might have been like had the Roman empire somehow been reconstituted, or had any imperial form taken its place! Pre-industrial empires were

[42]   Crone, *Pre-Industrial Societies*, ch. 8.

too centralized for their logistical capacity, and thus produced capstone government based on their appreciation that secondary organizations were dangerous. Empires usually sought to encourage the economy, but never gave the economy sufficient leeway for it to gather self-sustaining momentum. Why should an imperial Europe have been any different? As it was, a decentralized market system came into place between 800 and 1000 when there was no state which could interfere with its workings, but an organization which nevertheless gave people a sense of belonging to a single civilization. A re-established imperial form would very probably have sought to control such "natural" processes; but no such restoration ever took place, meaning that no single center was thereafter able to control capitalism – whose reach has always been more extensive than that of any single state. The point is perhaps best illustrated by a consideration of the European city. Historians think Max Weber correct in the more materialist part of the theory concerning the rise of the West, namely in his contention that only in Europe did the city gain full autonomy. It invented a new civilization, that of the Renaissance, whose political theory contributed vitally to the rest of European history; it provided a space in which the merchant was king and in which bourgeois values could jell and solidify.[43] Specifically, north Italian cities gained their autonomy as the result of a power vacuum between pope and emperor, such that they were able, as is often the case in Third World countries today, to get the best for themselves by opportunistically chopping and changing their allegiance.[44] How much they owed to their freedom from interference is simply seen: once they become part of the Spanish mini-empire they contributed virtually nothing new to European civilization. And there is a further way in which multipolarity proved beneficial for economic growth. A state system always has an in-built escape system. This is most obviously true in human matters. The expulsion of the Jews from Spain and the Huguenots from France benefited, and was seen to benefit, other countries,

[43]   J. Baechler, *The Origins of Capitalism*, Blackwell, Oxford, 1975.
[44]   This point, derived from Jacob Burckhardt, is made striking in P. Burke, "City States," in J. A. Hall, ed., *States in History*, Blackwell, Oxford, 1986. Cf. W. Blockmans, "Voracious States and Obstructing Cities," *Theory and Society*, vol. 18, 1989.

and this served in the long run as a limitation on arbitrary government. Capital was equally mobile. Thus Philip II's abuse of Antwerp led within a matter of years rather than decades to the rise of Amsterdam. In a brilliant passage making this point, W. H. McNeill has shown that time and again Philip II wanted to behave like an autocrat but the mobility of capital and capitalists sapped his ambition.[45] This was particularly true of his relationship with Liège, the foremost cannon producer of late sixteenth-century Europe. When Philip pressed too hard, artisans and capitalists simply upped and left. Contemporary theorists such as Kant and Gibbon realized that a certain measure of decent and regularized behavior was ensured by these means.

Now a moment's thought makes it clear that the absence of empire cannot in itself explain the triumph of capitalism. For both India and classical Islam had cultures which were usually more extensive than their polities: differently put, for all their periods of imperial rule, these civilizations often witnessed struggles between competing states. However, those states tended to have very shallow roots in society. In the case of Islam, tribal dissidence limited state power, whilst states in India were enfeebled by the caste system.[46] Both types of state were unable to provide much social infrastructure, whilst their tendency to be short-lived made them very likely to be exceedingly predatory. Some of these states were consciously opposed to capitalist developments, but it was their inability to provide basic protection that made capital something to hoard rather than to invest. However, it should be firmly stressed that the central thrust of these civilizations was not, as it was in the Occident, towards endless expansion and development. The point being made is accordingly more limited: had capitalist developments occurred in these civilizations, their political forms would likely have curtailed the dynamism inherent in capitalism.

European states are in striking contrast in being long-lasting and restrained, and thereby homes to capitalism. This gives us the clue to the distinctiveness of the European state: a limit to

---

[45] W. H. McNeill, *The Pursuit of Power*, Blackwell, Oxford, 1982, ch. 1.

[46] Hall, *Powers and Liberties*, chs 3 and 4.

arbitrariness combined with, indeed in part caused, considerable and ever-increasing infrastructural penetration. The European state evolved slowly and doggedly in the midst of a pre-existing civil society. It was no capstone or predatory organization in large part because it was not a conquest state. Rather its history is typified by the cautious policy whereby, for example, the king of France was slowly able to expand from his own domains in the Ile-de-France and gradually to build a bureaucratic state able to dominate the larger region we know today as France. That this process took a very long time is particularly clear in the linguistic field: although the French language had become dominant by the early modern period – through noble accession to a medium that gave advantage in law-suits as much as by sheer coercion – it took the French Revolution to extend it and conscription at the end of the nineteenth century to ensure its final triumph amongst the peasantry and over previously distinctive regions.[47]

All of this can be put in a different way. One other uniqueness of the West is the role that parliaments played in its history: indeed so unique has this role been that German historians have considered the *Standestaat*, the representation of the three functional estates, church, noble, and burgher, to be a particular stage in world history.[48] It is quite clear that the prominence of such assemblies owes a great deal to the church. Since it owned so much land, it was as jealous as any noble of the powers of the crown to tax. Hence it generalized two tags of canon law – "no taxation without representation" and "what touches all, must be approved by all" – and these became crucial to these estates. Strong organization of society came before the state: the ruler's only way of gaining money – so needed for warfare – was to co-operate with what was so firmly entrenched. The paradox of this situation is that restraint on government in the end generated a larger sum of power in society. Perhaps the most important mechanism in the process was the king's decision to make money by providing a certain infrastructure to the society. This is most

[47]   R. Balibar and D. Laporte, *Le Français national*, Hachette, Paris, 1974; E. Weber, *Peasants into Frenchmen*, Stanford University Press, Stanford, 1976.
[48]   A. R. Myers, *Parliaments and Estates in Europe to 1789*, Thames and Hudson, London, 1975.

clearly seen in the field of justice. The lawyer has a very central place in European society, and it results from the king's desire to gain profits from justice. Fees were charged for every legal transaction, and these came to provide an important part of the revenue of most monarchs after about 1200. This is not of course to say that the law was equally open for all to use; but it was present. Increasingly European states provided other sorts of infrastructural help. They became good at managing disasters of various sorts; by the eighteenth century, for example, considerable help was available to the victims of earthquakes, whilst disease was quite rigidly controlled by quarantine laws.[49]

The organic quality of the European state arose from its having to accept and co-operate with other elements in civil society. Why was it, however, that the more powerful European state did not turn inwards in order to establish something more like an imperial system? Roughly speaking, European absolutism represents just such a move, and it is important to stress how unsuccessful it was. It is conventional to compare absolutist France with constitutional Britain in order to give the impression of greater strength in the former case. This is mistaken, since British society generated more power without an absolutist façade; it proved this in defeating France in war on every occasion bar one in which they met in the eighteenth century.[50] This returns us to the question of competition. No state could afford to go it alone without risking defeat. It is hugely significant that by the middle of the eighteenth century France was sending its intellectuals to England, and was in other ways trying to copy her secrets. All this suggests that there must be a prime mover amongst the states in order to get competition to work in the first place. In fact, there were several prime movers in European history, the torch of progress being passed from Italy, to Holland and to Britain. The latter played a highly significant

[49] E. L. Jones, *The European Miracle*, Cambridge University Press, Cambridge, 1981, ch. 7.

[50] British success of course rested on its greater powers of fiscal extraction, on which see P. O'Brien and P. Mathias, "Taxation in Britain and France, 1715–1810," *Journal of European Economic History*, vol. 5, 1976 and P. O'Brien, "The Political Economy of British Taxation, 1660–1815," *Economic History Review*, vol. 41, 1988. The best fiscal sociology of early modern Europe is now R. Bonney, ed., *Economic Systems and State Finance*, Oxford University Press, Oxford, 1995.

part as such a torch-bearer, and it seems no accident that this state possessed a powerful and, crucially, centralized estates system which insisted on the state remaining organic during the absolutist period.[51] Britain managed both to build state machinery that could increase rates of fiscal extraction and to benefit from the revenues that came from an expanding economy.[52] It is important to stress this since the reaction to the discovery that imperial strength hides feet of clay has been to say that the European state was always more powerful.[53] Put like this the statement is misleading. Power operates on two dimensions and the real contrast is between arbitrary capstone government generating little power and civil society/organic government generating a great deal.

Let us turn finally from neutral, aseptic description of European exceptionalism towards moral assessment. Two negative points about European power need to be made to begin with so that they can thereafter stand in conjunction with two positive considerations. The precise balance to be struck between these factors can be left to the reader.

The balance of power that triumphed after Westphalia depended not just on the calculating abilities and skills of statesmen within a shared social world, but also on key agrarian baselines which limited developments, both economic and military. Within this homogeneous and relatively static social world, there is something to be said for outright contradiction of the famous thesis of John Nef, that is, there is definite sense in arguing that state competition positively aided human progress.[54] In the eighteenth century, socio-economic change began to place this achievement in doubt. Most obviously, the commercial breakthrough described by Adam Smith's *Wealth of Nations* came to

[51]   J. Brewer, *The Sinews of War*, Alfred Knopf, New York, 1989. For a brilliant geopolitically based, comparative account of the roots of democracy and autocracy in Europe see B. Downing, *The Military Revolution and Political Change*, Princeton University Press, Princeton, 1992.
[52]   C. Tilly, *Coercion, Capital and European States, A.D. 990–1990*, Blackwell, Oxford, 1990.
[53]   B. Turner, *For Weber*, Routledge and Kegan Paul, London, 1981.
[54]   J. U. Nef, *War and Human Progress*, Harvard University Press, Cambridge, MA, 1950.

characterize the highly specialized and urbanized world of Great Britain, lending it huge power advantages since taxation rates were made high not just thanks to political arrangement but also as a result of the greater ease of taxing movables.[55] These commercial developments were in fact harder to copy than the industrial revolution which soon followed, for all that particular sectors in other countries had similar characteristics. Still, what mattered was that these developments put France under such pressure that its state broke down, thereby allowing a revolutionary party to come to the fore. That revolution itself occasioned an escalation in warfare to the extremes. The nineteenth century witnessed, of course, the spread of an equally disturbing social force, that of industrialism, which in turn increased the destructive powers of war. A foretaste of industrialized mass military mobilization war was provided by civil war in the United States. As it happens, the lesson to be drawn from that war, that there was a need to subject war to greater control, was not learnt, and Europe created its own mass killing fields in 1914 – the effects of which were so socially destabilizing that they did much to occasion a second world war after a mere two decades. If the details of these developments can be left to the next chapter, a general moral point can be firmly made immediately. A social portfolio that produced progress in one set of circumstances could lead to disaster in another: instability was all very well within the limits of agrarian life and professionalized war, but it proved to be an altogether different matter in changed circumstances. Competition between states within a larger cultural frame brought Europe dynamism and development – but destruction too.

A second negative moral reflection comes from realizing the huge increase in power that came to the Western world as the result of capitalism.[56] One way of highlighting the change is to note the eighteenth-century revolution in political theory. The

[55]   E. A. Wrigley, "Urban Growth and Agricultural Change," in R. I. Rotberg and T. K. Rabb, eds, *Population and Economy*, Cambridge University Press, Cambridge, 1986.
[56]   P. Bairoch, "International Industrialisation Levels from 1750–1980," *Journal of European Economic History*, vol. 11, 1982 shows that European economies came to completely dominate the world fully only in the nineteenth century, as the result of demographic growth and industrialization. But before that time European state competition had pioneered military techniques that allowed for dominance overseas.

central paradigm of much Western political theory to that point had taken for granted that history moved in cycles, with the corruption endemic to urban, commercial, and civilized life sure eventually to lead to the fall of every great state. A key element in this viewpoint, derived from the presuppositions of Greek thought, was that virtue was derived from simplicity, whether of an independent peasantry or of barbarians whose harsh existence bred in them military virtues. Enlightenment figures such as Montesquieu, Gibbon, Smith, and Hume abandoned the tradition of republican civic virtue, preferring instead to celebrate a world of wealth.[57] One fundamental reason for their confidence was military. Gibbon's "General Observations on the Fall of the Roman Empire in the West" made it particularly clear that the everlasting cycle of decline and fall had now been broken: the wealth of commercial societies meant that they could defeat barbarian nations, however strong their military virtue.[58]

It is no longer possible, given the benefits of hindsight, to be complacent about this development. For the consequence of the intensification of power resources within Europe was domination of the rest of the world. If the European incursion into the Americas and Asia had initially been small and for purposes of trade, it soon became an altogether more powerful force. Settler society in North America established a completely new social world; equally, the Battle of Plassey in 1757 marks the moment at which Europeans in Asia moved from trade to the acquisition of territorial empire. By the end of the eighteenth century, only Japan and China remained free from interference – but, as we know, only for a short time. European domination rested on two intertwined forces. Early European trade had often, despite the extortion of protection monies, proved to be compatible with and complementary to the activities of Islamic and Chinese traders.[59]

[57]   I. Hont and M. Ignatieff, eds, *Wealth and Virtue*, Cambridge University Press, Cambridge, 1983.
[58]   E. Gibbon, *The Decline and Fall of the Roman Empire*, Oxford University Press, Oxford, vol. 4, 1904, pp. 191–202. Cf. J. W. Burrow, *Edward Gibbon*, Oxford University Press, Oxford, 1985, chs 6 and 7.
[59]   P. D. Curtin, *Cross Cultural Trade in World History*, Cambridge University Press, Cambridge, 1984, chs 6–9; K. N. Chaudhuri, *Trade and Civilization in the Indian Ocean*, Cambridge University Press, Cambridge, 1985.

Furthermore, much of the trade was initially conducted by capitalist traders, albeit such traders – most notably, of course, the East India Companies of the Dutch and the English – were licensed by states.[60] But the presence of competing capitalist organizations did not create a stable situation, with the dynamic of development in the periphery proving to be the same as that in Europe itself. State competition variously between Portugal, Spain, Holland, France, and Britain encouraged a search for security. The fear that others might permanently acquire territory led each state to pre-emptive territorial strikes. European state competition, rather than capitalism *per se*, encouraged the building of empires. It is worth stressing, in all this, that European economic development was not in any sense economically dependent upon its peripheries.[61] Perhaps that makes the moral consideration to be stressed all the more awful. Bluntly, the European impact on the rest of the world was both brutal and devastating. Some of this was the result of accident rather than design, as in the fearful demographic consequences of diseases that ravaged the Americas.[62] But still more striking is the casual barbarism of European society. Millions of Africans died in the slave trade's "middle passage" between West Africa and the West Indies, whilst whole cultures were destroyed by the ruthlessness with which European settlers quenched their hunger for land. It is well worth emphasizing that liberal Anglo-Saxon societies had their hands steeped in blood quite as much and perhaps more than European authoritarian regimes; this needs to be set against the decencies of liberal states towards each other quite as much as that intensity of their organized violence against non-liberal states remarked upon by Doyle in his celebrated article on liberalism and foreign affairs.[63] But the record of all Europeans is terrible, and the moral accordingly simple: no triumphalism should be occasioned by any

---

[60]   J. Thomson, *Mercenaries, Pirates and Sovereigns*, Princeton University Press, Princeton, 1994.

[61]   P. O'Brien, "European Economic Development," *Economic History Review*, vol. 35, 1982.

[62]   W. H. McNeill, *Plagues and People*, Blackwell, Oxford, 1977, ch. 5.

[63]   M. Doyle, "Kant, Liberal Legacies and Foreign Affairs," *Philosophy and Public Affairs*, vol. 12, 1983.

account of the rise of the West for that rise was written in the blood of others.

Nonetheless, a measured position needs to take into consideration two positive factors. The first of these is simply that of economic development. Life chances were not always poor in pre-industrial circumstances, especially for hunter-gatherers, but they often had that character. Short life spans, death of one's children, and the chance of starvation together with disease, pain and social humiliation characterized the life of the vast majority before modernization – as they characterize the lives of hundreds of millions not yet reached by the social benefits of the modern world. Those who lack such benefits are not often in any doubt of their worth. The social portfolio of the West, which allowed for the emergence of key elements of modernity, accordingly deserves some moral approbation.

But the real European miracle, secondly, is altogether different. Consider these words of Edward Gibbon:

> The division of Europe into a number of independent states, connected, however, with each other, by the general resemblance of religion, language, and manners, is productive of the most beneficial consequences to the liberty of mankind. A modern tyrant, who should find no resistance either in his own breast or in his people, would soon experience a gentle restraint from the example of his equals, and the dread of present censure, the advice of his allies, and the apprehension of his enemies. The object of his displeasure, escaping from the narrow limits of his dominions, would easily obtain, in a happier climate, a secure refuge, a new fortune adequate to his merit, the freedom of complaint, and perhaps the means of revenge.[64]

Adam Smith went to the heart of the key mechanism that was involved here when he noted that "commerce went with liberty."[65] Furthermore, the earliest arguments in favour of capitalism endorsed it for the essentially pragmatic reason that money-making was a soft passion capable of controlling the more violent

---

[64]   Gibbon, *The Decline and Fall of the Roman Empire*, vol. 1, 1903, p. 93.
[65]   D. Winch, *Adam Smith's Politics*, Cambridge University Press, Cambridge, 1978.

desire for political domination.[66] Of course, we must qualify these views: capitalism has proved able to ally itself all too easily with authoritarian rule. Still, there is truth to the notion that the first emergence of capitalism went hand in hand with relatively soft political rule. European states tended to be rather more organic and co-operative internally than were the more predatory states of other civilizations. This in turn was partly caused, as argued, by that multipolar character of the European system that made it madness to be too brutal to sections of your population given that their skills, should they move, might significantly enrich your enemy neighbours. This returns us to the condition liked by both Edward Gibbon and Hedley Bull in which a competitive world filled with escape hatches and marked by a culture of civility furthered human life chances. This condition was a significant moral achievement, and it can stand as an exemplar for all that it was the result of accident rather than design.

CONCLUSION

This chapter has offered an account of the emergence of the European system. The European polity differed utterly from the agrarian empires of China and Rome in providing a larger frame, of Christianity and the market, within which states had to move and find their way. In conclusion, let me spell out the ways in which the events of the period discussed relate to the ideal types of international order introduced in the opening chapter.

Strong support is lent to sophisticated realism by the evidence considered, as is scarcely surprising given that many of the most important realist theorists derived their theories from this social world. The vicious escalation to extremes during the Thirty Years War provides support of a negative kind: social heterogeneity combined with fragmented states to ensure geopolitical chaos. Equally, the fact that the agreement to differ about religion

[66] A. Hirschman, *The Passions and the Interests*, Princeton University Press, Princeton, 1977.

together with strengthening of state power allowed international order to flourish after Westphalia provides clear positive support for sophisticated realism. I do not wish to be romantic about this period of order: room in which to calculate most certainly did not always translate into skill in calculation. The vanities of rulers, most notably those of Louis XIV, continued to occasion endless wars.

Eighteenth-century order had nothing to do with any concert of powers; nor was it based on economic interdependence or on liberal principles. Further, the events of this period seem almost irrelevant for hegemonic stability theory. Perhaps that is not quite so: hegemonic stability theory has the merit of placing states and markets at the center of its attention, and thereby of making it clear that realism worked within a relatively economically static world. Yet if fundamental economic change was to challenge realism, so too was the entry of the people onto the political stage.

3

The Age of Revolutions

The age of measured equipoise did not last long, and this chapter accordingly confronts three very different periods within the history of war and peace. The War of the Atlantic peaked, or, rather, took on different stakes, in the revolutionary and Napoleonic wars – wars which France and Britain felt to be so crucial that they extracted unprecedented sums from their national economies.[1] Concentration on fiscal matters should not be allowed to mask the actual sufferings of these major wars, brought to mind both by the terrible anti-war paintings of Goya, inspired by the cycle of atrocities of the first popular war of national resistance, and by the horrors of Napoleon's retreat from Moscow.[2] A second broad moment is that of the long peace of the nineteenth century. It may be that tensions increased towards the end of the nineteenth century, although this view probably reflects our view of what happened soon afterwards, but it remains a fact that mass slaughter (in comparison to short wars and numerous suppressions of popular movements) did not deface the European landmass for a century – although the behavior of Europeans overseas was, of course, a very different matter. By the end of

---

[1]   M. Mann, *Sources of Social Power*, Cambridge University Press, Cambridge, vol. 2, 1993, ch. 11.
[2]   These horrors receive marvellous fictional evocation in J. Winterson, *The Passion*, Penguin, Harmondsworth, 1987.

this period, many commentators had come to believe that geopolitics had finally been vanquished, that it was an illusion to
believe that war was even possible.[3] These hopes were codified as
presuppositions by mainstream sociological theory. Marx and
Durkheim (but not Weber) had few concepts to deal with war,
not surprisingly, given that their own experience had been one of
peace. In a sense this book is an attempt to remedy the gaping
whole in the center of sociological studies occasioned by the third
moment, the era of visceral geopolitical struggle that produced
the two world wars, the greatest and most abominable in human
history.

In order to fill that gap it is necessary to consider the relationship between states and the social forces that surrounded them.
Capitalism took on an enhanced, urbanized form in eighteenth-
century England, and this was soon followed by the industrial
revolution. More than ever states had to copy if they were to
survive; and if the secrets of commercial capitalism had been hard
to imitate, the character of modern industry lent itself easily to
state planning.[4] The way in which states affected economic life
can be seen in the fact that all the nineteenth-century powers
ended up with the same industries, this common portfolio being
dictated by the demands of geopolitical autonomy.[5] The nature of
the regimes in charge of the very varied state structures were
challenged even more. For the eighteenth century marks the
beginning of the entry of the people onto the political stage –
which is to emphasize an important and neglected point, namely
that popular politics gain real bite before industrialization, for all
that the latter adds to their importance. It is worth pointing out
immediately that industrialization did not occasion any absolute
destruction of all previous social structures: rather, many old
regimes tried to modernize in order to avoid Jacobin horrors,
making the nineteenth century a breathing space of social stability

[3]   N. Angell, *Europe's Optical Illusion*, Simpkin, Marshall, Hamilton, Kent and Company, London, 1909.
[4]   E. A. Wrigley, *Continuity, Chance and Change*, Cambridge University Press, Cambridge, 1988.
[5]   G. Sen, *The Military Origins of Industrialisation and International Trade Rivalry*,
Pinter, London, 1984.

before the onset of the two great social revolutions of the twentieth century.[6]

The reference to modern industry naturally brings to mind the concept of class which has so dominated modern social science. But "the people" came, so to speak, in two forms. The idea of the nation has proved to be an ever more important mobilizing force, and it accordingly demands immediate definition. Nationalism is considered here very conventionally. It is the belief in the primacy of a particular nation, real or constructed; further, nationalism often moves from a cultural to a political form, that is, a culture often seeks the protective shell of its own state, and this habitually entails popular mobilization. This omnibus definition contains two presuppositions which deserve highlighting. First, there is everything to be said, despite the works of Armstrong and Smith, for the view that nationalism is modern.[7] There have always, of course, been distinctive cultures, and particular upper classes have had some sense of sharing by blood an ethnic solidarity. But the power of the nationalist idea – that all people within a particular territory should share a culture and be ruled only by someone co-cultural with themselves – is historically novel. The second presupposition concerns the claim that there have been three great ages of nationalism: the foundation of new states in early nineteenth-century Latin America, the Central European enlargement engineered by Wilson at Versailles, and the still greater expansion of the international order as the result of decolonization. There is indeed much to be said for the view that nationalism flourishes as the result of the collapse of empires, a view which makes us realize that the collapse of the Russian and Soviet empire means that we are now faced with a fourth great moment in the history of nationalism. Nonetheless, the definition should not be linked to the idea that nationalism is in any absolute sense committed to separatism. One obvious consideration counting against this is that nationalism can dominate established states.[8]

[6] A. Mayer, *The Persistence of the Old Regime*, Croom Helm, London, 1981; Mann, *Sources of Social Power*, vol. 2, chs 6 and 20.

[7] J. Armstrong, *Nations before Nationalism*, University of North Carolina Press, Chapel Hill, 1982; A. D. Smith, *The Ethnic Origin of Nations*, Blackwell, Oxford, 1986.

[8] It is worth issuing a promissory note here: a second consideration – that national identity can be assured within a multinational state if its regime is liberal – will become ever more important as the argument proceeds.

If the contemporary United States, as is possible, becomes mobilized, either as the result of incautious elite manipulation or of sentiment genuinely coming from below, around the conviction that Japan is an economic enemy, then this will deserve to be considered an example of nationalism.

Obviously, nations, states, regimes and classes are in constant interaction with each other. Less appreciated but still more important is the fact that these forces have, to adopt Sartrian terminology, particular existences rather than pre-ordained, permanently fixed essences, with nations and classes being, to use the language of Freud when characterizing the libido, particularly labile, capable of attaching themselves to very different social projects. Capitalists can be genuinely transnational actors, for example, for all that they sometimes tie their fortunes to a particular state. To make this point means that we are faced with a complicated task: general claims about, say, war and capitalism or war and nationalism need to be broken down into detailed analyses of the behavior of particular classes and particular nations at particular historical moments. It is worth stressing that modern history has seen different types of nationalism, several of which are noted below.[9] Nonetheless, it is possible to say something about human psychology by way of general orientation.

Much social science, notably when under the spell of modern American rational choice theory, takes it for granted that social inequality causes discontent and social mobilization. Matters are not so simple. Political exclusion breeds radicalism far more effectively, with inclusion inducing a combination of content and passivity; in the different terms of Albert Hirschman, when voice is denied, exit becomes attractive, whereas the possibility of influence and the experience of participation makes for loyalty.[10] One point to be noticed here is that the very fact of exclusion often makes it necessary to take on the state, that is, attention becomes focused at the political level because the state prevents social life proceeding according to its own logic. A further

---

[9]   For the typology on which I draw, see J. A. Hall, *Coercion and Consent*, Polity Press, Cambridge, 1994, ch. 6.
[10]   A. Hirschman, *Exit, Voice and Loyalty*, Harvard University Press, Cambridge, MA, 1978.

consideration is that ideological innovation tends to take place from a position of resentment. Thus authoritarian and autocratic regimes managed the extraordinary feat of making their working classes genuinely socialist.[11] It is equally important to note that the universalism of great ideologies is often based on a character-ization of social enemies: just as Christianity utilized the Roman power previously exercised against it so as to persecute its own heretics, so have modern ideologies sought to rule out of the world those considered to be traitors to their causes. All this stands in great contrast to the social world created by political liberalism. The possibility of organizing in society tends to diffuse social conflict. This is not for a moment to deny that there are many conflicts in societies ruled by liberal regimes: but such manifold conflicts tend not to create any monolithic social catas-trophe since their different purposes balance each other out. This contrasts with the exacerbation of conflict that occurs when authoritarian regimes superimpose different grievances on top of each other.[12]

Encapsulating this last point in the maxim that "civil society when left to itself will not develop political ambitions" usefully suggests some final definitional points.[13] Most immediately, the notion of civil society needs to be defined tightly. Whilst it is entirely proper to analyze civil society in terms of social self-organization, and accordingly to stress those eighteenth-century forces which allowed for this to be enhanced, the full weight of the term civil society should lay as much emphasis on civility as upon societal force.[14] A civil society is one of active human beings

[11] There is now a substantial literature on this point; see, inter alia: C. Waisman, Modernisation and the Working Class, University of Texas Press, Austin, 1982; D. Geary, European Labour Protest, 1848–1945, Methuen, London, 1984; T. McDaniel, Autocracy, Capitalism and Revolution in Russia, University of California Press, Berkeley, 1987; I. Katznelson and A. Zolberg, eds, Working Class Formation, Princeton University Press, Princeton, 1986; R. McKibbin, The Ideologies of Class, Oxford University Press, Oxford, 1990; Mann, Sources of Social Power, vol. 2, chs 15 and 17–19.

[12] R. Dahrendorf, Class and Class Conflict in Industrial Society, Stanford University Press, Stanford, 1959.

[13] The maxim is my formulation, but the idea runs through Mann's Sources of Social Power, vol. 2.

[14] J. A. Hall, "In Search of Civil Society," in J. A. Hall, ed., Civil Society, Polity Press, Cambridge, 1995.

prepared to limit conflict by tolerating difference – as took place in Europe, as noted, once the idea of toleration was embraced in the wake of visceral religious division. The notion of civility can help us understand the character of nationalism quite as much. Nationalist studies quite often draw a contrast between civic and ethnic nationalism, habitually endorsing the potential inclusiveness of the former in comparison to the visceral exclusiveness of the latter – seen so strikingly in the Balkans today.[15] Whilst there is sense to this distinction, it is important to remember that civic nationalism is not necessarily pleasant and innocuous. Consider the thundering admonitions about linguistic homogenization in the *Moniteur* of January 28, 1794:

> Citizens! the language of a free people ought to be one and the same for all ... free men are all alike, and the vigorous attitude of liberty and equality is the same whether it comes from the mouth of an inhabitant of the Alps, the Vosges, or the Pyrenees ... We have observed that the dialect called the Bas-Breton, the Basque dialect, and the German and Italian languages have perpetuated the reign of fanaticism and superstition, secured the domination of priests and aristocrats ... It is treason to the fatherland to leave the citizens in ignorance of their national language.[16]

The drive to create a homogenized society so as to have a unified national will can be exceptionally intolerant of difference, for all that blood is not called for in order to gain belonging. The concept of civil nationalism is needed to refer to an ideology endorsing a large political frame within which difference is allowed, even appreciated.

---

[15]   E. Hobsbawm, *Nations and Nationalism in Europe since 1980*, Cambridge University Press, Cambridge, 1990; R. Brubaker, *Nationhood and Citizenship in France and Germany*, Harvard University Press, Cambridge, MA, 1992.
[16]   C. A. Macartney, *National States and National Minorities*, Russell and Russell, New York, 1968, p. 110.

FALSE DAWN

The title of this section is a play on the famous lines of Wordsworth welcoming the coming of the French Revolution. "Bliss
was it in that dawn to be alive," he assured us, "whilst to be
young was very heaven." Tracing the defeat of this dream of
Enlightenment, that is, of a new world of democracy and rationality in which peace would be assured is the task of this section.
An appropriate place to begin is with the celebrated claim that the
late eighteenth century was the age of democratic revolutions, the
two most important of which were linked by the peripatetic figure
of Tom Paine.[17] If there is much to recommend in this thesis, it
will also be necessary to point to its limits. Let us start with the
Anglo-Saxon world before turning to France, and to its impact on
world politics.

North American colonial society was uniquely egalitarian, and
it witnessed huge developments in levels of communication and
self-organization. This was a world of coffee houses, periodicals,
and of notably high levels of literacy.[18] Still, the break with
London was not inevitable, nor was it one led by revolutionaries
wishing to change the nature of social order. The occasion for
revolt has everything to do with the pressures of state competition:
the War of the Atlantic, for all its profits, caused severe fiscal
problems for the British state and led it to demand of its colonies
a rather minimal amount of burden-sharing. In general, representative struggles in the eighteenth century gathered pace precisely
because states were forced by nearly continual warfare to extract
larger shares of wealth from their societies; social movements
responded to prior activity on the part of states. Those colonists
who were opposed to Britain began by proffering the traditional
and respectable argument that there should be no taxation without representation, something which had especial salience for

[17]   R. Palmer, *The Age of the Democratic Revolutions*, Princeton University Press,
Princeton, 1959. J. Keane, *Thomas Paine*, Little, Brown, Montreal, 1995, provides a
sympathetic portrait of the great radical and of his age.
[18]   M. Warner, *The Letters of the Republic*, Harvard University Press, Cambridge, MA,
1990.

them, given their complete lack of representation at Westminster.[19] The leaders of the revolt in the colonies were then forced into making universal claims, first about the people but soon about the nation, because of the intransigence of the British. The resulting ideological intensity, for all its civic form, led to the expulsion of those who had supported the British.

There still remains doubt about the revolutionary status of American achievements. There is certainly a sense in which the initial universalism was tongue-in-cheek. Once British diplomatic stupidity in fighting a war without allies had given the colonies independence, the respectable planters sought to control popular passions.[20] One continuing legacy of their deliberations was a constitution which established a second chamber and a separation of powers – to which was added, in 1803, judicial review. A second legacy, that of the party system, was not the product of conscious design in the same way. The regulation of conflict by peaceful transfers of power between parties prepared to treat their opponents as loyal oppositions depended heavily upon solidarity within the elite.[21] But additional factors mattered quite as much. The revolutionary process had not seen the violence that was to characterize that of its sister republic, and the resort to arms was made thereby less likely. As important was the fact that the revolution had been made against the state, since this meant that no standing army was available to suppress political rivals; this course of action was anyway ruled out for the Federalists given that their opponents had a geographically cohesive power base in Virginia. Underlying this was the vital fact that the initial years of consolidation were free from any fundamentally divisive issue:

[19]   H. G. Koenigsberger, "Composite States, Representative Institutions and the America Revolution," *Historical Research*, no. 148, 1989.
[20]   A general analysis of devices to limit passion and misjudgement in democracy is provided by J. Elster, "Majority Rule and Individual Rights," in S. Shute and S. Hurley, eds, *On Human Rights*, Basic Books, New York, 1993. Elster's argument, that many of these devices were created by the Founding Fathers of the United States, is reiterated in J. Shklar's "Montesquieu and the new republicanism," in G. Bock, Q. Skinner, and M. Viroli, eds, *Machiavelli and Republicanism*, Cambridge University Press, Cambridge, 1992, a brilliant analysis contrasting the moderating impact of Montesquieu in the United States with the radical drive for political unity associated with Rousseau in revolutionary France.
[21]   R. Hofstader, *The Idea of a Party System*, University of California Press, Berkeley, 1969. Cf. Hall, *Coercion and Consent*, ch. 5.

most obviously, no geopolitical pressures affected the United States, given that Europe was embroiled in the Napoleonic wars. In any case, politics was not everything: this was a social world replete with opportunity, and there were avenues of social mobility open to those who lost political power. Whatever the exact weighting of these factors, there can be no doubt of the importance of the achievement. The fact that liberalism came before full democratization, that is, that traditions of limits to political contest preceded majority rule, did something to make politics civil thereafter.[22]

Nonetheless, what mattered even more was early political inclusion. This was probably made inevitable both by the wide diffusion of property in early American society and by the fact that popular military involvement had been crucial in the fight for independence. By the end of Jackson's administrations in the mid-1830s all white males had the vote. It is well worth underscoring the consequence of this development: inclusion diminished political radicalism. Whilst there were fights thereafter in the industrial realm, they gained little further political edge: gaining a voice within the system permanently diminished the oppositional force of American popular politics.[23] There were no domestic pressures dictating involvement with the world, rather a revulsion against European corruption, and Americans were accordingly free to develop their own frontier. Only much later was the consequence of these attitudes – an all-or-nothing moralism applied to foreign policy – to affect international relations.

The situation in Britain was at once similar and different. On the one hand, the immediate occasion for citizenship movements resembled that in the colonies, as the loyalty of many to the American cause attests, for taxation in Britain was then almost certainly the highest in the world.[24] Equally, the social base for the creation of novel extensive identities was quite as developed. The extraordinary efficiency of the agricultural base had created

22 R. Dahl, *Polyarchy*, Yale University Press, New Haven, 1971.
23 I. Katznelson, *City Trenches*, Pantheon, New York, 1981.
24 P. O'Brien and P. Mathias, "Taxation in Britain and France; 1715–1810," *Journal of European Economic History*, vol. 5, 1976; P. O'Brien, 'The Political Economy of British Taxation, 1660–1815," *Economic History Review*, vol. 41, 1988.

an urbanized and commercialized society far different from those of the continent.[25] But Britain was not geopolitically isolated, and so could not enjoy the luxurious option offered by Washington in his farewell address, namely that of leaving Europe to its own devices.[26] To the contrary, the continuing War of the Atlantic endlessly increased rates of fiscal extraction. In these circumstances, continued popular struggles were inevitable. The loss of the colonies led an element of the elite to join with popular forces in order to achieve some "economical reform" at the expense of "Old Corruption." But the fact that monies were demanded for war meant that collective identity was defined as much in national as in class terms.

Nationalism was complex.[27] A British nationalism had certainly existed earlier on, founded on the notion of a Protestant people under attack from Europe's Catholic monarchies. But there was also an English nationalism, often directed against the Scots – not least as they did so well out of their connection with Britain. In many ways, John Wilkes is the best exemplar of the conjoined popular politics of the time. He was an apologist for the blunt ways of John Bull, for roast beef and Yorkshire pudding, and for the liberties established in 1688. It was entirely characteristic that a typical procession of Wilkite supporters in 1768 assembled at a tavern named after William of Orange before setting out to vote for their hero under banners of Magna Carta and the Bill of Rights; equally many Wilkite songs were sung to the tunes of "Rule Britannia" and "God Save the King."[28] All this was of course contrasted first to the mannered artificialities of the French aristocracy and then to the terrors of "Boney." The result of such sentiments was a huge increase in the strength of the British state, for all that its ruling elite initially cold-shouldered the blessings of legitimacy brought by popular feeling. Further, that elite remained politically liberal, despite toying with the notion of repression in the early nineteenth century, thereby ensuring its survival as it slowly opened the political system to majority rule.

[25]   Wrigley, *Continuity, Chance and Change*.
[26]   F. G. Gilbert, *To the Farewell Address*, Princeton University Press, Princeton, 1961.
[27]   L. Colley, *Britons*, Yale University Press, New Haven, 1992.
[28]   Colley, *Britons*, pp. 111–12.

Wordsworth's hopes had of course been pinned on France, and there can be no doubt whatever about the impact of its politics upon international society. The revolution was largely occasioned by the sort of power stand-off characteristic of absolutism: the fiscal crisis of the state, to be precise, resulted less from actual economic exhaustion than from failure to tax commercial dealings and from a system that allowed too many exemptions and too much corruption.[29] Once the state had broken down, genuine social revolution was imposed, largely by those new men, educated, intelligent and possessed of ideological force, whom the old regime had excluded.[30] It was no accident that their attempt to create a republic of virtue took Rousseau as a figurehead: the fear of the Genevan philosopher of all types of social division and complexity was echoed in the revolutionary drive for a singular and unitary national will – a drive which all too easily led to some being ruled out of the world altogether.[31] The best analysis of the revolution from this viewpoint remains "The Liberty of the Ancients Compared with that of the Moderns," an address given by Benjamin Constant in 1819:

> The aim of the ancients was the sharing of social power among the citizens of the same fatherland: this is what they called liberty. The aim of the moderns is the enjoyment of security in private pleasures; and they call liberty the guarantees accorded by institutions to these pleasures.
>
> I said at the beginning that, through their failure to perceive these differences, otherwise well-intentioned men caused infinite evils during our long and stormy revolution ... those men had derived several of their theories from the works of ... philosophers

[29] J. Goldstone, *Revolution and Rebellion in the Early Modern World*, University of California Press, Berkeley, 1991, especially pp. 202–9; D. Dessert and J. L. Journet, "Le Lobby Colbert," *Annales*, vol. 30, 1970; R. Mousnier, ed., *Un Nouveau Colbert*, C. D. U. and SEDES Réunis, Paris, 1985; R. Bonney, *The Limits of Absolutism in Ancien Régime France*, Variorum, Aldershot, 1995.

[30] The distinction between state breakdown and revolutionary outcome is made particularly clearly in Goldstone, *Revolution and Rebellion in the Early Modern World*. Mann's *Sources of Social Power*, vol. 2, ch. 6 offers an innovative account of the content of Jacobin ideological power.

[31] J. Shklar, *Men and Citizens*, Cambridge University Press, Cambridge, 1969; C. Blum, *Rousseau and the Republic of Virtue*, Cornell University Press, Ithaca, 1986; S. Schama, *Citizens*, Alfred Knopf, New York, 1989.

who had themselves failed to recognize the changes brought by two thousand years in the dispositions of mankind. I shall perhaps at some point examine the system of the most illustrious of these philosophers, of Jean-Jacques Rousseau, and I shall show that, by transposing into our modern age an extent of social power, of collective sovereignty, which belonged to other centuries, this sublime genius, animated by the purest love of liberty, has never-theless furnished deadly pretexts for more than one kind of tyranny.[32]

This last sentiment was prescient: *polis* envy was to reappear, albeit in markedly different form, in later European history.

There was much debate amongst the revolutionary leaders as to the proper revolutionary approach to foreign policy, with the Jacobins interestingly initially being opposed to the expansion recommended by the Girondins.[33] Attacking a revolution is always dangerous, as has been seen most recently in the case of Iran, and it led to the creation of a new type of war.[34] The character of the new warfare was apparent very soon after the revolution had been saved by citizen-soldiers at the battle of Valmy:

> ... a force appeared that beggared all imagination. Suddenly war again became the business of the people – a people of thirty millions, all of whom considered themselves to be citizens ... The people became a participant in war; instead of governments and armies as heretofore, the full weight of the nation was thrown into the balance. The resources and efforts now available for use surpassed all conventional limits: nothing now impeded the vigor with which war could be waged ...[35]

This is the young Clausewitz writing in 1793. When Napoleon added to popular feelings the perfection of such military tech-niques as that of having his troops move fast whilst living off

[32]   *Benjamin Constant: Political Writings*, ed. B. Fontana, Cambridge University Press, Cambridge, 1988, pp. 317–18 and passim. Cf. S. Holmes, *Benjamin Constant and the Making of Modern Liberalism*, Yale University Press, New Haven, 1984.
[33]   I. Hont, "The Permanent Crisis of a Divided Mankind," *Political Studies*, vol. 42, 1994.
[34]   T. Skocpol, "Social Revolutions and Mass Military Mobilization," *World Politics*, vol. 40, 1988.
[35]   C. von Clausewitz, *On War*, Princeton University Press, Princeton, 1976, pp. 591–2.

the land, a hugely formidable conquering machine was set in place.[36]

Whilst it is obvious that France is the prime mover behind the escalation of war to the extreme, traditional views as to the nature of the novelties pioneered by France are somewhat mistaken. More particularly, it will not do to see France as simply promoting the cause of the people all over Europe, and thereby threatening old regimes in the process – and this despite the new heroic individualism, exemplified in the heroes of Stendhal's novels, that set the cultural tenor of the age. First, it is far too simple to contrast popular politics, on the one hand, with unchanging old regimes on the other. The ideas of the Enlightenment were in fact twofold: if some of them flowed through and fitted popular channels, others were favored by and developed for enlightened absolutism. Justification of rule in terms of efficiency had characterized European international society for some time: the partitions of Poland had begun before the incursions of the French, and Austria, Prussia, and Russia were more concerned with concluding them than they initially were with the revolution.[37] Napoleon was very much the inheritor of this side of Enlightenment doctrine, as the Napoleonic Code so clearly demonstrated; differently put, he was not quite the novel force he is often portrayed to be, and accordingly much easier for many old regimes to deal with than is often imagined.

Secondly, radical change often occurred for negative rather than positive reasons. One example of this is the break-up of the Spanish empire: Latin American nationalist movements were able to gain independence because the Peninsular War tied up metropolitan military forces. Of course, these movements are great idiosyncrasies within the history of nationalism as a whole since they were led by an elite which had been scared by rebellions directed at those of European background, most obviously in Haiti, and who sought thereafter to avoid the mobilization of the people – a view so generalized that it does much to explain the

---

[36]   M. van Creveld, *Supplying War*, Cambridge University Press, Cambridge, 1977.
[37]   D. Kaiser, *Politics and War*, Harvard University Press, Cambridge, MA, 1990, pp. 203–12 and part III passim.

relative absence of war in the region thereafter.[38] The situation in Europe was very different, as can be seen by noting the logistics of the French armies. The fiscal crisis of the French state, from late absolutism through to its Napoleonic form, meant that its armies plundered huge amounts from territories it was forced to conquer – and continued to do so for years as such territories were made to pay for occupying French troops.[39] This did a very great deal to undermine the popular governments that were established by local "patriots." Bluntly, this is to say that French rule, like that of Rome long before, was already imperial before Napoleon made it blatantly so. Of course, he showed no particular respect for national liberation, being prepared to carve up the map in any way that suited his larger purpose. This created a new type of nationalism, geopolitically induced and comprising a revolution from above, in which states with previous histories chose to change their social structures in order to survive. Characteristic figures of such nationalism include the Prussian reformers – Hardenberg, Scharnhorst, Gneisenau, and Stein – who sought to modernize their state after defeat by Napoleon at Jena and Auerstädt in 1806. Their sense of nationalism could run very deep: Clausewitz resigned his commission, so as to fight in the Russian army against the national enemy, even though this angered his king.[40]

All this is to say that the novel nature of French society and government occasioned similar responses elsewhere due to its entirely traditional drive for hegemony. Putting things in this way raises an interesting and puzzling question. Why was it that Napoleon could not call an end to his conquests? Even after Trafalgar, his Continental System damaged the British, whilst as late as 1813 it was apparent that the other great powers would have been perfectly prepared to make a traditional geopolitical deal which would have favored France, in the sense that its borders would have been enlarged to include the left bank of

[38]   B. Anderson, *Imagined Communities*, Verso, London, 1991, ch. 4.
[39]   S. Schama, *Patriots and Liberators*, Alfred Knopf, New York, 1977; T. W. C. Blanning, *The French Revolution in Germany*, Oxford University Press, Oxford, 1983.
[40]   P. Paret, *Clausewitz and the State*, Princeton University Press, Princeton, 1976.

the Rhine. One answer to this question is entirely personal. Napoleon had such a set of victories behind him that his confidence in his own genius was untouched. This was hubris. But a second answer has to do with the domestic character of the Napoleonic system.[41] Napoleon managed to solve France's internal problems by an aggressive policy of externalization. One obvious way in which this was true concerned taxation and conscription: armies were paid for by others, whilst troops over time ceased to be French – another way in which Napoleon came to resemble the old regime. Most importantly, the imperial system provided pickings for a whole new class, turned by Napoleon into a European-wide nobility. If the key component within that class was of course his generals, so too were others who had risen as suppliers of the war machine. Had Napoleon retreated in 1813 within France's pre-revolutionary boundaries he would have had to take his family, his generals, and the rest of this nobility with him. He feared to do so, trapped within the social order his war machine had created. His position was curiously like that of some feudal kings, successful as long as their expansion provided new land to give to the younger unemployed sons of their nobility, but dreadfully threatened by them if expansion ever came to an end.

A PAX BRITANNICA?

The escalation to the extremes occasioned by ideological innovation in conjunction with a fragmented state was followed by nearly a century free from major war. When we remember that this period saw both nation-building and industrialization, that is, the creation of the new social world described by sociology, it becomes apparent that this is a remarkable achievement. What sort of international order made this possible? The answer is not simple, for different types of order came to be layered on top of each other; disentangling these factors will make the task of the

---

[41] Kaiser, *Politics and War*, pp. 255–63.

next section, that of explaining the collapse of international order, that much easier.

In the years immediately after Napoleon's defeat international order was clearly provided by the Concert system. Rather different starting points lay behind the concerns of the leaders of the great powers. Metternich wanted above all to guard against revolution, knowing full well that the Habsburg Monarchy was in a structurally different position from the other great powers: it could scarcely strengthen itself by becoming a national state, let alone a nation-state, given that it was a classical composite monarchy, that is, a multinational arrangement within whose territories, themselves widely dispersed throughout Europe, no prior attempt had been made at linguistic homogenization or bureaucratic centralization. In contrast, Castlereagh was concerned simply to make sure that French ambitions could not again dominate the European polity. Nonetheless, the powers agreed to meet to resolve their difficulties, and all did so, not just in 1815 and 1818 but again in 1822.

It is conventional to say that these different starting points led to the break-up of the Concert. Britain did not attend further meetings, used by Metternich to legitimize Habsburg intervention against liberal and revolutionary forces: rather, Canning threatened the use of British naval power to ensure that the Spanish empire in Latin America was not restored. It is accordingly possible to say that the Concert ended after only a few years. But the other great powers continued to meet, and all continued to consult thereafter. This allowed for international recognition of Belgium in 1831, of German and Italian unification, and of the creation of a set of new states, all but one in the Balkans, in the later nineteenth and early twentieth centuries. Furthermore, this dense web of interaction encouraged the emergence of international regimes to control the navigation of the Danube and the elimination of the slave trade, as well as preventing some unilateral actions that might well have caused war; further, mere diplomatic pressure was sufficient to ensure at the Congress of Berlin that Russia disgorged territories already taken from the Ottomans. All this can be put very simply. The Concert system enhanced and underwrote the realist norms of the society of states. If the system was in full operation for only a few years, international society was notably strong until 1856, and not without some achievements to its credit even after 1875.[42]

If the spread of international society was one factor enabling peace, is it the case that the real novelty of the nineteenth century was the result of British power? Should we accept, in other words, the contention of hegemonic stability theory that the nineteenth century was made peaceful thanks to the general services – an insistence on open markets, the provision of a top currency and generalized defence for capitalism as a whole – rendered by a selfless norm-giver?

At first sight, there seems much to recommend this view. It is certainly true that the first three-quarters of the nineteenth century witnessed both the spread of free trade, in theory and in practice, and an increase, partly in consequence, of actual world trade. Tariffs fell throughout Europe, and liberalism gained in strength as an international force. It seemed as if the British dream, of peace through interdependence, of the spread of free trade and eventually of the parliamentary system, might be realizable. But was this happy situation the result of conscious British determination to spread the doctrines in which it believed and which were to its advantage? There seems little evidence to support the theory of hegemonic stability at this point. Britain was not especially aggressive in seeking to break down tariff barriers.[43] That such barriers did come down in Europe between the 1850s and 1870s was essentially because European states found such a policy in their immediate interest. Britain had found in the 1840s that a rationalization of tariff barriers actually increased state revenue. Prior to 1846 over 1,200 items had been subject to various levels of tariff, even though by far the greatest proportion of revenue derived from a mere nine items. The taking of hundreds of items off the books hurt smugglers badly and made it possible to police the remaining items in such a way that enhanced revenues were assured, even at lower tariff rates, whilst costs of collection were

---

[42]   K. Holsti, "Governance without Government," in J. N. Rosenau and E. O. Czempiel, eds, *Governance without Government*, Cambridge University Press, Cambridge, 1992.
[43]   T. McKeown, "'Hegemonic Stability Theory' and Nineteenth Century Tariff Levels in Europe," *International Organisation*, vol. 37, 1983.

dramatically slashed. Not surprisingly, other countries followed suit.[44]

Further reflection suggests that there is very little to recommend in connection with the other services supposedly rendered. It is probably a mistake to see the pre–1914 monetary system as genuinely hegemonic. The Germans and the French had their own monetary blocs, and the latter were able to invest in Russia in francs rather than in sterling. The crucial evidence for a monetary hegemony equivalent to that of the United States in the 1960s – when one power alone could so increase money in circulation as to extract seigniorage – would have been persistently large deficits of Britain with Paris, Berlin and New York, that is, evidence to show that Britain financed its deficit by making others hold sterling. But most scholars do not believe that this was so: "Britain is said to have had sufficient income from trade, investment, and services, plus the Indian milk cow, to remain in balance with the other major centres," whilst such sterling balances as were held resulted from economic calculation rather than from hegemonic coercion.[45] There may be an element of truth to the notion that the Royal Navy's policing of the sea lanes (and its mapping skills) was a public good, although against this should be set the fear that this military advantage could systematically be used against any other country that became dependent on the international market.[46] But in broader terms the notion that Britain provided the service of defense for capitalist society as a whole is nonsensical. Britain was one great power amongst others. In military terms, she most certainly never had the capacity to push the Russian army around, nor after 1870 was her army sufficiently large to have disciplined that of Germany.

In a nutshell, Britain was at no time in the nineteenth century a genuinely hegemonic power. Britain had certain advantages – an

[44]   P. O'Brien and G. Pigman, "Free Trade, British Hegemony and International Economic Order in the Nineteenth Century," conference paper, 1991.
[45]   D. Calleo, "The Historiography of the Interwar Period," in B. Rowland, ed., *Balance of Power or Hegemony?*, New York University Press, New York, 1975, p. 241. Cf. P. Lindert, *Key Currencies and Gold, 1900–1913*, Princeton University Press, Princeton, 1969.
[46]   A. Offer, "The British Empire, 1870–1914," *Economic History Review*, vol. 46, 1993 and *The First World War*, Cambridge University Press, Cambridge, 1989.

economic lead and the Royal Navy – but she was continually faced with continental powers whose armed forces were greater than her own. She was never in a position to dictate to genuine geopolitical rivals. That Britain played no positive hegemonic role does not, however, distract from the fact that the nineteenth century saw the spread of free trade and an increase in economic growth. Why then was this possible? Mercantilist policies in the century between 1713 and 1815 had been massively encouraged by the protracted conflict between France and Britain, especially in the War of the Atlantic. With the ending of those hostilities, together with the entry of both Germany and Russia onto the scene, basic European order could be maintained by the traditional means of a balance of power between the leading states. One source for that balance was undoubtedly the realization that Napoleon's drive for hegemony had led to exile in St Helena. Clausewitz's final definition of war certainly reflected this fact: gone was the admiration for the total nature of absolute war, to be replaced by a realization that the traditional, limited wars of Frederick the Great had in fact achieved more, by keeping the political aim of war in sight at all times. All this is to say that states calculated carefully as long as a negative exemplar was at the forefront of statesmen's minds. A second source helping the balance of power was the homogeneity of international society. Mutual understanding was based on the use of a common language, for the language of diplomacy was still French, and it was further enhanced for much of the century by dynastic links. The fact that fortunes were to be made internally as industrialization gathered pace perhaps distracted attention from geopolitical adventures; certainly states lost salience since their tax burdens decreased as a proportion of national product over the course of the century, thereby diminishing the likelihood of state breakdown and social revolution.[47] In a nutshell, this was a second age of equipoise. It proved to be equally short-lived.

[47]   Mann, *Sources of Social Power*, vol. 2, ch. 10.

TRADERS AND HEROES

Unraveling the tangled web of causation that led to the First World War is difficult but not impossible. I begin with the occasion for the war, that is, Gavrilo Princip's assassination of Archduke Franz Ferdinand in Sarajevo in June 1914 – or, in more general terms, with nationalism. The argument will be that this separatist nationalism did not cause war. It is necessary to spend some space in describing the nationalism represented by Princip so as to contrast it with a rather different type of nationalism whose salience for war was much greater. Analysis of this second type of nationalism takes us right into the heart of the Wilhelmine regime, wherein the fullest explanation for war is to be found.

The classic nationalism of nearly all of the nineteenth century deserves to be called risorgimento nationalism.[48] This variety of nationalism was liberal. Both John Stuart Mill and Mazzini were famously amongst its numbers, and the conjunction of their names makes it clear that the hope of the age was that the setting free of oppressed peoples would usher in a reign of peace. Hroch's famous treatment of this form of nationalism makes much of the movement, from the collectors of folklore, to the ideologists of nationalism, to the final moment at which cultural revival becomes political demand.[49] Two particular social forces fueled this development. First, there was a notable increase in the educated in nineteenth-century Europe, an increase which often began before states sought to ensure normative integration through their territories.[50] Second, economic development moved many from the countryside to the city: the destruction of the traditional segmentary cultures of such people made them available for nationalist propaganda.[51] These social forces were certainly there, but the

[48]   P. Alter, *Nationalism*, Edward Arnold, London, 1990.
[49]   M. Hroch, *The social preconditions of national revival in Europe*, Cambridge University Press, Cambridge, 1985.
[50]   L. O'Boyle, "The Problem of an Excess of Men in Western Europe, 1800–1850," *Journal of Modern History*, vol. 42, 1970.
[51]   Hroch, *The social preconditions of national revival in Europe*.

move beyond cultural awakening is best interpreted in political terms. Consider the career of Palacký, the Czech historian who followed Herder in seeing the Czechs as a peaceful people oppressed by both Magyars and Germans.[52] Palacký had begun working for the Bohemian Museum in the 1830s, and his great history was begun in German. Increasing anti-German feeling, consequent on the state's attempt to make German the language of officialdom, led him in the 1840s to start writing in Czech. But it was the events of 1848 which pushed him into politics. The Czechs refused to join the parliament at Frankfurt, and felt deeply threatened by plans concocted there that might have led to their cultural demise. They participated instead in a counter-meeting in Prague, which firmly stressed that the best hopes for the Slavs, given their geopolitical position between Russia and Germany, remained with the Habsburgs.[53] So the switch to political nationalism did not, in a sense, come from below: it was rather the desire of a modernizing state to conduct official business in a single language that suddenly placed some in the position of facing blocked or perhaps downward mobility. State intervention occasioned popular response.

The point being made can be put differently by asking whether the Habsburg enterprise was doomed by nationalism to collapse. General considerations suggest a negative answer, at least for a particular sort of Habsburg enterprise. By that I have in mind the Kremsier reform proposals of 1849, the key clause of which asserted that:

All peoples of the Empire are equal in rights. Each people has an inviolable right to preserve its nationality in general and its language in particular. The equality of rights in the school, administration and public life of every language in local usage is guaranteed by the state.[54]

[52]   J. Breuilly, *Nationalism and the State*, Manchester University Press, Manchester, 1985, pp. 99–103.
[53]   L. Orton, *The Prague Slav Congress of 1848*, Eastern European Monographs, Boulder, 1978.
[54]   This is cited in A. Sked, *The Decline and Fall of the Habsburg Empire, 1815–1918*, Edward Arnold, London, 1989, p. 143.

Had this been enacted, different nationalities might not have sought to escape the empire, resting content instead with national identity within it.

What is at issue here is the nature of state-building. Both France and Britain built their states in part, as noted, by pushing through linguistic homogenization before the modern era. The emergence of mass schooling systems did much to underwrite the languages of the regional cultures which composite monarchies had scarcely touched, thereby making linguistic homogenization of this sort far more difficult.[55] In these circumstances, state-building was probably only possible by absolutely alternate means, that is, by creating a sense of unity based on a respect for difference. Had it been possible for the national minorities to have voice inside the system, the attraction of exit might well have been diminished.[56] Differently put, the pop singer Sting did not realize that what follows from his insistence that "if you love someone, set them free" is often a voluntary decision to stay connected. So the nature of political regime matters: nationalism has historically habitually involved separation from authoritarian polities. Where the regime is liberal, multinationalism may be possible. Of course, there is great variation at this point. It is easy to grant linguistic rights when it is clear that the state language is that of a large majority, and thereby sure not to be threatened, as well as when a relatively neutral state language – say, English in India – does not obviously advantage one group against others. The situation was one of maximal difficulty at this point in Austro-Hungary, for the state language, German, was that of the dominant ethnic group – which thereby led to ceaseless demands not just for linguistic rights but for expansion in the number of officially recognized state languages.

Still, why did the Habsburgs not consistently try the liberal option?[57] Two points are of relevance. First, defeat in war against

[55]   D. Laitin, *Language repertoires and state construction in Africa*, Cambridge University Press, Cambridge, 1992.

[56]   A. O. Hirschman, *Exit, Voice and Loyalty*, Harvard University Press, Cambridge, MA, 1970.

[57]   O. Jaszi, *The Dissolution of the Habsburg Monarchy*, University of Chicago Press, Chicago, 1961. Cf. M. Mann, *Sources of Social Power*, vol. 2, ch. 10.

Germany made it possible for the Hungarians to gain their autonomy in 1867. This was disastrous, for within that half of the empire authoritarian cultural assimilation was practiced, to the ever greater anger of the southern Slav peoples. Secondly, the Habsburgs wished to remain a great power. It was this which encouraged them to modernize in a centralized rather than a more liberal and federal manner. Despite their problems, they were unwilling to let any territory go, not least because they feared that it would fall under Russia's sphere of influence, and indeed at this precise moment were entertaining hopes for imperial expansion at the expense of the Ottomans!

Nationalist demands were a severe problem for the Habsburgs in 1914. Nonetheless, such demands should not be exaggerated. The empire was holding together, not least because core groups like the Czechs still felt that their safety was best guaranteed, in a hostile geopolitical climate, by remaining within rather than seeking to leave the empire. It is extremely likely that a different Habsburg response to Serbia in 1914, calling on other powers to help condemn what had taken place, would have been accepted by the other great powers. A situation that might have been managed as successfully as had been previous Balkan crises was changed by German behavior. It is to that behavior that most attention must be given.

German decision-makers knew that to support the Habsburgs in such an aggressive manner was to risk war. This risk was accepted on the grounds that Germany's sole ally had to be supported and that a war deemed to be inevitable was best fought sooner rather than later – that is, before Russia had fully modernized her military machine. The key point in this position, rational in its reasoning but not, we will see, in its presuppositions, concerns the inevitability of war. A central factor involved was a nationalism very different from that of the risorgimento variety.

The ideology of nationalism changes at the end of the nineteenth century. What is best termed integral nationalism is politically illiberal. There is no longer room for the belief that human beings, seen as possessing inalienable rights, need the carapace of a nation, and that all nations can develop together in a positive-sum game. To the contrary, universalism is held to be a febrile myth: the fact that one should think with one's blood naturally turned nationalist quarrels into Darwinian zero-sum affairs. This form of nationalism was securely in place well before it received its ultimate form in German national socialism, and accordingly cannot be completely explained in terms of a reaction to Versailles. It can be seen, for example, in Max Weber's 1895 inaugural address to Freiburg University:

> We must grasp that the unification of Germany was a youthful spree, indulged in by the nation in its old age; it would have been better if it had never taken place, since it would have been a costly extravagance, if it was the conclusion rather than the starting-point for German power-politics on a global scale.[58]

In the context of his time, Weber's nationalism was of course liberal – although Poles familiar with Weber's wartime views as to how Germans should behave in the East are not likely to accord him that epithet.[59] Nonetheless, what is crucial is to stress that the context of that time included belief in imperial expansion. It is the coupling of integralist ideology with imperialism that stands at the back of the disasters of twentieth-century Europe. Again Max Weber is relevant. He was one of the "fleet professors" who insisted that Germany needed secure sources of supply and of outlet in order to retain sufficient autonomy to play a world role. In a nutshell, imperialism was necessary. It mattered a very great deal that Bethmann-Hollweg, the German Chancellor in 1914, believed this to be true.[60] Is it then simply enough to ascribe the First World War to Germany's insistence on "a place in the sun"? Answering this negatively will take us to the heart of an explanation for the European disaster.

One obvious reason for a negative answer is that not all German leaders felt the same way as did Bethmann-Hollweg. This was most notably true of Bismarck, although it also applied to Caprivi. The Iron Chancellor had been perfectly happy to allow a marriage between iron and rye in the 1870s, principally because tariffs

[58]   M. Weber, *Max Weber: Selections in Translation*, ed. W. G. Runciman, Cambridge University Press, Cambridge, 1978, p. 266.
[59]   For details, see W. Mommsen, *Max Weber and German Politics, 1890–1920*, Chicago University Press, Chicago, 1984, pp. 211–27.
[60]   K. Jarausch, *The Enigmatic Chancellor*, Yale University Press, New Haven, 1973.

increased the state's revenues at a time when developments in military technology demanded new expenditures. Further, Bismarck had made something of a bid for colonies in the 1880s. His motive on that occasion, as so often in his career, was most largely that of increasing his own power by splitting oppositional forces, in this case the National Liberals who were internally divided on the matter. But what mattered about Bismarck was his ability to drop something once local internal politics had been seen to. His banker Bleichröder had made him well aware of the key facts about formal imperialism, that it required heavy investment and produced poor profits.[61] Much more important to Bismarck was the geopolitical sense that Germany's best bet was to rest at peace within Europe, that is, to remain a satiated power rather than an aggressive one. More particularly, the core of his diplomacy rested on the insistent belief that Germany must never be completely isolated, and most particularly must never be in a position in which it faced war on two fronts.

But that is precisely what happened in 1914, with pre-emptive war being then considered necessary precisely so as to break out of encirclement. The determining step in the process of escalation involved occurred in 1897 when the decision to build a fleet launched a *Weltpolitik*; this new policy did not replace but rather co-existed with traditional expansionist goals directed towards the East. Thereafter, an alliance system came into being with France and Russia firmly opposing Austro-Hungary and Wilhelmine Germany, with Britain naturally leaning to France, given the potential threat to the Channel ports. Germany's leaders went to war in 1914 in a fatalistic mood, knowing that the odds were stacked against them. How could such a situation have arisen? Let us proceed by process of elimination so as eventually to reach the proper explanation.

It was and still is sometimes claimed that a *Weltpolitik* was necessary for German economic success. In terms of pure economic fact, there is no justification whatsoever for this claim. Whilst it is true that protectionist policies characterized Europe after the 1870s, the trade rivalries that ensued were mostly not

---

[61]   F. Stern, *Gold and Iron*, Alfred Knopf, New York, 1977.

very severe.[62] German economic expansion was certainly not arrested: her economy overtook that of Britain in 1913, and it was set, as several contemporaries realized, to dominate all of Europe. Moreover, Germany's closest trading partner was Great Britain, and the bulk of her products did not anyway go outside Europe. In addition, there was no real indication that protection was likely to be vastly enhanced inside Europe. It is true that one British Cabinet committee did indeed consider the possibility of imposing tariffs on Germany; but the way in which the United States negotiated a deal with Britain about tariffs before 1914 showed that compromise was possible – as it would have been with Germany, given that the Committee in question only considered protection for strategic reasons, that is, in order to open Germany's market.[63] Of fundamental importance was the explosion, by the Austrian economist Bohm-Bawerk, of the notion that imperialism was necessary because the home market would eventually become saturated – the logic of which criticism has been upheld ever since.[64] If these are facts, it remains vital, however, to see how they were interpreted by contemporaries – for what matters about the economic factor as an historical determinant is often less what is than what is believed to be the case. Were the social actors of the time so convinced of the need for empire that they forced the German state into a rash policy?

This seems not to apply to Germany's capitalist class as a whole. It is certainly true that particular sectors gained from an aggressive foreign policy, not least the steelmakers whose potential surpluses were absorbed by battleship production.[65] Further, particular capitalists, amongst them Krupp and Ballin, became convinced of the need for world markets. But this is distinctively

[62]   German–Russian tensions over grain were important, but there is little else to recommend the thesis of Sen, *The Military Origins of Industrialisation and International Trade Rivalry.*

[63]   A. Friedberg, *The Weary Titan,* Princeton University Press, Princeton, 1988; D. Lake, *Power, Protection and Free Trade,* Cornell University Press, Ithaca, 1988.

[64]   N. Stargardt, "Origins of the Constructivist Theory of the Nation," in S. Periwal, ed., *Notions of Nationalism,* Central European University Press, Budapest, 1995.

[65]   E. Kehr, *Battleship Building and Party Politics in Germany,* Chicago University Press, Chicago, 1975 and *Economic Interest, Militarism and Foreign Policy,* University of California Press, Berkeley, 1977.

only one side of the equation. If some did well from aggression, German trade as a whole benefited from access to British markets. And some great capitalists, most notably the Rothschilds, explicitly chose to argue against war, not least by taking space in *The Times* in July 1914.[66] But capitalism of this international type was not dominant. What was more normal was capitalist actors who had neither time for nor interest in geopolitics: they were far too busy making money to produce geopolitical visions of their own. Finally, it is worth noting that the German state was not in any case particularly open to influence by exerted by capitalists, even had they had a clear set of demands which they wished to push. The Kaiser and his entourage made up a court in which mundane business concerns had no place.

If the pure theory of economic imperialism, that is, the theory that capitalists controlled the state and forced it into doing its business holds little water, there is not much more to be said for an alternative theory. The theory of social imperialism suggests that expansionist adventures were undertaken so as to keep the social peace, and in particular so as to provide a means of integrating the working class.[67] This working class certainly needed integrating. German workers differed from their British counterparts in having the franchise; but it was a franchise without effect, for the Reichstag had no real powers. More importantly, workers between 1878 and 1890 were faced with anti-socialist laws; not surprisingly, exclusion bred a genuinely socialist political movement determined – or, rather forced – to combat the state. This radicalism was extremely important in domestic politics in that it prevented co-operative alliances with middle-class parties. Nonetheless, the extent of this radicalism can be exaggerated; much of it was a radical veneer, as Max Weber realized, which hid reformist tendencies.[68] The fact that the movement had some ideas about internationalism and militarism

---

[66] J. Joll, *The Origins of the First World War*, Longman, Harlow, 1984.

[67] H. U. Wehler, *The German Empire, 1871–1918*, Berg, Leamington Spa, 1985.

[68] Weber made his viewpoint – that political inclusion would produce a class loyal to the nation – particularly clearly in his wartime reflections on the historical sociology of Wilhelmine Germany. See M. Weber, "Parliament and Government in a Reconstructed Germany," in *Economy and Society*, University of California Press, Berkeley, 1978, p. 1391.

should not disguise the fact that workers had little overall interest in geopolitics. And against evidence that some elite members did think about the social benefits of imperialism, not least at the fateful meeting of 1912 which decided that war would soon be necessary, should be set data pointing in the opposite direction. Bethmann-Hollweg, for example, was terrified at the prospect of hostilities because he felt that it was likely to so undermine the position of the elite that social revolution might result.[69] In any case, there is a large difference between flag waving and starting a major war.

This is not to say that the German elite was completely autonomous. But before examining the pressures that did increasingly constrain them, let us turn to the nature of the regime itself. After all, modern Marxist theories make much of the fact that the state can be "the best capitalist," seeing beyond the immediate needs of capitalists. Might economic imperialism be best seen in these terms, as the state wishing to ensure long-term economic prosperity? Whilst it is certainly possible to conceptualize the state in these terms, reasons already adduced suggest that it makes little sense here, given that the actions of the German state, which led to a war fought on two fronts which was hugely destructive in social as much as material terms, most certainly did not help the long-term interests of German capital. Imperialism was certainly not necessary for the German economy. Any rational calculation between what one contemporary saw to be alternative strategies of trading and heroism should have come down against military action.[70] This suggests the key point: the German state could not calculate its own best interests.

Germany's actions can best be explained by considering the nature of its state. War on two fronts was guaranteed by Germany having two expansionist policies at one and the same time. The army and the Junkers favored a traditional Eastern policy whilst the Navy, some heavy industrialists, and the Social Democrats (who feared that an expanded army might be used for purposes

[69]   D. Kaiser, "Germany and the Origins of the First World War," *Journal of Modern History*, vol. 55, 1983.
[70]   W. Sombart, *Handler and Helden*, Dunckler und Humblot, Leipzig, 1915. Cf. R. Rosecrance, *The Rise of the Trading State*, Basic Books, New York, 1986.

of internal repression), favored *Weltpolitik*. What is really striking, especially in comparison with the subtle calculations of Bismarck, is the way in which it proved not to be possible, despite some significant efforts, to assign priorities so as not to offend most of the great powers at the same time. Perhaps the fundamental reason for this failure is the fact that Imperial Germany was effectively a court society dominated by the personality of the Kaiser.[71] The continuity and consistency lent to policy by Bismarck was not recaptured by his successors. If nineteenth-century German politics had always involved "divide-and-rule" tactics, the process of log-rolling between special interests was vastly increased by the entry of the people onto the political stage.[72] Both left and right mobilized support, and the ability of the state to gain some autonomy by constantly changing alliances accordingly decreased. Studies of the popular leagues pressing for expansion to the East and for world imperialism have shown us that these views were attractive to the educated, to those whose careers were associated with a German state of which they were proud, something which undermines Hobsbawm's view that nationalism turns nasty at the end of the nineteenth century because it comes to be rooted in the lesser bourgeoisie.[73] The nationalism of this popular bourgeois radical right played a much greater part in limiting the Wilhelmine state's room to manoeuver before 1914 than did any pressure from the left, and this factor helped occasion the outbreak of war. The rules of diplomacy work most easily, as noted, when state actors are part of an homogeneous international society: what radical nationalists at this time were demanding was an end to transnational identity so that national society could be favored, in a world seen largely in Darwinian terms.

[71]   J. Rohl and N. Sombart, eds, *Kaiser Wilhelm II*, Cambridge University Press, Cambridge, 1982.

[72]   J. Snyder, *Myths of Empire*, Cornell University Press, Ithaca, 1991. Note too that I am telling only a part of the story: Germany's lack of coherence owed quite as much to religion as it did to class, as is demonstrated in H. W. Smith, *German Nationalism and Religious Conflict*, Princeton University Press, Princeton, 1995.

[73]   E. Hobsbawm, *Nations and Nationalism since 1780*, Cambridge University Press, Cambridge, 1990, pp. 117–22; Mann, *Sources of Social Power*, vol. 2, pp. 575–88 and ch. 22.

The move to war was in consequence far more the result, in Walter Lippman's phrase, of drift than of mastery. After the famous meeting of 1912 that envisaged war, no thought was given to matters of general strategy. Furthermore, there is no evidence of much thought being devoted to economic affairs at all:

> ... to most members of Wilhelm's entourage, economic expansion and even world power were first and foremost means to maintain the domestic status quo. Their intrinsic advantages were secondary. They were meant to provide somehow enough prosperity and/or nationalist prestige to quell the pressure for reforms at home. How they managed this did not matter. *MittelAfrika*, *MittelEuropa*, it was all the same so long as the victory was large enough to sustain the power of the Junkers and their Kaiser. The means thus stood only in oblique relationship to the end, making it all the harder to fashion a consistent policy. The usual ways to measure success, economic growth, acquisition of territory, increase in influence, could not be used under such a system because the question was not "have we expanded" but "have we expanded enough" (to reach the greater goal).[74]

Nonetheless, what remains most striking about Germany's action is the extent to which no agreed notion of national interest had been hammered out. There is one particularly clear indicator of this point. The army had for some time embraced the "cult of the offensive," part military style, part necessity, given mobilization schedules.[75] The fact that war plans in consequence depended upon violating Belgian neutrality – which was almost certain to lead to a British declaration of war – was not revealed to the Chancellor until a very few days before the war became generalized. The various branches of the state did not know what their colleagues were up to, and the resulting inability to establish a clear set of priorities led precisely to the encirclement that German leaders feared. When nationalist passions in the Balkans presented an opportunity, Germany risked war in an attempt to break out of a situation largely of its own making.

---

[74] I. Hull, *The Entourage of Kaiser Wilhelm II, 1888–1918*, Cambridge University Press, Cambridge, 1983, pp. 253–4.
[75] S. van Evera, "The Cult of the Offensive and the Origins of the First World War," *International Security*, vol. 9, 1984.

What has been said needs summarizing. To begin with, there is no especial reason to accept the pessimistic view that the development of capitalism entails war between nations. Equally, war made no sense on realist grounds. Bismarck had understood this, although there remains much to be said for the view that his actions did much to undermine the social conditions on which realism depends. On the one hand, he did not hand down a liberal constitution which would have encouraged responsible government. War was eventually created by a half-modern authoritarian state, that is, an authoritarian state with a democratic façade, paralyzed by its internal contradictions and accordingly extremely unstable. There is everything to be said at this point for the distinction made by Snyder between late industrializers and late, late industrializers: where the authoritarian control of the latter over society is so complete that rational policy making is as possible as it was in eighteenth-century absolutism, the compromised coalition politics of the former made the weighting of policy impossible and mistaken geopolitical policy likely.[76] On the other hand, Bismarck did a great deal to encourage that neo-Darwinist political culture which so fractured the homogeneity of international society. Attempts to appease Germany at the end of the century foundered in part because of a lack of shared terms of discourse.

A contrast can be drawn between German confusion and the altogether more sensible setting of British priorities in the same period which further justifies concentration on Germany's responsibility for the onset of war. Britain was deeply threatened by German cruisers in the North Sea, and she had found herself overstretched internationally at the time of the Boer War, and unpopular to boot. A skillful and rational policy of retrenchment brought commitments into line with resources.[77] On the one hand, a peace treaty with Japan reduced commitments in the Far East and allowed for a relocation of the fleet. On the other hand, a more diffuse but fundamental agreement was reached with the United States, implicitly recognizing its position as the leading

[76] Snyder, *Myths of Empire*.
[77] A. Friedberg, *The Weary Titan*, Princeton University Press, Princeton, 1988; A. Offer, *The First World War*, Clarendon Press, Oxford, 1989.

power of the Anglo-Saxon world – and thereby allowing Britain once again to redeploy the fleet to home waters. Still, two points against Britain should be made. The first is that Britain was unwise to acquire such vast possessions in the first place. In 1805 William Playfair, friend and follower of Adam Smith, warned against grabbing too much of the world on the grounds that this would lead to resentment. Is there not a modicum of sense in his view that "if there were no such possessions, or if they were equally divided, there would be very little cause for war amongst nations"?[78] A second point concerns liberalism. If the rational character of the British state owed a good deal to the checks and balances of liberal institutions, against this must be set the fact that Sir Edward Grey, the foreign secretary in the run-up to war, was constrained in an altogether more unfortunate way by the members of his own Liberal party. A clear continental commitment to the French (which his officials had sought) or an absolute warning to Imperial Germany in early July 1914 that the invasion of Belgium would entail a British declaration of war would both probably have prevented war.[79] Such declarations were not issued since they would have led to many resignations from the Cabinet and mass liberal protest.

BONHOMIE AND BARBARISM

This long story of the failure to calculate and to understand would in itself matter little, if it had proved possible to pull back from war once it became obvious, as was clearly the case by 1916, that huge destruction was being wrought on the fabric of European civilization. Of course, one reason why this was not possible was that the German state showed no sign of being willing to disgorge conquered territory – and without that the allies might find

---

[78] W. Playfair, *An Inquiry into the Permanent Causes of the Decline and Fall of Wealthy Nations, Illustrated by four engraved Charts. Designed to show how the Prosperity of the British Empire may be Prolonged*, Greenland and Norris, London, 1805, p. 292.
[79] C. Nicolson, "Edwardian England and the Coming of the First World War," in A. O'Day, ed., *The Edwardian Age*, Macmillan, London, 1984.

themselves attacked later by a more favored but equally aggressive neighbor.[80] But something more general than this was at work. Modernity affected war in such a way that it ceased to be an instrument of politics. On the one hand, the application of industry to war created a juggernaut of such size that it seemed to take all the energy of politicians simply to keep it in motion. On the other hand, the war was fought by conscripts, who died in unprecedented numbers. It accordingly became necessary to assure them that they had died for something: in no time at all, a war – as far as England was concerned – for little Belgium became a war to end all wars, in which soldiers expected to return home to a land fit for heroes.[81] Rarely have hopes been so dismally destroyed. After a mere two decades war returned, and in a more extensive, brutal and destructive form.[82] I begin an explanation of renewed escalation by examining the emergence of those revolutionary forces which made this new war different from the first, and turn only after that to the failures of the liberal powers, both at Versailles and thereafter.

Analysis of the two great revolutions of the century can usefully be prefaced by explaining the title of this section, derived from a character in a Malcolm Bradbury novel who voices a preference for the society of anomie to that of bonhomie. Modern social thought has certainly focused intensively on anomie, that is, the alienation and loss of meaning consequent on the destruction of community and its replacement by life in an impersonal, "meaningless" urban environment. The message of most of this thought, which includes much of that of the founding fathers of sociology, is that the individual cannot manage alone, bereft of social support. The deep structure of this message is in fact far from new. The desire for unitary selves animated the ideas of Rousseau, and reflects a more general admiration for the Greek *polis*. Still, the isolation of modern intellectuals, deprived by the spread of mass literacy of their claim to status and trapped in the interstices

---

[80] F. Fischer, *Germany's Aims in the First World War*, Chatto and Windus, London, 1967.
[81] R. Aron, *The Century of Total War*, Derek Verschoyle, London, 1954.
[82] P. M. H. Bell, *The Origins of the Second World War in Europe*, Longman, Harlow, 1988.

of the market, does much to explain the higher pitch with which this viewpoint was rendered – which is to say, of course, that the social experience of modern intellectuals, if not of the vast majority of mankind, has indeed been debilitating.[83] One response to this situation, was that of Max Weber who called for stoicism in the face of the ineluctable fate of what he termed "the disenchantment of the world."[84] But Weber was not above lowering the lights on critical intelligence so as to allow for a little re-enchantment, as when calling for charismatic leaders for democratic societies, and many others showed no discrimination whatever when seeking moral revivals. It can be said immediately that Constant's point about the return of civic virtue amongst the Jacobins holds as true when applied to more modern catch-all ideologies which seek to combine science with the moral certainty of past societies: though planned by men of good intentions, they led to horrible disaster.[85]

The contours of Bolshevism, which made its mark first because the Russian state collapsed in the midst of war, are well known. Lenin's genius as a revolutionary was nowhere more apparent than in his being quite prepared to go against his deep ideas if it ensured the success of the revolution, as happened when property rights were extended to the peasants to ensure the stability of the new order. But deep ideas there were, and these seem to have two sources. Most important was the impact of Marx. What is noticeable about Marx is the insistence, seen in the early essays but present thereafter as a presupposition, that alienation can and must cease. Communist society will restore us to our unitary selves, to a world of self-expression and sharing.[86] It should be

[83]   M. Mann, "On the Ideology of Intellectuals and Other People in the Development of Capitalism," in L. Lindberg, ed., *Stress and Contradiction in Modern Capitalism*, Lexington Books, Lexington, 1975.

[84]   M. Weber, "Science as a Vocation," in *From Max Weber*, ed., H. H. Gerth and C. W. Mills, Oxford University Press, Oxford, 1946.

[85]   The notion of "catch-all" philosophies is that of O. Kirchheimer, "The Transformation of the Western European Party System," in J. LaPalombra and M. Weiner, eds, *Political Parties and Political Development*, Princeton University Press, Princeton, 1966.

[86]   The extent of Marx's debts to the Greeks is apparent from J. Booth, *Households*, Cornell University Press, Ithaca, 1993. The relations between Rousseau and Marx have not been the subject of a thorough examination, but suggestive arguments are contained in R. Wokler, "Rousseau and Marx," in D. Miller and L. Siedentop, eds, *The Nature of*

said immediately that there have in fact only been three types of society in the past when genuine sharing in the face of social complexity has been encountered.[87] Warrior communism was exemplified by Sparta, but has otherwise only rarely been present in the historical record.[88] More common but still rare, has been sharing inside religious communities, most of which pool their resources in the belief that the millennium is at hand.[89] Finally, communism has flourished amongst intellectuals, albeit usually at the ideational rather than the practical level, and particularly amongst monks or those attracted to monasticism. All this can be put very differently by saying that communism does not, as Marx believed, come naturally on the backs of peasants or workers as the result of socio-economic conditions and practices of production: it rather requires a considerable break in settled social life for it ever to gain significance. Spontaneous forces were never likely to maintain communism in any large society; not surprisingly, the realization of Marxism in practice has always depended upon brutal authoritarianism. More particularly, Lenin hugely admired the Jacobins, and it is accordingly appropriate to see the Bolsheviks as their descendants. But the socialist heroism to which Lenin was naturally attracted had still further sources. For one thing, the allied attack on the nascent revolution encouraged war communism, and this initially allowed expansion to the West. For another, the sense of isolation intensified a decade later when the Kuomintang turned on the Chinese communists, creating an atmosphere in which forced and speedy industrialization seemed to have geopolitical logic on its side.

If the combination of these factors created a brutal totalitarian system, this revolution in power did not have the aggressive and expansionist quality of its French precursor. The early period of war communism was in fact followed by a step backwards, made as much as anything else in pure confusion, away from a com-

---

Political Theory, Oxford University Press, Oxford, 1983 and G. della Volpe, *Rousseau and Marx*, Lawrence and Wishart, London, 1978.

[87]   J. A. Hall, "A View of a Death: on Communism, Ancient and Modern," unpublished paper, 1995.

[88]   D. Dawson, *Cities of the Gods*, Oxford University Press, Oxford, 1992.

[89]   N. Cohn, *The Pursuit of the Millennium*, Harper and Row, New York, 1961.

mand economy. More importantly, the genuinely international revolutionary sentiments of this early period ceased – as European fascists realized, *pace* their propaganda – at a time when the Soviet Union was fully under the dictatorial control of Stalin. One reason for this was simply that the Soviet Union was sufficiently large to allow industrialization to take place internally, that is, without the need to seek supplies or markets outside its borders. A second reason is that the fact of late, late development placed policy making in a single set of hands, free from the need to gain legitimacy by foreign adventure. For the most part, Stalin was exceedingly cautious: he made it clear that socialism could proceed in one country, and he was quite prepared to sacrifice the interests of an international movement so as to forward those of the Soviet Union, as was true of his behavior in Spain and still more so when the infamous pact was made with Hitler in 1939. Of course, the ability of the state to calculate clearly does not guarantee good policy: there remains no good explanation as to why Stalin trusted Hitler so completely and for so long.

The German case is more complex because crisis in the state came only a decade after the war, with the Nazis gaining power only through a backstairs deal. Crisis of the state did not result wholly from the presence of the Nazis: to the contrary, what mattered most was the inability of the political center to hold. The earliest actions of the Social Democrats in power were directed towards the suppression of their greatest political rivals, the communists, and co-operation on the left was thereafter impossible. Further, the leftist social policy of the Social Democrats made for passive disloyalty on the part of capital, for all that few businessmen actually bankrolled the Nazi climb to power.[90] Most importantly, the fledgling democracy faced the horrendous problems of the Versailles settlement, that is, the problems of reparations and national humiliation – the former encouraging economic profligacy, the latter ensuring that Germany would not be on good terms with her neighbors. What mattered most was that the country continued to lack basic coherence, thereby

[90]   H. A. Turner, *German Big Business and the Rise of Hitler*, Oxford University Press, Oxford, 1985.

becoming ungovernable – or, rather, being governable only by means of presidential decree. Any government that could agree on constitutional issues differed about social issues, whilst any alliance in favor of capitalist demands could not agree on foreign policy.[91] It was in these circumstances that members of the traditional right turned to Hitler, thinking that he could be controlled for their own purposes. We know this not to have been possible, and it is worth spelling out the revolutionary nature of the radical right.

Fascism was distinctively an international movement, eventually spreading nearly everywhere east of France's borders. Probably the key general factor at work was that the collapse of old regimes and empires meant the destruction of key institutions of social control; differently put, there was often very little at work beneath authoritarian façades, not least because divide-and-rule policies had played on the divided nature of these societies to make the coalitions of normal politics exceptionally hard to build.[92] Still, the international movement depended very much on the German exemplar. Here the rise of Nazism immediately owed much to defeat in war because of the feelings of betrayal and disillusion of ex-soldiers. Such personnel formed the early core support of the movement, and also provided the myth, personified by Hitler himself, of shared brotherhood. More generally, this is the world of state servants and of lesser intellectuals who were especially hurt by economic chaos. These were the great ideologists of fascism.[93] Such thinkers were deeply attracted to the ideal of a unitary and warm society, marked by social harmony, and they hated liberalism quite as much as did the Bolsheviks.[94] But this ideology was aggressive from the start, not least since it was completely convinced of the need, given Darwinian presuppositions, to have secure sources of supply

[91]   R. Lepsius, "From Fragmented Party Democracy to Government by Emergency Decree and National Socialist Takeover," in J. Linz and A. Stepan, eds, *The Breakdown of Democratic Regimes*, Johns Hopkins University Press, Baltimore, 1978.
[92]   J. Linz, "Some Notes Toward a Comparative Study of Fascism in Sociological Historical Perspective," in W. Laqueur, ed., *Fascism*, Wildwood House, New York, 1976.
[93]   Z. Sternhell, "Fascist Ideology," in Laqueur, *Fascism*.
[94]   J. Herf, *Reactionary Modernism*, Cambridge University Press, Cambridge, 1984.

and market outlets.[95] There was in fact no more economic necessity for imperialism in the 1930s than there had been two decades before, as could have been seen from the successful trading policy pursued by the Weimar republic. Still, increasing tensions created a self-made trap such that aggression to the east probably became economically necessary and certainly economically profitable.[96]

The most immediate point to be made about the allies is that the peace made at Versailles was fundamentally flawed, with the reparations clauses mattering far less than the very idea of national self-determination. The trouble lay in the fact that no set of territories could be created to replace the Austrian and Ottoman empires which would be socially homogeneous; this applied in social, linguistic, and religious terms but above all in terms of nationality. Within every new state there were minorities, whose views depended both on the way in which they were treated and on the promixity and political flavoring of any external national homeland. It was extremely easy to create discontent and distrust. Thus Masaryk's comment, made on December 22, 1918, that Germans were colonists and immigrants was never forgotten by the Sudeten population of the western rim of Bohemia – and this despite the fact that a good deal of liberalism was present inside Czechoslovakia.[97]

Liberal practices were less apparent, to take a second case, in Poland.[98] The national homogenizing practices of the Poles can be seen as directed against Ukrainians, Jews, and Germans. The former were sufficiently few, rural and economically powerless to be considered the proper object of assimilation. In contrast, it was held that the Jews should not be assimilated, and a whole series of measures – from banning trading on Sundays to forced boycotts

[95] D. Kaiser, *Economic Diplomacy and the Origins of the Second World War*, Princeton University Press, Princeton, 1980.
[96] See the debate on this point between T. Mason, R. J. Overy and D. Kaiser in *Past and Present*, no. 122, 1989.
[97] R. M. Smelser, *The Sudeten Problem, 1933–38*, Wesleyan University Press, Middletown, 1975, p. 8.
[98] R. Blanke, *Orphans of Versailles*, University Press of Kentucky, Lexington, 1993. My attention was drawn to this reference by R. Brubaker, "Nationalising States in the Old 'New Europe' – and the New," *Ethnic and Racial Studies*, vol. 19, 1995.

of Jewish stores – was designed to assure dissimilation. Germans were regarded in a still worse light, as people who could not be assimilated, since they were seen as representing a Fifth Column given German efforts to revise borders, and most notably to acquire the Polish Corridor splitting East Prussia from the rest of Germany; and they were further disliked both because of their economic power and as the creators of Germanizing policies in the pre-war period which had caused massive resentment. In consequence, no mail was delivered if a German name was used, discriminatory land reform policies were created specifically to hurt Germans, attempts were made to destroy schools, and interference with religious practices became widespread. The result was mass emigration back to Germany: by the mid-1920s about 85 percent of urban and 55 percent of rural Germans had left. These practices were quite probably self-defeating in that they caused the attitudes which were disliked, whereas without them the ethnic Germans might well have been quite happy to be loyal Poles.

At this point, it is well worth noting a French memorandum of December 24, 1918 which noted that "the more we enlarge Poland at the expense of Germany, the more certain we shall be that she will remain her enemy."[99] Added to this was the fact that plebiscites were only allowed in areas that were likely to go to Poland, none being allowed in Poznania for fear that many Poles might have voted for economic reasons to join Germany. So some of the tensions were geopolitically designed rather than being the necessary result of ethnic hatred. All in all, though, it was no accident that war started in Eastern Europe: the area was a sort of power vacuum, in which states that were deeply internally divided and incapable of action, were anyway hostile to each other. The policies pursued by the new states were particularly misguided of course, given the presence of a powerful neighboring state likely to wish to protect its minorities abroad. German concern began under Weimar, and escalated under Hitler first to *Volkstumpolitik* and then to *Aussenpolitik*.

If the notion of self-determination that was so central at

[99]   Blanke, *Orphans of Versailles*, p. 10.

Versailles proved disastrous, a second point about the allies remains as important. It should be clear by this point that the conduct of international relations requires strong nerves and clear thought. In a situation of only partial defeat, two sensible logical possibilities stood before the allies. One of these was that of creating a harsh peace together with the determination to ensure that it was obeyed. The other would have been that of a soft peace designed to reintegrate a great power within international society as effectively as possible. In fact, the allies ended up with a harsh peace without the determination to enforce it. France and Britain were unwilling to fight, both because they feared casualties and were overstretched by nationalist demands in empires that had expanded still further in 1919. The United States retired to isolation, in largest part because Wilson showed so little political skill in the fight to ratify the Treaty.[100] In any case, a situation arose in which endless blackmail could take place. If this was begun by Stresemann, the genius of the policy was Hitler. Thus his first move in foreign policy, that of leaving the League, was combined with a non-aggression pact with Poland, even though this meant abandoning the ethnic Germans there more thoroughly than had Weimar politicians.

The failure to enforce the peace resulted, at the deepest level, from adopting a policy of illusion, although a loss of confidence consequent on Nazism and Bolshevism seeming to have the answers to the problems of the depression mattered as well. The allied states had been understandably revolted by war, with many blaming its incidence on the operations of special interests. This in turn led to a general belief that collective security could be assured through the League of Nations. But the League depended upon harmony, presumed to be a natural state, and it proved to be utterly useless when no common ground was to be found. The League had no teeth, and nobody was really prepared to go to war to defend it.[101] It may even be that the presence of the United States on the European scene would have made little difference,

[100]   W. Widenor, *Henry Cabot Lodge and the Search for an American Foreign Policy*, University of California Press, Berkeley, 1980.
[101]   The classic account of the naivety of the majority of liberals in these years remains E. H. Carr, *The Twenty Years Crisis, 1919–1939*, Macmillan, London, 1939.

pace the tenets of hegemonic stability theory, that is, if it had remained true to the impractical ideals of Wilson seen so disastrously at work in the League he had done so much to design.[102] The point being made can be put in an alternative, more philosophical form. The background assumption for very many in the liberal democracies was that every human being was rational and sensible, and that just beneath the surface agreement was present, waiting to be discovered. The trouble with this position was that it did not realize that values can differ absolutely, and that endless appeasement was less a route to peace than a failure to defend oneself. The slowness to respond that Tocqueville felt to be characteristic of democracy played some part in the origins of the Second World War. Still, the liberal democracies did eventually abandon supine prostration for war.

Two points about Hitler's policy need to be made in order to conclude analysis. Whilst it is certainly true that Hitler grew up in the political culture of Wilhelmine Germany, thereby absorbing its views about the need for economic imperialism, the decisions that led to war were his and his alone, that is, the result of pure and untrammelled ideology rather than of a divided state unable to calculate rationally.[103] Secondly, the international order that Hitler had created in Europe by 1941 might have survived if he had stuck to the West. But Hitler sought grandeur, with the invasion of Russia and the declaration of war on the United States thereby creating logistical conditions bound to lead to defeat.

CONCLUSION

The findings of this chapter certainly reinforce my caution towards the insistence of Gibbon and Bull that benefits are to be derived from state competition within a larger frame of civilization. If the very thought of Nazi hegemony makes endorsement of an open international system virtually mandatory, the ability of European

---

[102]   L. E. Ambrosius, *Woodrow Wilson and the American Diplomatic Tradition*, Cambridge University Press, Cambridge, 1987, p. 291.
[103]   Snyder, *Myths of Empire*, pp. 105–8.

multipolarity to engender disaster is hugely unsettling. Bull further failed to appreciate the problems that can result from forcible homogenization within the units of the system: if states act too viciously international order is likely to break down.

Let me turn from this reflection so as again to relate historical events to the ideal types of international order introduced in the first chapter. The contentions of hegemonic stability theory were not supported by detailed consideration of the long peace that followed the Congress of Vienna, although there may be something to the view that America's retreat into isolationism undermined the stability of capitalist society. The theory of interdependence proved no more powerful a guide. For one thing, economic factors habitually reflect rather than cause geopolitical conditions: thus the international economic rivalry of the interwar period is best seen as the consequence of geopolitical tensions. For another, just as the sad fact is that marital infidelities occur between people who already know each other well, so too is it often the case that war has often broken out between states involved in trade.

Positively, the principle of Concert did help international order, most importantly, given the very short duration of the Concert system, by so increasing homogeneity that realist calculations were much enhanced. This leads into what has been stressed most of all: conflict was kept within bounds when intelligent states existed within an ideologically homogeneous world; equally, to stress the other side of the same coin, war escalated to extremes when states lacked the capacity to calculate within a world fissured by visceral ideological hatreds. The generalization about the diminution of conflict is supported by pre-revolutionary eighteenth-century experience as well as by that of the nineteenth century as a whole; on both occasions a balance of power working within the frame of a single civilization enabled conflict to be kept within bounds. In contrast, the revolutionary cataclysms of the Napoleonic period and the neo-Darwinist atmosphere of the late nineteenth century led to distrust and fear, with the presence of states made incapable by domestic pressure groups of weighing priorities generating still further misunderstanding.

This is a good point at which to subject sophisticated realism to more pointed critical analysis. Can anything be done to separate or to weight the two separate variables conjoined inside this single theory? Is it ideological homogeneity or the presence of intelligent states that matters most to the proper functioning of realism? In some of the cases at work, both factors have been present. Negatively, the Wilhelmine state could not calculate its best interests whilst the ideological atmosphere of Europe was anyway poisoned by neo-Darwinian rhetoric. Positively, the ability of Britain and the United States to reach agreement in the years before 1914 depended on Anglo-Saxon solidarity and realist calculation. It may well be that detailed historical investigation will eventually disentangle the two variables in these particular cases. Still the argument as a whole can be much advanced by saying something now about situations when only one of the variables is present. In these admittedly muddied circumstances, it seems that the ability to calculate is of greater import than ideological homogeneity. Domestic pressures on Napoleon ruled out the accord that was reachable by, say, 1813, rather than ideological division; equally, we will soon see that the conflict against capitalism did not lead to total war since the late, late developmentalist pattern of Soviet history gave it a state able to calculate, with rationality being further mandated by the facts of the nuclear age.

This last argument might suggest ultimate reversion to some version or other of realism.[104] But no such step backwards is being taken. Rather, what matters is the realism/liberalism mix. The crucial descriptive discovery has been that liberalism can enhance the intelligence of states. Wilhelmine Germany lacked the ability to calculate in this way, instead appeasing every constituency of a semi-mobilized late developing society. In contrast, a cabinet system ensured that Britain brought its commitments into line with its capabilities in the early years of this century. Liberalism can and has helped realism by so freeing the state from pressure groups that it gains the capacity to calculate. It is only fair to point out that liberalism's record at this point is imperfect, given that domestic pressures placed some limits on diplomatic action

---

[104] Despite many wise cautionary words, such reversion pervades that brilliant general account of modern *Realpolitik*, Henry Kissinger's *Diplomacy*, Simon and Schuster, New York, 1994.

in Britain in the years before 1914. But more than this is anyway at issue. The record of states led by dictators able to make policy all by themselves is disastrous, as the behavior of Hitler and of Stalin when trusting him most clearly indicate, and a key benefit of liberalism that accordingly deserves especial underscoring is its capacity to improve policy by so privileging deliberate counsel as to control adventurism.[105] Furthermore, the world of late, late development is no longer as stable as it once was, and this suggests the desirability of extending liberalism, given that the people are bound to be ever more central to the modern social contract.

This appreciation of liberalism has stressed institutional mechanisms that allow priorities to be set and which correct the vanities and passions which have caused elites and people to err. But liberalism is complex, and two other of its facets should at least be mentioned. One such facet, that of international solidarity between human beings, was noted when first putting forward the ideal type of liberalism: it was not much in evidence in the period covered by this chapter, albeit the putative solidarity of naive liberal norms was present, and did much harm. But much has been made of a second facet, relatively unknown to international relations experts. The potential challenge of nations and classes can be contained by polities which try to incorporate rather than to exclude. Liberal states ensured their own stability in the period that has been examined by paying attention to this principle.

[105]   Snyder, *Myths of Empire*, chs 5 and 7, discusses the self-correcting mechanism of liberal regimes in mid-Victorian Britain and the postwar United States. For a similar argument, see C. Kupchan, *The Vulnerability of Empire*, Cornell University Press, Ithaca, 1994.

4

La Paix Belliqueuse

The title of this chapter is that given by Raymond Aron to the postwar international order.[1] The great French theorist's precise and judicious mind preferred this term to that of Cold War because violent conflict between the United States and the Soviet Union did not occur, despite preparations, mud-slinging, proxy wars, blackmail, and the intense rivalry generated by each power being the representative of complete ways of life. If the first task of this chapter is that of characterizing and understanding this principal pillar of postwar international order, the second is that of analyzing its consequences for the "Third World." Sovereignty gained by late-developing countries did not prove to be development achieved, and this gave rise to a set of sustained challenges to an order which disadvantaged the South quite as much as it benefited the North: despite much sound and fury, it will be argued that these challenges did not fundamentally disrupt international order. But stability *was* eventually undermined. For many commentators what mattered most was the putative hegemonic decline of the United States.[2] We shall see that there was (and is) very little to recommend this received wisdom. Of course, one reason for doubting the school of decline became overwhelmingly

[1]   R. Aron, *Le Grand Schisme*, Gallimard, Paris, 1948.
[2]   The clearest statement remains R. Gilpin, "American Foreign Policy in the Post-Reagan Era," *Daedalus*, vol. 116, 1987.

obvious immediately after dire predictions for the future of the
United States had been made. To near-universal surprise, the
Soviet Union collapsed, dramatically and completely, in 1989 or
1991 – that is, according to choice, on the occasion of the fall of
the Berlin Wall or the defeat of the August coup which signaled
both the end of communism and the territorial break-up of the
union. This collapse represented a tectonic shift in the international system, and it naturally closes the period with which this
chapter is concerned, leaving its consequences to be investigated
in the final chapter.

POWER AND THE PURSUIT OF PEACE

The origins of the Cold War have been the subject of intense
controversy.[3] This is particularly true of the United States, in any
case the home to the majority of scholars concerned with the
issue. The classic argument has been between a traditional view
which lays the blame on Stalin's expansionism and revisionists
who condemn aggression on the part of the United States – with
that in turn habitually being explained in terms of the needs of
America's capitalist economy.[4] The vitriol with which this controversy was conducted derived from political commitments: the
traditional view differed little from the self-justification of the
actual makers of postwar American grand strategy, and this
irritated the revisionists whose *marxisant* views owed a very great
deal to opposition to the war in Vietnam.[5] More recently, post-
revisionist authors such as John Gaddis, Daniel Yergin, and, most

[3]   T. G. Paterson and R. J. McMahon, eds, *The Origins of the Cold War*, D. C. Heath,
Lexington, 1974.
[4]   Representative statements of the traditional view include W. W. Rostow, *The United
States in the World Arena*, Harper, New York, 1960, L. J. Halle, *The Cold War as History*,
Harper and Row, New York, 1967 and A. Ulam, *The Rivals*, Viking Press, New York,
1971. Key revisionist claims are contained in W. LaFeber, *America, Russia and the Cold
War, 1945–75*, John Wiley, New York, 1976, J. and G. Kolko, *The Limits of Power*,
Harper and Row, New York, 1972, and G. Alperowitz, *Atomic Diplomacy*, Vintage, New
York, 1967.
[5]   R. W. Tucker, *The Radical Left and American Foreign Policy*, Johns Hopkins
University Press, Baltimore, 1971.

recently, Melvyn Leffler have offered a more measured view, made weighty by extensive archival research.[6] Though the synthesis offered here follows the post-revisionists in finding truth on both sides of the initial controversy, it should be admitted immediately that closure to the debate is unlikely. One reason for this is straightforward. The archives of the former Soviet Union are only beginning to be opened to historians; until their contents are fully digested, no definitive history of the origins of the Cold War is possible. Secondly, it is hard to be dispassionate about the character of both the United States and the Soviet Union. Hence it may be useful to note that one of the earliest treatments of the subject, W. H. McNeill's *America, Britain and Russia*, remains one of the best.[7] From the lofty vantage point of a world historian, it was apparent that the nature of the conflict between the two powers which decisively won the war was historically normal, so much what one would expect that no particularly novel interpretation was required. That said, some elements of an analytic history can now usefully be highlighted.

As the Second World War drew to an end Roosevelt became ever more aware, most notably as the result of Soviet behavior in Poland, that Stalin had a decided view of his own interests. As 28 million Soviet citizens died in the war, in comparison to less than half a million Americans, Stalin's insistence on increased security is scarcely surprising. Further, the war seems to have been interpreted in Moscow less as Hitler's than that of rampant, aggressive capitalism, thereby suggesting the necessity of a *cordon sanitaire*. Still, Roosevelt refused – both from fear that a stand-off causing Stalin to go slow in the East would increase American casualties in the Pacific and as the result of his own sheer physical debility – to send American policy down any new track. He had always floated between liberalism and realism, as is evident in the way in which his brainchild the United Nations combines a

[6]   J. L. Gaddis, "The Emerging Post-Revisionist Synthesis," *Diplomatic History*, vol. 7, 1983, offers an overview of this school, whose key works include J. L. Gaddis, *The United States and the Origins of the Cold War*, Columbia University Press, New York, 1972 and *Strategies of Containment*, Oxford University Press, Oxford, 1982, D. Yergin, *Shattered Peace*, André Deutsch, London, 1978, and M. Leffler, *A Preponderance of Power*, Stanford University Press, Stanford, 1992.
[7]   Oxford University Press, Oxford, 1955.

general assembly with a security council of great powers, and he seemed to hope that his personal skills would be able to paper over the cracks in relations with the Soviet Union. This delay and indecisiveness contrasted with Churchill's insistence on the need for a clear understanding of spheres of influence. This was a language that Stalin understood, and the British and Soviet leaders had no trouble reaching a notional agreement as to the division of the world. It may well be that early and forceful realist policy – something which was not, despite the myth, forthcoming at Yalta – would have limited Soviet gains in East and Central Europe.[8]

Nonetheless, upon Roosevelt's death there was a decisive change in tempo that resulted in a new and powerful grand strategy, not just concerned with geopolitical balance but also hugely creative in international economics – as the emphasis on free trade and multilateralism, the founding of the World Bank and the International Monetary Fund, and the creation of a dollar standard so clearly demonstrated. No account of this grand strategy will be satisfactory unless it recognizes the autonomous impact of four factors. First, the revisionists are surely right to stress that the American state, due to its liberal character and its historic lack of geopolitical involvement, was especially permeable, largely through the Council for Foreign Relations, to the wishes and demands of its domestic capitalists.[9] It was during this period, for example, that involvement in Vietnam became likely as south-east Asia became defined as part of "the national interest."[10]

But the revisionist account is incomplete. In particular, secondly, we must note that many state leaders had, from the turn of the century, geopolitical visions of their own, a remarkable number of which had been formed by the Kiplingesque enthusiasms key members absorbed when at school together at Groton.[11]

[8]   V. Mastny, *Russia's Road to the Cold War*, Columbia University Press, New York, 1979.

[9]   J. Frieden, "Sectoral Conflict and US Foreign Economic Policy, 1914–40," *International Organization*, vol. 41, 1988.

[10]   W. Domhoff, *The Power Elite and the State*, Aldine de Gruyter, New York, 1990, especially chs 5 and 6.

[11]   H. K. Beale, *Theodore Roosevelt and the Rise of America to World Power*, Collier Books, New York, 1967; W. Widenor, *Henry Cabot Lodge and the Search for an American*

This elite enjoyed the power it discovered during the war, and embraced empire willingly. There was of course a considerable overlap between the first and second sets of actors; this was scarcely surprising since the latter saw multilateralism as a means to ensure peace, although they stressed quite as much those necessities for hegemonic leadership later to receive codification in academic prose. Nonetheless, if the statements of the political elite, public and private, are to be believed, they were far more worried by questions of security than by the needs of the American economy, whether seen from their own point of view or as interpreted for them by capitalists and their experts. It was traditional balance of power reasoning that underlay the Truman administration's decisions to allow the multilateral norms they preferred to be diluted and to accept involvement in NATO. Further, various economic policies, in particular the Marshall Plan, were created and accepted in order to shore up the geo-political situation.[12]

A third set of actors was not American at all. The collapse of Britain, joined with the vigorous if defensively inclined security demands of Stalin, meant that many Europeans, most notably Bevin, actively sought an American presence.[13] This was an "empire by invitation," and some part of its dynamic came from allied actions.[14] Finally, the actual character of the grand strategy was markedly influenced by the nature of American institutions and experience. The American people – and in particular voters with ethnic ancestries in Ireland and Germany – had long been suspicious of foreign entanglements, and it did not prove easy to gain support for a global policy.[15] The Truman administration in

Foreign Policy, University of California Press, Berkeley, 1980; W. Isaacson and E. Thomas, The Wise Men, Simon and Schuster, New York, 1986; J. L. Gaddis, Strategies of Containment.

12   R. Pollard, Economic Security and the Origins of the Cold War, Columbia University Press, New York, 1985.

13   W. F. Hanreider, Germany, America and Europe, Yale University Press, New Haven, 1989 makes clear the desire to contain both Russia and Germany. The best summary of the European position noted that it sought to keep the Russians out, the Americans in, and the Germans down.

14   G. Lundestad, "Empire by Invitation?" Journal of Peace Research, vol. 23, 1986.

15   F. Gilbert, To the Farewell Address, Princeton University Press, Princeton, 1961; Gaddis, The United States and the Origins of the Cold War, 1941–47.

1946 was faced with a Congress dominated by the Republicans which was at once anti-communist and keen to balance the budget. It proved possible to turn anti-communist Republicans like Vandenberg, who himself faced re-election from mid-Western Polish-American voters, in an internationalist direction, and to split them from that fiscally cautious mainstream headed by Taft which remained suspicious of foreign involvement. Historians disagree as to the exact input of public opinion on policy formation at this time. Whilst a realist "spheres of influence" deal might have been possible before public opinion was aroused, this became difficult once arousal had taken place, given the moralistic terms applied to foreign policy.[16] Involvement became total, by crusade alone, much to the embarrassment of realist sophisticates such as Acheson and Kennan. This all-or-nothing approach finally became cemented by the Korean war which seemed to justify the charges made by McCarthy about the "loss" of China. Thereafter fear of electoral retribution, perhaps exaggerated in fact, made politicians reluctant to see the world in other than bipolar terms. This led to overextension – not in Europe but in the Third World, where bipolar tunnel-vision prevented proper appreciation of local contexts and where there were few strategic interests of any real significance.[17]

Some reflections on the debate about the origins of the Cold War are suggested by this review of American grand strategy. To begin with, the threat faced by Western Europe was both real and substantial. If the revisionists are wrong to ignore that, they may well be right, however, when insisting that the manner in which danger was met, that is, by means of an ideological crusade, created movement to the extremes, as in a game of mirrors in which processes of perception and misperception overtook calmer, more rational calculation.[18] Beyond this, complexities abound:

[16]   K. Klingberg, "Cyclical Trends in American Foreign Policy Moods and Their Policy Implications," in C. W. Kegley and P. McGowan, eds, *Challenges to America*, Sage, Beverly Hills, 1979; S. Hoffmann, *Gulliver's Troubles, or, The Setting of American Foreign Policy*, McGraw Hill, New York, 1968.

[17]   S. van Evera, "American Strategic Interests: Why Europe Matters, Why the Third World Doesn't," Testimony prepared for hearings before the Panel on Defense Burden Sharing, Committee on Armed Forces, US House of Representatives, 2 March, 1988.

[18]   S. Hoffmann, "On the Origins of the Cold War," in L. H. Miller and R. W. Preussen, eds, *Reflections on the Cold War*, Temple University Press, Philadelphia, 1974.

key actors changed their minds, with Kennan initially favoring a spheres of influence deal whilst yet creating a climate of crusade through his analyses of Soviet conduct.[19] Nonetheless, a clear judgement about the end result can be made. An international order was created, albeit in a piecemeal manner given the absence of any formal conference, that achieved stability – even if, as is likely, the complete freezing of history was overdone. In order to understand the actual workings of the system created, attention must first be given to the external agreement between the two superpowers, before then seeing how they maintained order within the spheres over which they exercised hegemony.

The postwar settlement created stability most obviously because its terms reflected the realities of power in the bluntest possible way.[20] Utterly unlike Versailles and its aftermath, nationalism mattered so little that both Korea and Germany were divided. The realities of power, moreover, made this a simple system to operate. The system was effectively bipolar from the start, and definitively so with the advent of nuclear weapons; if the former made calculation easy, the prospect of absolute destruction created by the latter necessarily concentrated minds – not least that of Khrushchev whose famous declaration, that the atomic bomb did not distinguish between social classes, makes the point beautifully. And if these were states which could calculate, they were equally "enemy partners."[21] This may seem a strange claim. But the fact that the opposition between the superpowers was between different and competing principles of civilization in itself did something to induce a clarity of thought that had been missing in the inter-war period.[22] More importantly, an awareness of a common destiny was soon equally present, and this became institutionalized via "hot-lines" of communication and, on the part of the United States, an absolute realization (in fact though not in rhetoric) that there would be no rollback – that is, no aid would ever be given to any people in Eastern Europe attempting to be

[19]   J. L. Gaddis, *The Long Peace*, Oxford University Press, Oxford, 1987, ch. 3.
[20]   Gaddis, *The Long Peace*, p. 220 and ch. 8 passim.
[21]   The expression "enemy partners" is taken from R. Aron, *Peace and War*, Weidenfeld and Nicolson, London, 1966, ch. 18.
[22]   Gaddis, *The Long Peace*, pp. 233–7.

free. Differently put, propaganda hid the fact that the leaders of the superpowers understood each other very well indeed.

The United States most certainly dominated capitalist society within this international order in a way that Britain never did at its moment of greatest strength. Hegemony resulted from the United States being dominant in all the key sources of power that affect world politics – monetary, ideological, military, and economic.[23] Further, the ending of the war showed American leaders grasping new opportunities with enthusiasm: Keynes's plan for a clearing union was dismissed since it ran counter to American interests, and financial power was used very decidedly to make Britain realize who was now number one.[24] Three points are of especial importance in order to appreciate the more general impact of the United States. First, the United States provided a model of how to overcome internal social struggles. The politics of productivity, soon to be (loosely) described as Keynesian, meant that zero-sum redistributive conflicts could be avoided.[25] Secondly, if the sheer fact of winning the war meant the destruction of the extreme right, the United States also helped undermine the extreme left.[26] The promotion of centrist parties, particularly those of Christian Democracy in Europe, was far from difficult: the allies were essentially knocking at an open door, since wholesale conversion to a new order based on social redistribution had already been made. The end result was a type of "embedded liberalism," designed to cushion societies so that market forces might work better.[27] Thirdly, the American presence solved the security dilemmas of Japan and Europe, thereby making genuine interdependence based on trade rather than any search for self-sufficiency the norm within a world threatened by communism. It is this which explains the high levels of private investment in Europe immediately after the war, with Japan benefiting more

[23]   J. Nye, *Bound to Lead*, Basic Books, New York, 1990.
[24]   R. Gardner, *Sterling–Dollar Diplomacy*, Macmillan, London, 1969.
[25]   C. Maier, "The Politics of Productivity," *International Organization*, vol. 31, 1977.
[26]   C. Maier, "The Two Postwar Eras and the Conditions for Stability in Twentieth Century Western Europe," *American Historical Review*, vol. 86, 1981.
[27]   J. G. Ruggie, "International Regimes, Transactions and Change," *International Organization*, vol. 36, 1982.

directly when it became a source of military supplies during the Korean war.

Still, the hegemonic leader did not absolutely have its way even at the height of its power. The United States failed to realize its greatest hope, namely that of Britain, divested of its colonies, leading a move to a supranational capitalist Europe capable of its own defense.[28] Marshall Aid was not sufficient to give powerful leverage towards this end, and American designs for reconstruction through the Committee of European Economic Co-operation were seen to have failed by 1949, the year in which America went into recession.[29] The near-collapse of Britain in that year forced the United States to endorse France's attempt to lead in a Europe that would be opposed to multilateral norms, as well as to recognize, for security reasons, the sterling area. The Bretton Woods system died the earliest of deaths, to be resuscitated only between 1958 and 1971. In contrast, successful reconstruction was based initially on the European Payments Union and then upon the European Coal and Steel Community – which famously provided a model for the European Economic Community. The detailed history of the European Coal and Steel Community shows the most important creative element at work to have been that of French bureaucrats seeking to control Germany less by force than co-operation.[30] But if one element of most initiatives for integration has been that of wishing to control Germany, another has been that they serve the interests of other states.[31] Thus for Belgium, the European Coal and Steel Community underwrote the sort of welfare arrangements to which it was already committed. Belgium eventually received large payments that allowed for retraining of its miners, for market forces eventually led to the collapse of the industry, as the government had in fact wanted.[32] Exactly the same point must be made about the Common Agricultural Policy. It is of course entirely correct to see the policy as a

[28] I draw here on A. Milward's revisionist *The Reconstruction of Western Europe, 1945–51*, University of California Press, Berkeley, 1984. See too his magisterial *The European Rescue of the Nation-State*, University of California Press, Berkeley, 1992.
[29] Milward, *The Reconstruction of Western Europe, 1945–51*, chs 1 and 3.
[30] J. Duchêne, *Jean Monnet*, W. W. Norton, New York, 1994.
[31] Milward, *The European Rescue of the Nation-State*, p. 443.
[32] Milward, *The European Rescue of the Nation-State*, ch. 3.

huge protectionist affair, but its historic role nonetheless has been that of escorting huge numbers of peasants and agricultural workers off the land.[33] More important than either of these, however, was the opening of opportunities for internal European trade. It proved possible for Europe to prosper in 1949 despite depression in the United States because the German market was expanding so fast. The secret to the European boom and to the phenomenal growth of the postwar years is that of production for high-technology markets.[34] Great support is lent to this proposition by the fate of Great Britain: left outside Europe, trading with the empire (partly in order to repay the sterling balances), she lost more and more market share, and became ever less dynamic an economy.[35]

Two analytic points implicit in this account deserve emphasis. The first concerns the states of advanced capitalism. Many countries sought from the end of the nineteenth century to be everything, to become complete "power-containers," worlds unto themselves.[36] This policy went disastrously awry. A first thought when trying to summarize the character of postwar states is that little has changed: what is obviously true of Japan is as true of Western Europe once we remember that the European Union (and its various predecessors) is an area of high diplomacy between states rather than the organ of a supranational society.[37] Nonetheless, this first thought would be far too narrow. The key reality that needs to be remembered is that these countries are now successful. Two sides of what is a single coin need to be stressed. On the one hand, these countries both integrated their people into a settled way of life, marked by welfare provisions and continual economic growth, and provided consociational and federal arrangements for national minorities which look set, as we shall see in the next chapter, to ensure their loyalty. On the other hand, these states now exist within a larger frame, meaning that zero-sum, no-holds-barred, beggar-my-neighbour competition has

[33]   Milward, *The European Rescue of the Nation-State*, ch. 5.
[34]   Milward, *The European Rescue of the Nation-State*, ch. 4.
[35]   Milward, *The European Rescue of the Nation-State*, ch. 7.
[36]   A. Giddens, *The Nation-State and Violence*, Polity Press, Cambridge, 1985.
[37]   S. Hoffmann, "Europe's Identity Crisis Revisited," *Daedalus*, vol. 123, 1994.

ceased – albeit, with the exception, to be analyzed later, of the ever more predatory demands of the hegemon itself. Regular meetings within the context of shared objectives has created a very particular, partially institutionally integrated society of states: one element of this has been the creation of an international community of policy experts, another has been the emergence of something like an international upper class.[38] In a nutshell, the states of capitalist society have finally become successful: doing less has enabled them to achieve more. Their powers, internal and external, have been increased rather than diminished by co-operation – not surprisingly since genuine state strength lies, to adopt Samuels's suggestive phrase about Japan, in the politics of reciprocal consent.[39]

Secondly, it is well worth highlighting what may anyway have been noticed, namely that two separate forces – political liberalism and the improved economic well-being consequent on growth, full employment, and welfare – contributed to stability in advanced capitalism. Key reformers felt that the two forces went together, and they certainly provided each other with mutual support. But some attempt to weight the two factors can be made. For by the end of the 1970s academics and commentators on both the left and right habitually agreed that the mix of political freedom with social inequality was no longer stable. Pundits began to speak of a crisis of governability caused above all by a loss of deference in working classes and a consequential secular tendency to inflation, particularly as politicians sought to win elections by means of economically irresponsible policies that gained votes.[40] Most of these prognostications were utterly confounded. For the great postwar inflation was eventually defeated, with many of the politicians responsible for this reaping electoral reward for placing long-term considerations above immediate advantage. It is worth noting in this context that countries with corporatist arrange-

[38] G. J. Ikenberry, "Creating Yesterday's New World Order," in J. Goldstein and R. Keohane, eds, *Ideas and Foreign Policy*, Cornell University Press, Ithaca, 1992; K. van der Pijl, *The Making of an Atlantic Ruling Class*, New Left Books, London, 1984.
[39] R. J. Samuels, *The Business of the Japanese State*, Cornell University Press, Ithaca, 1987.
[40] E. A. Gellner, "A Social Contract in Search of an Idiom," *Political Quarterly*, vol. 46, 1975.

ments, heralded in the 1970s as a source of stability and so of growth, have not performed particularly well; this is not surprising once we realize that the great inflation was not caused by working-class pressure in the first place.[41] All this suggests that liberal politics may have been more important as a source of stability than more material considerations; differently put, the generalization that liberalism diffuses conflicts through society seems intact. Still, it would be naive, as we shall see, to begin to take social stability for granted. For one thing, one wonders whether liberalism would continue to diminish conflict in the face of long-term absolute decline of material standards – something which has not been the experience of the majority, even in Britain and the United States. For another, the great postwar inflation was caused in large part by the behavior of the leading power: Lyndon Johnson preferred to print money rather than to tax the American people so as to pay for the Great Society in tandem with involvement in Vietnam, thereby creating an inflation that allied powers were then bound to import.[42] This is a classic instance of hegemonic predation.

Just as various social and political logics intertwined within the West, so too at least three social forces – socialist heroism for sure, but also militarism (powerful under Trotsky and still more so later because of the defeat of Hitler in the Great Patriotic War), and a model of development – mingled together to create the social formation characteristic of the socialist bloc.[43] Further, it is both conventional and accurate to distinguish between two periods within the history of state-organized socialism. The first period might be termed that of heroism and terror, the latter that of economic stagnation and softer political rule. But this change scarcely matters here. Given that the intention is that of explaining order within the socialist bloc, brevity is all too possible. "Actually-existing-socialism" was an exceptionally brutal power-system. More is meant here than such Stalinist institutions, applied to every country in the bloc, as show trials, secret police, and

---

[41]   M. Smith, *Power, Norms and Inflation*, Aldine de Gruyter, New York, 1992.

[42]   Smith, *Power, Norms and Inflation*.

[43]   A. Janos, "Social Science, Communism and the Dynamics of Political Change," *World Politics*, vol. 44, 1991.

prison camps. The system was exceptionally centralized, and the postwar period showed on several occasions that little deviation from policy established in Moscow was to be allowed. Order within socialism was maintained by fear, with the invasions of 1956 and 1968 designed as exemplars for others. Two points deserve to be emphasized here. Firstly, hindsight makes it clear that socialist society was brittle because authoritarian power concentrated and increased the intensity of conflict. Socialist rule meant that a strike was – necessarily had to be – a move against the regime, in contrast to the West where economic conflict did not necessarily take on political coloring. Secondly, life chances within state socialism always depended upon what happened in Moscow. It will accordingly be to that city that we will look later when seeking to explain the demise of the second world.

THE RISE AND FALL OF THE THIRD WORLD

The notion of a "Third World" following industrial capitalism and the model applied inside the Soviet empire first gained prominence in postwar France. The concept initially suggested great hope. The poor wartime performance of the European empires, particularly in the East, hastened decolonization, and to increasing numbers of new states was added an ideology of non-alignment and developmentalism, held to include nation-building as well as economic modernization – the best route to which for many was some form of socialist planning. The measure of disillusion that followed from the realization that statehood did not automatically translate into wealth, that is, that political independence could mask economic dependence, occasioned greater challenge to the advanced world: on the one hand stood revolutionaries such as Che Guevara and the Vietcong, on the other economic radicals, first at the United Nations then within the Organization for Petroleum Exporting Countries, insisting on a New International Economic Order. This greater assertiveness was a failure, and this is one reason why it now certainly makes sense to abandon the very notion of a Third World.

One brute indicator of the troubles of the less-developed world since 1945 is the fact that at least 20 million people have died there through violence under an international order held – quite properly since a world war with nuclear weapons was avoided – to have created a long peace. As a good deal will necessarily be made of the failings of the advanced world, it makes sense to begin by disputing the notion that the rivalry between the super-powers brought nothing but harm to the Third World. Most importantly, the fact of stalemate at the systemic level gave the Third World – or at least those parts of it not clearly incorporated into superpower spheres of influence – some room for maneuver. A country such as Egypt had the possibility of accepting bids for its favors, and of changing alliances at will. Differently put, some autonomy was given to the less-developed world by the fear of both superpowers that massive external interventions might entail nuclear confrontation: it was this background situation that allowed oil exporters to increase oil prices in the 1970s. This fact does much to explain the very great allegiance given to the norms of non-intervention and sovereignty enshrined in the United Nations' Charter – although those norms were embraced with especial warmth by the leaders of many states, notably in Africa, aware that attempts to change admittedly absurd borders might well lead to something worse. That something more than mere ideology was involved here can be seen in the amazing fact that decolonization and the collapse of the Soviet Union account for virtually all changes in territorial borders since 1945. Further, the superpowers favored decolonization. The contribution of the Soviet Union was, given shortage of capital, ideological more than practical, that is, the power of example wedded to the insistence on the justice of wars of national liberation; still, this contribution was made powerful by quite general acceptance of the view that empires were "necessary" for capitalism. In contrast, the United States was in a position in which it could directly influence certain of its allies. This was a crucial factor explaining the speed with which Dutch colonial possessions were granted independence, and it had some influence on British policy makers. Still, probably the key factor in the British decision to relinquish empire without a fight was the realization that the loss of the Indian army made the costs of empire far outweigh their benefits.

The factor at work in this last consideration is of such importance that it deserves to be both highlighted and generalized. The wealth of European nations never depended, as argued, upon the exploitation of poor countries, and a logical possibility, especially in the face of costs generated by nationalist movements, was that of abandoning territorial empire.[44] The loss of empire in the postwar period did not so much dictate European economic decline as open the way to the greatest period of economic growth in European history. Capitalism proved to be flexible enough to deal with changes in economic networks – in fact benefiting from a move out of small and backward markets to larger, more competitive arenas. The realization that territorial expansion is not necessary for economic well-being was appreciated at differential speeds, with France, perhaps due to a mistaken interpretation of Spanish decline, being far slower than Britain to make the final move from heroism to trading. The United States remains still reluctant to replace the logic of military with that of economic power.

This last judgement may seem strange. On the one hand, the United States has not, at least until very recently, traded much with the world as a whole, let alone with the Third World – that is, trade has been small as a proportion of national product, for all that this gave the United States the largest single share of world trade. On the other hand, the international regimes created by the United States in the aftermath of war habitually applied the crassest economic logic to the developing world; this is in marked contrast to the political sensitivity with which the embedded liberalism of advanced countries was endorsed, and this despite the fact that nation-building and state-building are absolutely essential for economic development.[45] But statist policies tended to be seen as communist, and this proved terrifying, especially given ever more uncritical acceptance of the domino theory, that is, the view that the loss of a single country might mean nothing less than the end of the free world as a whole.[46] This view had little to

[44]   A characteristically brilliant and influential statement of this position was R. Aron, *La tragédie algérienne*, Plon, Paris, 1957.
[45]   Ruggie, "International Regimes, Transactions, and Change."
[46]   S. Krasner, *Defending the National Interest*, Princeton University Press, Princeton, 1978.

recommend it: resentment in Iran caused by the removal of Mossadeq in 1953 helped prepare the way for the Ayatollah Khomeini
two decades later, whilst the spread of nationalism was always
likely, as Kennan realized in the late 1940s and as ought to have
been generally obvious after the Sino-Soviet split, to dilute the
cohesion of the communist movement.[47] Whilst there is some truth
to the view that this rigid position was maintained due to fear of
electoral punishment, it was equally the result of the intellectual
laziness that came with visceral anti-communism, that is, of lesser
minds than those who had created the postwar strategy refusing
to think their own times. One reason for saying this is that Nixon's
diplomatic revolution was the result of fundamental intelligence
for all that it was a move easier for a Republican than for a
Democrat. The analytic point to be made about the abandonment
of Vietnam together with the opening to China is that it massively
strengthened the position of the United States. The predominant
tone of American foreign policy for the last quarter of the century
has been that of resolute lack of involvement in the Third World,
with the partial exception of those engagements made suitable for
television by the fact that American casualties are avoided. Heroism has been abandoned in practice, but not in theory, and the
United States has certainly not made a full transition to any
generalized trading strategy. The picture as a whole is complicated. If one facet of the power of the United States lay in the self-
sufficiency which allowed it to divest itself of commitments,
another lay in the economic muscle that followed from possessing
huge amounts of capital. This structural power was seen in the
debt crisis: for most of the 1980s Latin America lowered its living
standards so as to send huge amounts of capital to the richest
country in the world. But there is complexity here too. Against
such exploitation should be set the surprising fact that the United
States, largely as the result of initiatives taken by President Carter,
has sometimes promoted democracy in regions where it once
favored mere strong men.[48] Whether this support for democrati-

[47]   S. Hoffmann, *Duties Beyond Borders*, Syracuse University Press, Syracuse, 1981; van
Evera, "American Strategic Interests"; Gaddis, *Strategies of Containment*.
[48]   K. Sikkink, "The Power of Principled Ideas," in Goldstein and Keohane, *Ideas and
Foreign Policy*.

zation can withstand the economic pressures entailed by speedy debt repayment is a moot point.

If the self-sufficiency and economic power of the West did much to counter the challenge mounted by developing countries, a full account of the fall of Third World assertiveness must give equal attention to a second reason, that of increasing fragmentation within that putatively unitary social world. Even though much of the dynamic of this latter process is internally generated, larger structures of power still impinge upon it; to understand this entails moving beyond Eurocentric assumptions about states, wars, and nations. This point can initially best be advanced by noting the nature of wars experienced by the developing world.

The Vietnam war can be seen in Clausewitzian, European terms, despite its origins in guerilla war and the fact that one side lost less than 60,000 soldiers in contrast to more than two million Vietnamese deaths. Other engagements within the Third World whose rationale is essentially local are similarly classical in their character, for all that their logistics depend upon supplies from the outside. This judgement applies to the wars between Israel and the Arab states, between India and Pakistan, and, more recently and most savagely, between Iran and Iraq. But the largest number both of deaths and of wars within the developing world have been internal rather than inter-state. Many of these were proxy wars. This was particularly true in the 1970s when the Soviet Union threw its previous geopolitical caution to the winds, thereby allowing the United States to arm the Islamic rebels of Afghanistan just as the Soviets themselves had once supported the Vietcong. The harm inflicted by some of these wars is hard to exaggerate: Mozambique has now become one of the poorest of all states, a situation from which recovery is horribly difficult since the countryside is still littered with mines. Nonetheless, much civil strife, especially in Africa, is entirely the result of internal circumstance. What needs to be noticed most of all in this connection is the weakness of many states: these are "quasi-states" held together by international agreement rather than by their being able to provide a Hobbesian minimum of internal order.[49]

---

[49]   R. H. Jackson, *Quasi-States*, Cambridge University Press, Cambridge, 1990; J. Herbst, "War and the State in Africa," *International Security*, vol. 14, 1990.

This difference between the advanced and the less-developed world might not seem to amount to much. After all, European states were once equally artificial, and centuries were required before they could establish and normatively integrate within set boundaries. But the pattern of the past is unlikely to be repeated. The most fundamental reason for this is implicit in what has already been said. Endless competition between states, that is, that Darwinian pressure which necessitated interaction between state and society, forced social rationalization in Europe. Normative agreements to limit inter-state war, in Latin America after independence and much more generally now, rule out this historic route to state-building. And this is not the only abstract consideration suggesting that states in the Third World are likely to remain weak. Three further factors deserve notice in their own right. These will make it possible to demonstrate the fragmentation of the Third World by showing how their presence or absence accounts for different developmental records of varied political economies.

The first factor at issue is nationalism, about which key points can be made by concentrating on language. In the European past, the emergence of linguistically homogeneous communities was the result of violence and of time, that is, rulers insisted on a single language which came slowly to dominate as leading members of regional cultures acceded to a medium from which they could benefit. Whilst some developing states are blessed by homogeneity, many are not. Their pattern of state-building will differ from that of early modern Europe.[50] On the one hand, modern state-building takes place, as was apparent even when discussing Austro-Hungary at the end of the nineteenth century, in an era of mass education. This matters enormously since linguistic diversity is now encoded in society thanks to the infrastructure provided by mass education systems – making it harder to homogenize or nationalize, not least since such policies face the television cameras of the world. On the other hand, the state's servants have more clearly articulated self-interest than their forebears in royal house-

---

[50] This paragraph follows D. Laitin, *Language repertoires and state construction in Africa*, Cambridge University Press, Cambridge, 1992.

holds. Quite often their claim to status rests on mastery of a foreign language, and they are accordingly unwilling to support any nationalizing process which would diminish this. Forcible homogenization in the face of these two conditions has required – and, more importantly, has bred – great violence. In this context, it is worth noting that economic development, especially in Africa, has not been much helped by vicious policies of homogenization resulting in endless social exclusion. The alternative solution that has been sometimes tried, and which is hugely preferable in prescriptive terms, is that of state-building by means of accommodation. A stable formula has perhaps been reached in India in which the individual needs to master "three plus or minus one languages," that is, the central state languages of Hindi and English (for Indian nationalism could not overcome the vested interest of bureaucrats trained in English) together with the language of the provincial state, with the minus referring to someone living in a Hindi-speaking state and the plus to a member of a minority within any provincial state.

This leads to a second point. It has often been suggested that imitative industrialization cannot be achieved under liberal democratic rule.[51] The rationale for this view is that speedy structural change requires concentration of power so that a society can, so to speak, be given an entirely different direction. John Stuart Mill felt such concentration of power for developmental purposes to be justified, and it equally stands behind the ideas of Friedrich List, the practice of communism in power, and the advantages of backwardness more generally.[52] Whilst this is a complicated issue, dictatorial powers should not be recommended too easily, that is, on the assumption that they will automatically result in economic development. For one thing, many states became dictatorial without the leaders then trying to rationalize or change societies at all. Mobutu is a good example of this: aid money is spent on

---

[51]   E. Gellner, "Democracy and Industrialisation," *European Journal of Sociology*, vol. 8, 1967.

[52]   J. S. Mill, *Considerations on Representative Government*, Harper, New York, 1862, ch. 23; R. Szporluk, *Communism and Nationalism*, Oxford University Press, Oxford, 1988; A. Gershenkron, "Economic Backwardness in Historical Perspective," in B. Hoselitz, ed., *The Progress of Underdeveloped Areas*, Chicago University Press, Chicago, 1952.

arms, but the larger society is ignored, one consequence of which has been fundamental societal regression. For another, many have tried – especially under the hugely deleterious influence of the Soviet model – absolutely disastrous policies which have caused dreadful problems. Moreover, the reaction to dictatorial power has often been to create social movements of great political intensity, thereby ruling out the give and take of "normal politics," in a game in which the winner takes all. For the most part, however, developing states simply do not have the capacity to put into effect central plans, however well designed and intentioned. But if one hesitates to recommend giving power to corrupt and unwieldy states, states with "bounded autonomy" – that is, states which are free from upper-class pressure, demagogic democracy and blessed with geopolitical aid whilst being constrained to perform by nationalist demands and external pressure – can and do foster development.[53]

Thirdly and finally, there is indeed a measure of truth to dependency theory. That measure does not consist in the view that capitalism cannot manage without formal or informal empire: trade and investment figures, with the important exception of oil, go against this, suggesting rather that large parts of the Third World could drop off the map without materially damaging the workings of the world political economy. However, participation in a developed world does have deleterious and distorting effects on new countries, making them dependent where the advanced world is not. One example of this is that of Indian skilled labour, whose free movement inside capitalist society may well be to the detriment of the home country; another is the fact that a truly interdependent world economy makes start-up costs higher, thereby militating against development by means of local crafts.

One political economy to which many of these generalizations do not apply is that of East Asia. National product in South Korea increased by an average 8.5 percent per year between 1962 and

---

[53]   The notion of "bounded autonomy" is fully spelt out in D. Zhao and J. A. Hall, "State Power and Patterns of Late Development," *Sociology*, vol. 28, 1994. The remainder of this section draws on material first presented in this article.

1980; similar rates were achieved only by Taiwan, Singapore, and Hong Kong.[54] Leaving aside the two city states, it is easy to see that South Korea and Taiwan experienced similar phases of economic development: from import-substitution industrialization in the 1950s, to export expansion in the 1960s, followed in turn by heavy but technology-intensive industries after the 1970s – which these states now hope to use for further progress up the product cycle. Each of these policy shifts was engineered by the state by monetary and by non-monetary means such as subsidies, foreign exchange controls, export tax incentives, and tariff barriers.[55] What is striking about the East Asian pattern is less the tools themselves, many of which have been tried elsewhere, than the general political ethic which lies behind their use: the essence of strategy is not protection but rather a policy of "direct and escort," that is, a determination to nourish industrial sectors perceived as important only until they acquired competitive advantage in the world market.

Such state-led developmentalism has been made possible by several factors. Historically, both states were ruled for a long time by unified agrarian empires. Before the arrival of Western powers, these societies already had a unified written language, a dominant religion, and ethnic homogeneity, whilst they more or less shared a common market. The two states possessed high levels of literacy as early as the 1950s, when they were still very poor; this was a direct result of Japanese colonial rule and an indirect result of general East Asian Confucian culture.[56] This advanced political and cultural development encouraged the development of strong nationalist feelings directed against Japanese colonizers. Further, old regime structures were destroyed as the consequence of geopolitical events. The 1948–50 land reform in South Korea had only a limited success because the Rhee government was so entwined with the landed upper class. But invasion and occupa-

[54]   C. Johnson, "Political Institutions and Economic Performance," in F. C. Deyo, ed., *The Political Economy of the New Asian Industrialism*, Cornell University Press, Ithaca, 1987.
[55]   R. Wade, *Governing the Market*, Princeton University Press, Princeton, 1990; A. Amsden, *Asia's Next Giant*, Oxford University Press, Oxford, 1989.
[56]   B. Cumings, "The Origins and Development of the Northeast Asian Political Economy," *International Organisation*, vol. 38, 1984.

tion destroyed the old class structure.[57] The fact that Taiwan's government was imported from mainland China and that it was backed up by pervasive military force meant that the interests of local elites could be completely ignored. The rather poor but egalitarian society that resulted proved to be good developmental material: the state had sufficient room to organize a society which had high levels of consumption and abundant, highly disciplined cheap labour. Finally, the extent of American help can scarcely be exaggerated. Aid monies other than those directly for military purposes financed 40 and 70 percent of gross domestic capital formation between 1952 and 1960 in Taiwan and South Korea respectively.[58] The strategic importance of the region forced America to tolerate both early import substitution policies and the high trade deficit that came when the two states adopted an export-led strategy. The United States also provided many direct economic opportunities to the region, notably when at war with Vietnam.[59] Furthermore, American pressure has more recently supported the emergence first of a softer authoritarianism, firmly oriented to the world market, and then of a controlled move towards democracy. This matters a great deal for foreign policy: the Korean state has real achievements and legitimacy, and is less prone than before to volatile behavior which might have negative consequences for international affairs.

The level of economic development (and of indebtedness) of Latin America was very similar at the time of the first oil shock, and a comparison of differential routes thereafter is accordingly suggestive.[60] What seems to matter most is a very different historical background. Crucially, Latin American states gained independence in the early nineteenth century, and experienced political democracy before industrialization.[61] Their early economic development was based on direct foreign investment so as to

[57] H. Koo, "The Interplay of State, Social Class, and World System in East Asian Development," in Deyo, *The Political Economy of the New Asian Industrialism*, p. 170.
[58] S. Haggard, *Pathways from the Periphery*, Cornell University Press, Ithaca, 1990, p. 196.
[59] Cumings, "The Origins and Development of the Northeast Asian Political Economy."
[60] A. Fishlow, "Latin American Failure against the Backdrop of Asian Success," *Annals of the American Academy*, vol. 55, 1989.
[61] N. Mouzelis, *Politics in the Semi-Periphery*, Macmillan, London, 1986.

allow the export of a few primary products. This pattern made Latin America the hinterland of the core of advanced capitalism, thereby creating an unbalanced economic profile. Indigenous industrialization only really began in the 1930s, and the diminution of international trade at that time ensured that such development was import-substituting in character. This policy had initial successes, but it never gained sufficient salience to bring structural change to society. Large latifundias and native village communities remain the dominant form of landholding in most countries.[62] No fundamental land reform has been undertaken, and Latin America accordingly suffers from massive inequalities.[63] This distributional fact limited both the size and level of integration of the domestic market, and ensured such low levels of literacy and skill that industrial products could find no market niche despite low labour costs. For many reasons, Latin American states were unable to make a successful policy shift from import substitution to export-led growth.[64] Most obviously, states had no autonomy from their landed upper classes. Accordingly, the stagnation that afflicted their economies after the 1960s brought in its tail a series of military coups. These repressive governments did not change the economic situation – except, perhaps, for exacerbating it by borrowing huge amounts of petrodollars in the wake of the second oil shock. When democracy once again become the dominant ideology in world politics in the 1980s, Latin American politics changed their tenor once again. But this has not made any real difference to the economic situation, and democratization remains precarious.

The relative failure of late development in Latin America is

---

[62]   J. Lambert, *Latin America*, University of California Press, Berkeley, 1967; W. Taylor, "Landed Society in New Spain," *Hispanic American Historical Review*, vol. 54, 1974.

[63]   The presence of petroleum, whose revenues could be used to buy off the upper classes, made Venezuela an exception to the rule. In this connection, see T. Karl, "Dilemmas of Democratisation in Latin America," *Comparative Politics*, vol. 22, 1990.

[64]   Neoclassical accounts – for example I. Little, F. Scitovsky and M. Scott, *Industry and Trade in Some Developing Countries*, Oxford University Press, Oxford, 1970 – ascribe the failures of Latin American development to the adoption of import substitution. This is misleading for several reasons. Most obviously, development did occur by means of this strategy, most notably in East Asia. What matters is the ability to move away from this strategy to a new one based on export. This step, taken successfully in East Asia, has proved beyond the capacities of Latin American states.

most obviously explained by the idiosyncratic character of its nationalism, that is, by the fact that the movement for independence sought to contain rather than to mobilize the people.[65] The continuing marked inequalities already noted curtailed successful nation-building. Further, Latin American elites identified themselves with Europe, doubting that their tropical and racially diverse countries could ever achieve a distinctive civilization, as had the United States.[66] It is scarcely surprising that this elite adopted liberal free trade policies, and that its opponents invented dependency theory.[67] One piece of evidence demonstrating that Latin America is still at an early stage both of nation- and state-building is the fact that ideological cycles, from democracy to fascism to the rediscovery of democracy, always went in tandem with those of Europe. Importing a foreign ideology is not without cost. On the one hand, liberalism encouraged Latin American states to involve themselves uncritically in the world market. In comparison with East Asia, Latin America had no period of withdrawal from the international market in order to establish infant industries. Foreign multinationals could accordingly completely dominate the economies of Latin American societies, whereas in East Asia they were forced to become, as the result of the establishment of a national industrial structure, mere junior partners.[68] On the other hand, early democracy brought political instability to the region. The lack of institutional means of expression combined with radicalism, (caused by attempted political exclusion)

[65]   T. S. Skidmore and P. H. Smith, *Modern Latin America*, Oxford University Press, Oxford, 1984.

[66]   Argentina enjoyed a lower level of ethnic diversity than most other Latin American states, principally because most of its population was European in origin. However, Argentina still suffered from a low sense of nationalism, in large part because immigrants came, within a very short time-span, from a variety of European countries – a pattern which is the opposite of that of Australia and New Zealand. In this connection, see C. Waisman, *Reversal of Development in Argentina*, Princeton University Press, Princeton, 1987, pp. 51–8.

[67]   For example, R. Prebisch, *The Economic Development of Latin America and Its Principal Problems*, United Nations, New York, 1950; A. G. Frank, *Capitalism and Underdevelopment in Latin America*, Monthly Review Press, New York, 1967.

[68]   P. Evans, "Class, State and Dependence in East Asia," in Deyo, *The Political Economy of the New Asian Industrialism*. This paper also makes it clear that geopolitical security meant that little free-floating aid was forthcoming.

so as to create impossibilist populist demands from below. Latin America has in consequence suffered from a continuing cyclical movement, with democracy leading to populist demands that ensure the installation of authoritarianism – whose mistakes then allow the whole cycle to begin again.[69]

Conventional wisdom about another contrast, that between the great population centers of the Third World, is that the chances for success in China are far greater than those of India. Whilst there is some justification for this view, mostly because of being blessed by more favorable initial conditions, some scepticism is in order.

The People's Republic of China shares much with South Korea and Taiwan. Four thousand years of continuous civilization and rule by a meritocratic bureaucracy since AD 7 ensured that the country has high homogeneity in terms of language, culture, religious belief, ethnicity, and market relations. China's nation-building process was advanced in other ways before the arrival of European imperialists. Traditional Chinese political thinking called for a strong state, able both to penetrate society and to gather social energy so as to repel foreign invasions: such sentiments lay behind the overthrow of both the Qing dynasty in 1911 and the nationalist government in 1949. An additional reason for loss of faith in the nationalist government was that the extent of its ties to the traditional landed elites made it unable to institute land and tax reform.[70] These tasks were completed by the communist revolution, together with nationalization and collectivization of industry. The old regime structure was, in a nutshell, completely destroyed.

However, China's economic performance under communism compares badly with that of its East Asian counterparts. After forty years China has established a systematic industrial system, but not an economy efficient enough to bring affluence. Crucially, communist rule brought political instability. If the state has

[69]   S. Huntington, *Political Order in Changing Societies*, Oxford University Press, Oxford, 1968.
[70]   B. Moore, *Social Origins of Dictatorship and Democracy*, Beacon Press, Boston, 1966; T. Skocpol, *States and Social Revolutions*, Cambridge University Press, Cambridge, 1979.

achieved agricultural self-sufficiency, basic literacy and higher life expectancy, its policy failures have brought stunning death tolls, notably in the great famine of 1959 to 1961 when between 20 and 30 million people died.[71] This poor economic performance was the result of three factors. First, China suffered geopolitically until at least the mid-1970s. The Cold War strategy of the United States totally isolated China from the first world; equally, open Sino-Soviet conflict shortly after the death of Stalin meant that China lost all hope of aid and technical assistance from the second world. This situation pushed China towards import substitution, that is, the strategy of "self-reliance," rather than towards the American sphere for the simplest of reasons: China was sufficiently large and confident to shrug off pressures from the outside. This long isolation from the world market, together with the character of the planned economy, made Chinese industry run at a low level of efficiency: even when the growth rate was high, industrial development did not bring economic dynamism since products were either of low quality or disproportionate to demand.[72] Secondly, in contrast to an anarchic past dominated by war and invasion, the early communist success in economic recovery, land reform, and the extension of social welfare, together with success in the Korean war, brought the communists great legitimacy. Finally, ideological factors also played an important role in poor Chinese performance. Utopianism encouraged the communist party to adopt radical economic development policies that brought disasters. Furthermore, ideological rigidity led the Chinese leadership to challenge changes in Eastern Europe that followed the death of Stalin: they rejected "revisionism," and thereby occasioned political movements aimed at *deepening* the revolution. The state-led movement which peaked during the Cultural Revolution ended with political turmoil, near economic bankruptcy, and a high cost in human life.

This analysis gains support by comparing Chinese economic performance before and after 1978 – the year in which the state

[71] S. W. Lavely, J. Lee, and F. Wang, "Chinese Demography," *Journal of Asian Studies*, vol. 49, 1990.
[72] V. Nee and D. Stark, eds, *Remaking the Economic Institutions of Socialism*, Stanford University Press, Stanford, 1989.

elite was forced by the disasters noted to adopt a hugely modified developmental strategy. China has allowed restructuring with minimal political liberalization, *perestroika* with limited *glasnost*. The marked successes of this strategy are very striking. In the 1980s, China's national product has grown at an annual rate of 9.5 percent.[73] Huge trade surpluses since 1989 have made the currency almost completely convertible, and have enabled the state both to lift tariffs and to remove licenses for industries no longer judged to be "infant" so as to force them to compete internationally.[74] In the mid-1980s almost 100 percent of industrial prices were controlled by the state; the fact that this has shrunk to only 44 percent makes it senseless to think of this social formation as a command economy.[75] None of this is to say, however, that Chinese success is assured. For economic development has not been matched by political modernization. Whilst a platform of economic success would certainly help any controlled socialist political decompression, that route has not yet properly been tried, for all that it has been contemplated. Political instability would harm China's economy, and it may produce erratic and aggressive international behavior as an insecure elite tries to operate in a semi-mobilized political environment by means of political adventurism.

India's remarkable history of virtually non-interrupted democracy since independence has been combined with slow but steady economic development. By the end of the 1980s, India had

[73]   The contrasting failure of reform in the Soviet Union tends to be ascribed to the destruction of the peasantry and the presence of a more entrenched and centralized party apparatus. Examples of this argument are A. Aslund, *Gorbachov's Struggle for Economic Reform*, Cornell University Press, Ithaca, 1989, pp. 181–3 and N. R. Lardy, "Is China Different?" in D. Chirot, ed., *The Crisis of Leninism and the Decline of the Left*, University of Washington Press, Seattle, 1989, pp. 148–53. In a nutshell, the success of contemporary Chinese strategy does not make it any the less doubtful that economic reform could have been achieved in the Soviet Union without full democratization. Note too that it would have been difficult to introduce free economic zones in the USSR. Such zones have caused severe regional imbalances in China "which would be much more dangerous in the Soviet Union with its nationality problems; the vast majority of foreign capital in [China's] free economic zones is invested by Chinese abroad, and the USSR would not benefit from such an effect" (Aslund, *Gorbachov's Struggle for Economic Reform*, p. 183).
[74]   *The People's Daily*, Overseas Edition, January 28, 1992 and March 16, 1992.
[75]   *The People's Daily*, Overseas Edition, January 21, 1992.

established a fully-fledged industrial system, capable of producing both basic necessities and high-technology goods; in addition, the "green revolution" has allowed agricultural self-sufficiency. India has never, despite population pressure, had large-scale famine after independence. In these ways, India has belied the pessimistic predictions made about its future.[76] Nonetheless, India remains one of the poorest countries in the world. Agricultural output still constitutes the major part of its national product, whilst a third of the world's "absolute poor" still lives in India.[77] At present, India enjoys more political freedom than China but suffers from greater economic inequality, slower economic development, lower status of women, and lower levels of literacy and life expectancy. If India has never had a famine equivalent to that of 1959 to 1961 in China, each eight years there are an equivalent number of fatalities in India due to low life expectancy.[78] More significantly, if India's growth rate averaged 5 percent during the 1980s, that of China was 9.5 percent in the same period. Furthermore, Indian growth was largely due, in contrast to that of China, to rapid expansion of the service sector rather than to improvements in agricultural and industrial sectors. The peaceful transition to independence together with early democracy meant such old regime structures as caste, the landed elite, and village control of local affairs were not destroyed. Furthermore, the strength of the business class at the time of independence limited the state's strategy for late development: in comparison with East Asia, the state has been powerless to discipline industry. Rather, the state subsidies are given away to those with good political connections, the consequence of which has been continual support for uneconomic "lame ducks." The state has been no more able to carry out fundamental land reform: rural areas are still controlled by local elites. Such organization as there has been locally has often been against the state; at times this has been so effective as to deny the state basic revenues.[79] It is worth noting finally, that India has not

[76]   For example, Moore, *Social Origins of Dictatorship and Democracy*.
[77]   *The Economist's Intelligence Unit*, Country Report: India, Nepal, 1991.
[78]   J. Drèze and A. Sen, *Hunger and Public Action*, Oxford University Press, Oxford, 1989.
[79]   P. Bardham, *The Political Economy of Development in India*, Oxford University Press, New Delhi, 1984.

been favored in geopolitical terms. India has a population 17 times that of South Korea, but between 1946 and 1978 it only received 50 percent more aid from the United States; if military aid was included, India's total aid from the United States did not even equal that sent to South Korea.[80]

Two considerations need to be set against these pessimistic remarks. First, there is an increasing awareness within the Indian elite of the relative failure of its model of import-substituting industrialization. Whilst the attempt to change this is by no means complete or secure, the momentum for an alternative is beginning to seem unstoppable. Secondly, the Indian state has considerable achievements to its credit. India lacked strong mass nationalism in comparison to China and Korea. There are long historical patterns at work here. In ancient China, Confucius and the system of civil examinations encouraged territorial cohesion. In contrast, the key Indian institutions, the caste system and the jati division of labour, divided society. In consequence, political unity was basically alien to Indian civilization before independence; its politics have rather been dominated by the caste-based village council.[81] But if India remains an extremely fragmented society in terms of language, culture, religious belief, ethnicity, and market relations, its adherence to liberal democracy has succeeded in allowing a multinational state to survive.[82] It may well be that the modernity of India's political arrangements gives it some comparative advantage, and particularly so in the international arena.

None of these difficulties of assessment face us when turning to sub-Saharan Africa.[83] After a few seemingly beneficent years, development was arrested in the 1970s and declined in the 1980s. Together with economic crisis went population explosion, large-

---

[80]   Cumings, "The Origins and Development of the Northeast Asian Political Economy."
[81]   Moore, *Social Origins of Dictatorship and Democracy*; K. W. Kapp and D. Kapp, *Hindu Culture, Economic Development, and Economic Planning in India*, Asian Publishing House, New Delhi, 1963.
[82]   Kashmir is an exception to this generalization. But this really is an exception which proves the rule: secession is encouraged on this occasion precisely because it is a site of illiberal Indian policies.
[83]   D. Bigo, "Is there hope for Sub-Saharan Africa?" *Contention*, vol. 1, 1986; N. Chazan, "Engaging the State," in J. Migdal, A. Kohli, and V. Shue, eds, *State Power and Social Forces*, Cambridge University Press, Cambridge, 1994.

scale famine, deforestation, and indebtedness. The catastrophic politics of the region – particularly the wars in the Horn of Africa that so disrupted food production and supply – account for a good deal of this awful situation. State elites tend to be so internally divided that military coups became the common mode of transferring power. In addition, the political system suffered from a lack of national homogeneity, the persistence of old social structures, a low general level of state- and nation-building and a poor location within the world political system. All this prevented the emergence of states sufficiently autonomous to pioneer successful late development.

The low level of state- and nation-building is ascribable to the fact that, before colonialism, the region was tribal – which is to say that it was marked by a very high level of ethnic, cultural, and linguistic diversity.[84] Only a few areas with settled and intensive agriculture experienced rule by states: but such states were puny, gaining revenue less from taxation of their own people than from long-distance trade in war captives and luxury goods.[85] European rule changed far less in Africa than it had in Latin America. Tribes were organized into administrative units less with reference to existing ethnic or market boundaries but rather to facilitate the extraction of resources. This was normally achieved by establishing a coastline trading post and then declaring its direct hinterland a legitimate sphere of influence.[86] As a result, tribes were arbitrarily divided between different colonies. Such an easy partition of sub-Saharan Africa curtailed state- and nation-building thereafter. Furthermore, independence was led by native elites trained in Europe.[87] Whilst this was an expression of nationalism, it was clearly of a lesser order than that of, say, China: where the former could only unite urban dwellers in fighting for independence, the latter reached all social strata, and thereafter drew on their energy for developmental purposes. The

---

[84]   Many of the languages in question were, of course, oral rather than written.

[85]   E. Terray, "Long-distance Exchange and the Formation of the State," *Economy and Society*, vol. 3, 1974; C. Coquery-Vidrovitch, "Research on an African Mode of Production," in M. A. Klein and W. G. Johnson, eds, *Perspectives on the African Past*, Little, Brown, New York, 1972.

[86]   I. L. Griffiths, *An Atlas of African Affairs*, Methuen, London, 1984, pp. 56–7.

[87]   D. K. Fieldhouse, *Black Africa, 1945–80*, Allen and Unwin, London, 1986.

precarious nature of rule made the elites of sub-Saharan Africa less interested in development than in grabbing power. This has been particularly true of attempts to secure power by forcibly homogenizing very varied populations: such nationalizing policies have produced tragedies, most recently in Rwanda, and they have led one commentator to insist that the attempt to create European-style nation-states in Africa is a final curse left behind by imperial powers.[88]

It might seem as if the moral to be drawn from the discussion as a whole, that is, from the analysis of Western strength and the fragmentation of the Third World, is that what happens outside the North is of less and less importance to international order. Further considerations point in the same direction. It is not the case, for instance, that the Third World has been the site of continual social revolutions: to the contrary, revolutions have been contained either by liberalism or by the presence of a bureaucratic and efficient army – Costa Rica exemplifying the first and El Salvador the second in Central America, with Nicaragua alone suffering revolution because its rulers were both vicious and nepotistic when dealing with the armed forces.[89] Still, the fact that the Iranian revolution, whose incidence was utterly unexpected since it occurred without defeat in war and in the presence of an army created in large part to prevent it, should not be forgotten. Nor too should the pressures placed on Islamic states by fundamentalist movements, many of them quite prepared to push through revolutions if granted power. The possibility of revolutionary zeal being allied to the economic power that derives from the possession of oil is one which necessitates caution and circumspection.

[88]   B. Davidson, *The Black Man's Burden*, Random House, New York, 1992.
[89]   I draw here on the path-breaking work of J. Goodwin, notably "Old Regimes and Revolutions in the Second and Third Worlds," *Social Science History*, vol. 18, 1994 and "Explaining Revolutions in the Contemporary Third World" (with T. Skocpol), *Politics and Society*, vol. 17, 1989.

THE END OF AMERICAN HEGEMONY?

Two tasks confront us in considering the claim that the United States was losing its hegemonic position by the late 1970s. On the one hand, skepticism must be directed at this view.[90] On the other hand, the processes explaining such limited decline as there was need to be examined so as to see whether hegemony is necessarily self-liquidating. The best way of getting a handle on both questions is to bring light to bear on the claim that American decline is following a path first traveled by Great Britain.[91]

The analogy between Great Britain and the United States has almost nothing to be said in its favor. Britain never possessed hegemonic power within the world polity: its short-lived economic lead at no time, as we have seen, gave it geopolitical predominance. A logical consequence of this is that decline cannot have been caused by the hegemonic provision of services for the system as a whole. Further, no real evidence can be found to support that thesis if we pretend for a moment that Britain had been a hegemon. Britain was certainly not exhausted by excessive defense spending: the burden of all defense expenditures, that is, including monies for imperial defense, was less than that of France, Russia, and Germany just before the outbreak of the First World War.[92] Nor should much credence be given to the view that British industry was hurt by allowing continued access to its own markets whilst its own products were banned by its major economic rivals, although Arthur Balfour was led by this consideration to argue for what one contemporary theorist calls "specific reciprocity" – that is, that Britain should have tried to force open protected

---

[90]   Important early contributions to this necessary skepticism included B. Russett, "The Mysterious Case of Vanishing Hegemony, or, Is Mark Twain Really Dead?" *International Organization*, vol. 39, 1985 and S. Strange, *Casino Capitalism*, Blackwell, Oxford, 1986.

[91]   P. Kennedy, *The Rise and Fall of the Great Powers*, Random House, New York, 1987. Kennedy is a very distinguished historian of late nineteenth-century British foreign policy, and there is a sense – seen in his recent practice of referring to "our" problems when writing in *The New York Review of Books* – in which he is seeking to provide Washington with advice to allow it to avoid repeating Britain's mistakes.

[92]   A full and precise account of the burden of defense for the major powers between 1870 and 1913 can be found in J. A. Hall, *Coercion and Consent*, Polity Press, Cambridge, 1994, ch. 8.

markets by threatening to close off its own.[93] Relative economic decline was always likely given the advantages of backwardness, with Germany in particular pioneering a second industrial revolution, based on technical education and on chemicals, that was difficult for Britain to emulate since its own industrial structure had gelled around its earlier moment of triumph. Nonetheless, the British economy did not perform badly before 1914, as its development of service and leisure industries demonstrated.[94] Hence the fundamental factor responsible for decline is simply that of exhaustion brought on by fighting Germany in two world wars. Furthermore, Britain had become exhausted as the result of state competition more generally. It was the challenge from other states, and particularly the fear that imperial rule by other powers might close off markets, that led to the acquisition of formal empire towards the end of the nineteenth century – albeit the extension of empire in 1919 was not so forced, and was altogether unwise. This was a sign of weakness rather than of strength, as became generally obvious once nationalist movements destroyed such limited profits as had ever accrued from empire.[95]

Relative decline is normal. But if Britain had poor cards could they have been better played? The answer for the most part must be negative. It is extremely unlikely for instance that the radical modernizing strategy of Joseph Chamberlain, favored by later critics, would have improved matters. The fundamental weakness of the policy was less working-class hatred of expensive food than the reluctance of Canada and Australia to be forced to remain primary producers; these states wanted genuine rather than dependent development.[96] Most importantly, the challenge from Germany was real, a factor beyond national control, and it could not be appeased. Still, it would be grossly mistaken to argue that

[93]   A. Friedberg, *The Weary Titan*, Princeton University Press, Princeton, 1988; R. Keohane, "Reciprocity in International Relations," *International Organization*, vol. 40, 1986.
[94]   S. Pollard, *Britain's Prime and Britain's Decline*, Edward Arnold, London, 1989.
[95]   L. Davis and R. Huttenback, *Mammon and the Pursuit of Empire*, Cambridge University Press, Cambridge, 1986; P. O'Brien, "The Costs and Benefits of British Imperialism," *Past and Present*, no. 120, 1988.
[96]   B. Semmel, *Imperialism and Social Reform*, Routledge and Kegan Paul, London, 1960.

every avenue of change was closed over nearly a century. It became clear after 1945, for example, that British decline was no longer simply the effect of other states catching up as the transfer of people from agriculture to industry enhanced their growth rates: that did help account for the strengthening of the position of both France and Germany, but it failed to account for the continued low rates of British economic growth.[97] Why was the British state unable to engage in the politics of modernization?

Responsibility for this failure is often attributed to a militant working class which is held to have caused inflation and to have prevented economic restructuring. This view has dominated recent British politics and much academic debate. It is largely wrong.[98] The British working class has only rarely been politically militant, and this was habitually the result rather than the cause of economic decline. For a very long period the British elite had considerable autonomy from working-class pressure; the failure to create an economically dynamic economy is accordingly to be laid at its door. If attention is to be given to internal social blockages, to distributional coalitions standing in the way of societal flexibility, it makes much more sense, as many scholars now realize, to ask whether the policies of the British state were determined by the interests of the financial sector of capital.[99]

There can no longer be any doubt of the deleterious impact of the unholy trinity of City–Treasury–Bank of England upon British industry. First, the great sophistication of the equity market has meant that profits have been made through trading in money, rather than through investing in domestic industry. In consequence, British industry has suffered from low levels of capital formation;[100]

[97]   Milward, *The Reconstruction of Western Europe, 1945–51*; P. Hall, *Governing the Economy*, Polity Press, Cambridge, 1986.
[98]   Smith, *Power, Norms and Inflation*; S. Blank, "Britain," in P. Katzenstein, ed., *Between Power and Plenty*, University of Wisconsin Press, Madison, 1978.
[99]   S. Strange, *Sterling and British Policy*, Oxford University Press, Oxford, 1971; G. Ingham, *Capitalism Divided*, Macmillan, London, 1984; A. Gamble, *Britain in Decline*, Macmillan, London, 1985; P. Anderson, "The Figures of Descent," *New Left Review*, no. 161, 1987.
[100]   An interesting example recounted by Pollard (*Britain's Prime and Britain's Decline*, pp. 98–9) concerns a company started in the Edwardian years by Fred Hopper. This enterprise successfully expanded from bicycles to motor cycles and eventually to cycle cars, and it had a flourishing export component. Nonetheless, its potential growth into car production was stymied by such a lack of capital that the firm was eventually driven into liquidation.

this goes much further in explaining paltry rates of worker productivity than *de haut en bas* comments about the laziness of British workers.[101] In addition, industrialists have constantly had to concern themselves with the provision of short-term profits so as to pay out dividends to shareholders – inattention to whose interests can easily lead to takeover bids. Secondly, the City has consistently argued in favor of high exchange rates. This lay behind the catastrophic return to gold in 1925, and the stop-go policies of the period from 1945 to 1971; the growth of the Eurodollar market in London in more recent times has, if anything, enhanced the City's power. The judgement to be made about this is simple: the single biggest obstacle to British industrial recovery for most of the postwar period has been the excessive strength of sterling and of the volatility of interest rates necessary to ensure that strength.[102] Thirdly, the triumvirate of City, Bank, and Treasury has consistently argued against the adoption of industrial policies, a factor which reflects the idiosyncratic, "budgetary" nature of British state capacity. Indeed, the best way in which the spirit of this whole package of policies can be summarized is that of slavish adherence to economic liberalism. Such policies were a source of strength when Britain had a strong industrial lead, but they led to less than optimal industrial performance when other nation-states developed strong banking–industrial links and to genuine catastrophe when, between 1925 and 1931 and for most of the period since 1945, they caused Britain's exports to be priced out of the world market.

One way in which the importance of the financial sector can be appreciated is by reference to the work of Rubinstein.[103] His finding – that the very rich in Britain have been landowners and financiers rather than, at any time, industrialists – allows considerable scepticism to be cast on the "Wiener thesis," that is, on the view that an aristocratic embrace undermined bourgeois virtue, sending the sons of businessmen to semi-rural retreat in the spirit of William Morris and Laura Ashley.[104] In fact, the British elite had no aversion

[101] T. Nichols, *The British Worker Question*, Routledge and Kegan Paul, London, 1986.
[102] Strange, *Sterling and British Policy*.
[103] W. D. Rubinstein, *Men of Wealth*, Croom Helm, London, 1981.
[104] M. Wiener, *English Culture and the Decline of the Industrial Spirit*, Cambridge University Press, Cambridge, 1981.

to money-making; to the contrary, it discovered the best avenue to riches that was available.

Nonetheless, we do need a theory which stresses the sleepiness of the British elite. There remains much to be said for the contention that the financial sector constrained rather than controlled the political elite. An autonomous elite sought to restore sterling's international role because it was obsessed by the politics of prestige; thus we should not accept the view of Harold Wilson in the early 1960s as a determined opponent brought to heel by finance capital; it makes no sense to say that he was defeated when he and his party had no real alternative strategy of their own. If continual loyalty to finance rather than to industry is one side of the coin of complacency created by geopolitical victory, the other is continued adherence to the tradition of national militarism: a full 50 percent of Britain's research and development funding went towards weapons in the 1980s, an absolute madness given the short production runs involved.[105] All in all the best summary judgement on British decline remains that of A. J. P. Taylor: "the English people of the twentieth century were a fine people and deserved better leaders than on the whole they got."[106]

With this picture in mind, let us turn to the United States. Theorists of decline occasionally give the impression that the United States once could do as it wished, but now is more or less impotent. The image of a golden age is certainly exaggerated since, as noted, the United States failed to establish multilateral liberal economic norms and became entangled with a continental commitment to Europe that it had sought to avoid. More important in this context is the resilience of the main sources of American power. The military power of the United States was never in question: it alone stood in rivalry to the Soviet Union, although its lead in nearly every key military technology made it very much first among equals. But an economy whose weakening was symbolized by America becoming a net debtor to the rest of the world in the later 1980s

---

[105]   J. Kingman, "Science and the Public Purse," *Government and Opposition*, vol. 21, 1986.
[106]   A. J. P. Taylor, "Accident Prone, or, What Happened Next," *Journal of Modern History*, vol. 49, 1977, p. 18.

meant, so the argument ran, that the huge burden of defense could not be borne in the long run.

Skepticism about American economic decline is very necessary. Figures of indebtedness to the rest of the world are exaggerated by the fact that the book value of American assets overseas is given at purchase price rather than current worth; recent debt is, of course, more the result of the policies of Ronald Reagan than of any long-term process of secular decline. Further, the claim of hegemonic stability theory that a decline in economic strength would lead to a demand for tariffs is clearly false, for all that informal quotas have been imposed in particular sectors.[107] For protectionism has only been half-hearted: the 1988 Trade Bill demanded, as have American negotiators at GATT over many years, increasing *openness* in services, agriculture, and shipping, that is, in areas in which America has a powerful economic edge. It is anyway important to be suspicious of what trade figures reveal given the huge increase in intra-firm trade, by now perhaps a third of all world trade. A more accurate index of American economic power, given that American investment is less through portfolios than through its multinationals, is the share of world product controlled by American companies. This shows continued strength: the loss of absolute pre-eminence naturally caused by the recovery of debilitated economies bottomed out in the early 1970s, with the United States thereafter holding more or less the same share.[108] It seems, further, that America is regaining competitive edge in middle-sized companies;[109] the most recent study suggests that the United States continues to dominate in the newest areas of high-technology goods.[110] Finally, the financial power of the United States remains very great, despite the fact that the seigniorial privilege of the dollar standard, that is, the unilateral right to expand the money supply, was removed with the floating exchange rate system instituted in

[107] S. Strange, "Protectionism and World Politics," *International Organization*, vol. 39, 1985.
[108] S. Strange, "The Persistent Myth of Lost Hegemony," *International Organization*, vol. 41, 1987; Nye, *Bound to Lead*.
[109] "A Portrait of America's New Competitiveness," *The Economist*, 4 June, 1988.
[110] R. McCulloch, *The Challenge to US Leadership in High Technology Industries (Can the US Maintain Its Lead? Should It Try?)*, National Bureau of Economic Research, Cambridge, 1988. *Cf.* "Back on Top?," *The Economist*, September 16, 1995.

1973. The dollar remained the world's top currency, and when Germany ceased to be its key supporter its place was taken by Saudi Arabia and then by Japan. The United States certainly retains enormous power within the monetary system as a whole: American policy created a strong dollar in the early 1980s, and it was again American policy at the Plaza Accords which made for a weaker dollar – in both cases, the largest player determined the rules of the game at the expense of the interests of smaller powers.[111] It is further worth recalling that one of the services that a hegemonic power was supposed to provide, at least in Kindleberger's original theory, was that of exporting capital to the rest of the world. In fact, world capital flew to the United States in the 1980s, largely as the result of Reaganomics. This was the brutal exercise of great power, particularly at the expense of Latin America, and it makes the Third World's paltry attempt to control its minerals and commodities pale into insignificance.[112] This is predatory extraction by a hegemonic power.

The question of decline was not resolved by this sort of analysis, since much of this could be admitted whilst maintaining that worse was still to come. But key features of the world polity made the position of the United States unlike that of Britain at the end of the nineteenth century. An initial point worth making is that the United States has not suffered a major defeat in war. This is not to deny the importance of Vietnam. But the United States was able to pass on part of the costs of the war to its allies by sending its inflation through capitalist society. Much more importantly, there was no equivalent to Imperial Germany facing the United States: its geopolitical rival stood outside capitalist society, whilst its economic rivals within capitalism were geopolitically dependent upon it. It was quite obvious that the former was suffering from internal economic problems, and that Nixon's opening to China had weakened it geopolitically. The situation that faced the United States within capitalist society was quite as advantageous, and it was so in an historically novel manner. There were good reasons for

[111] S. Strange, "Still an Extraordinary Power," in E. E. Lombra and W. E. Witte, eds, *Political Economy of International and Domestic Monetary Relations*, Ames, Iowa, 1982; Strange, *Casino Capitalism*.
[112] S. Krasner, *Structural Conflict*, University of California Press, Berkeley, 1984.

believing that, in addition to the fact that Germany and Japan were forced to become trading states and allies, the world economy would not return completely to a no-holds-barred conflict between trading blocs.[113] The speed of technological change makes it catastrophic to withdraw from the world market, something realized by most state leaders and enshrined by them and their leading industries in the sudden spread of joint ventures of very varied sorts.[114] In addition, there was an increasing awareness that traditional protectionist policies were no longer likely to work: how could one protect one's industries against, say, Japan, if that country chose to assemble Thai and Taiwanese parts in South Korea and then to import them into the United States via Mexico? In the case of the United States, the impact of free trade institutions and mentalities, both internally and externally, made it difficult to adopt any pure protectionist stance.[115] Finally, it is clear that the postwar settlement was popular among many states, and that they would go to considerable lengths to preserve it: that settlement solved the "German problem" and the "Japan problem," whilst there was widespread awareness that bipolarity in a nuclear age had a great deal to recommend it.

This general situation gave the United States certain clear advantages. The weakness of its geopolitical rival and the absence of challenges from within capitalist society meant that it did not have to acquire a formal territorial empire, despite the commitment given to Vietnam for two decades. But what proved to be important about that debacle was that it has not been repeated, thereby ruling out the necessity for other states to acquire their own territory for reasons of market security. Crucially, the United States had very considerable leverage over its allied economic rivals, both because it provided their defense and because their economic success was partly dependent on the sheer size of the American market – which the United States could, unlike most other states, close, given the

---

[113]   R. Gilpin, *The Political Economy of International Relations*, Princeton University Press, Princeton, 1987.

[114]   R. Rosecrance, *The Rise of the Trading State*, Basic Books, New York, 1986.

[115]   I. M. Destler and J. M. Odell, *Anti-Protection*, Institute for International Economics, Washington, 1987; H. Milner, "Resisting the Protectionist Temptation," *International Organisation*, vol. 41, 1987.

huge resource base its continental status afforded it. At times, seigniorage was obvious, as in the passing on of inflation under the Bretton Woods system; but it was present later, from the necessity of supporting the dollar to Japan's enforced abandonment of its plans to build fighter planes, a geopolitical form of industrial subsidy.

The situation of the United States differed from that of Britain in a further and absolutely fundamental way. Paul Kennedy was right to argue that Britain's decline had to be great since it had so massively reached beyond its natural power ranking, that is, the portfolio of demographic, geopolitical, and natural resource endowment.[116] Nonetheless, there certainly was *relative* American decline, and it is time to assess its causes. Let us begin by asking whether we should accept the claims of hegemonic stability theory in this case. Did the United States become exhausted because of the burden of defense it provided for capitalist society as a whole and by its obeisance to multilateralism in the face of formal and informal protectionism elsewhere?

There was some truth to both these claims, but each was subject to exaggeration. Figures that indicate that the United States' economy was being undermined by high defence expenditure, both absolutely and in comparison with her allies, need to be treated with the utmost care. The burden of defense was not particularly high by historical standards, and it is hard to credit it with causing economic decline given the economic success of South Korea and Sweden, both of which paid at least as large a share of national product for defense. Equally, defense expenditure was not an unrelieved burden for the American economy. The trade-off between defense spending and economic performance is extremely complex,[117] but it is clear that the United States, with long production runs and research at the frontiers of technology, gained something: certainly the Japanese and the Europeans regarded defense spending – especially when overseen by the Defense Advanced Research Projects Agency – as more or less equivalent to an

---

[116]   Kennedy, *The Rise and Fall of the Great Powers*, p. 553.
[117]   S. Chan, "The Impact of Defence Spending on Economic Performance," *Orbis*, vol. 29, 1985.

industrial policy.[118] Further, concentration on defense had no particularly deleterious effects on domestic industrial capital formation;[119] the National Research Council added to this the discovery that there was sufficient engineering talent left after concentration on defense for the health of domestic productive industry.[120] Figures for allied defense expenditures were equally distorted:[121] they did not include "offset payments," nor did they allow for hidden allied costs such as those of conscription and the provision of physical assets.[122] A proper accounting suggested that the major members of NATO – and France – paid nearly as large a share of national product for defense as did the United States for *its worldwide interests*; Japan, of course, was constitutionally mandated to pay very significantly less. Importantly, all these figures do not include the informal economic privileges that accrued, as argued, to the United States as military rent and as bribes to ensure that its markets remained open. It is this which led the advanced states to prop up the dollar and, in Japan's case, massively to increase its aid budget rather than to establish its own aerospace industry; in these ways, the allies informally paid for the cost of defense. Equally skeptical points must be made about the claim that decline resulted from the protectionism of others. German economic success at the end of the nineteenth century may have been helped by tariff walls, but it was not fundamentally ascribable to that; the same seems true of Japan today. Bergsten and Cline argued that if Japan had had no import barriers at all, America's 1985 near-50 billion dollars trade deficit with Japan would only have been reduced by five to eight billion dollars, and that five billion dollars would have been added to the deficit if the

[118]   R. Reich, *Tales of a New America*, Vintage Books, New York, 1988.
[119]   D. Greenwood, "Note on the Impact of Military Expenditures on Economic Growth and Performance," in C. Schmidt, ed., *The Economics of Military Expenditures*, St Martin's Press, New York, 1987; K. Rasler and W. R. Thompson, "Defence Burdens, Capital Formation and Economic Growth," *Journal of Conflict Resolution*, vol. 32, 1988.
[120]   National Labour Council, *The Impact of Defense Spending on Nondefense Engineering Labor Markets*, National Academy Press, Washington, 1986.
[121]   K. Knorr, "Burden Sharing in NATO," *Orbis*, vol. 29, 1985; D. Wightman, "United States Balance of Payments Policies in the 1960s," unpublished paper; K. Dunn, "NATO's Enduring Value," *Foreign Policy*, vol. 71, 1988.
[122]   G. Treverton, *The "Dollar Drain" and US Forces in Germany*, Ohio University Press, Columbus, 1978; Knorr, "Burden Sharing."

United States had removed its own considerable barriers to Japanese imports.[123]

Although they are hard to prove in any decisive manner, traditional theories of decline seem to offer a more plausible account of what is happening to the United States. If the Vietnam debacle represented a mere moment of military overextension, it had serious costs for the workings of capitalist society. More generally, just as Britain institutionalized its moment of economic success, so too has America allowed a set of institutions to gell around those Fordist politics of productivity that came to the fore under Roosevelt.[124] Such industrial giantism seems ill-adapted to the flexible trading system of the contemporary world economy – to whose logic the United States may find it hard to adapt, given the relative weakness of its social infrastructure.[125] Further, American failure to adapt partly reflects its sheer size; it has often chosen to use its power to change international norms rather than to make its society flexible enough to compete – an option which may have diminishing returns. Equally important, however, may well be the importance of finance capital within American society; if this sector has not yet reached the historic importance it gained in British history, the ways in which finance is currently favored over industry, as in the fact that "junk bonds" are tax deductible, offer obvious resonances. The whole point at issue can be summarized by saying that one reason for distrusting the "decline by service provision" thesis of hegemonic stability theory is that it fails to pay proper attention to the inventiveness, diligence, and adaptability of modern trading states.[126] Imitating such virtues would require lowering the extraordinarily high levels of national product given to consumption by means of increased taxation, less perhaps for direct industrial policy and more for the creation of suitable social infrastructures. If such

[123]   F. Bergsten and W. Cline, *The United States–Japan Economic Problem*, Institute for International Economics, Washington, 1987.
[124]   Maier, "The Politics of Productivity."
[125]   M. Piore and C. Sabel, *The Second Industrial Divide*, Basic Books, New York, 1984; L. Weiss, *Creating Capitalism*, Blackwell, Oxford, 1988.
[126]   R. Dore, *Flexible Rigidities*, Athlone Press, London, 1986; R. Dore, *Taking Japan Seriously*, Athlone Press, London, 1987; D. Okimoto, *Between MITI and the Market*, Stanford University Press, Stanford, 1988; F. C. Deyo, ed., *The Political Economy of the New Asian Industrialism*, Cornell University Press, Ithaca, 1987.

policies are resisted, this can only be ascribed to the particular character of Anglo-Saxon liberalism. More generally, the United States was born out of a revolt against the state, and this legacy seems again dominant after the idiosyncratic interlude of New Deal reformism. Without the setting of priorities it may, incredibly, be the case that the United States will yet suffer significant and unnecessary decline.

AN ABSOLUTE COLLAPSE

The best way to understand the collapse of the other political economy of industrialism is by recalling three general interpretations of state socialism.[127] The first of these was that of totalitarianism. The revolutionary regime was seen, in authors such as Arendt, as all-powerful – able at once to destroy extant social institutions and to rule effectively by means of terror. The second position, that of modernization or liberalization, insisted that the moment of high totalitarianism had passed, and that a much more technocratic elite sought to gain the allegiance and co-operation of those key sectors of society which would help in economic development. Where these theories concentrated on elite politics, the approach that gained popularity in the 1980s tended to give priority to social forces operating from below. The notion of civil society, that is, of the putatively increasing capacity of varied types of groups to organize themselves in opposition to the state, was designed to address the fact that it was becoming ever more difficult for the party-state to arrange compacts between state and society.[128]

It long seemed to me that good reasons existed for endorsing the second position.[129] Central Europe was certainly a world

[127]   B. Misztal, "Understanding Political Change in Eastern Europe," *Sociology*, vol. 27, 1993 distinguishes four explanatory modes, two of which are here combined in a single category.
[128]   Note that the definition of civil society offered by these scholars differs from that used in this book, namely in emphasizing societal self-organization rather than the agreement amongst strong and autonomous groups to live together with civility.
[129]   J. A. Hall, *Powers and Liberties*, Penguin, Harmondsworth, 1986, ch. 7.

without legitimacy, as was so graphically demonstrated in 1956, 1968 and 1981, and it seemed likely that it would somewhere, somehow, sooner or later change, for essentially socially evolutionary reasons. The heroic period of Bolshevism had managed to industrialize, albeit in a brutal manner, but it was clearly proving to be less and less effective everywhere in economic terms as a transition to a third industrial age took place. Imperial rule is as capable of debilitating the economy in the modern era as we have seen it to have been in pre-modern China! The nature of computers seemed to make the point most effectively. Widespread possession of printers quite as much as the machines themselves was surely necessary if a society was to thrive in the late industrial era, and this seemed to make a new social contract necessary. Gone would be the days in which the attempt to break the bounds of censorship involved spreading samizdat documents by retyping them using ten carbon papers at a go! Crucially, it was possible to see in most ruling parties of socialist societies a positively schizophrenic gap between the technocrats and the Bolsheviks, between those who wished to give the party new life by assuring economic growth and those who were prepared to maintain socialism as an ideocracy, a power-system based on an unsullied and unquestioned total ideology. In a sense, the moment in 1968 when Kadar, himself imposed by the Russians in 1956, announced that the rules of the system were to change – so that not to be against the system was acceptable rather than having to enthusiastically endorse it at every moment – signaled the formal start of softer political rule. Liberalization was already under way, and the era of high totalitarianism accordingly at an end. It seemed very likely that liberalization would continue. Modernizing leaders might be able to work with the technically competent, who had enough sense of international comparison to know that their mobility had been blocked, to create a more vigorous economy in tandem with softer political rule. Ernest Gellner put the case as a whole with characteristic verve:

> ... an advanced industrial society requires a large scientific, technical, administrative, educational stratum, with genuine competence based on prolonged training. In other words, it cannot rely on rigid ideologues and servile classes alone. It is reasonable to assume that this kind of educated middle class, owing its position

to technical competence rather than to subservience, and inher-
ently, so to speak professionally, capable of distinguishing reality
and thought from verbiage and incantation, will develop or has
developed the kind of tastes we associate with its life-style – a need
for security, a recognition of competence rather than subservience,
a regard for efficiency and integrity rather than patronage and
loyalty in professional life . . . This class is large, and it cannot be
penalised effectively without a cost to the economy which may no
longer be acceptable.[130]

Great skill would be needed to make the most of favorable
opportunity, to ask for reasonable change so that alliances could
be made between frustrated educated labor and technocrats inside
the ruling elite. Above all, to ask too much too fast created the
risk of an endangered elite calling in Russian tanks.

There seemed here an overlap with the burgeoning literature of
the early 1980s on transitions from authoritarian capitalist rule.[131]
That literature always emphasized the need to make pacts so as to
reassure the powerful that change would not be at their expense.
More recently, a leading member of this school has noted that
successful transitions from authoritarian capitalism have been
those initiated and controlled from above; transitions initiated by
pressures from below have tended to fail.[132] The nature of
socialism – the fact that domination was so concentrated, that is,
that different regimes had single parties rather than a dominant
landed class and, crucially, that the fate of those regimes depended
absolutely upon perceptions in Moscow – seemed to make an
emphasis on liberalization *rather* than democratization still more
necessary. Processes of reassurance seemed especially necessary
given that liberalization had been defeated in Hungary, Czechoslovakia, and Poland at the precise moment that liberalizing reforms,
often in the economy, had come to call the party-state into
question.

It is as well to own up to the fact that these considerations led

[130]   E. Gellner, "Plaidoyer pour une libéralisation manquée," *Government and Opposition*, vol. 14, 1979, pp. 63–4.
[131]   G. O'Donnell, P. Schmitter, and L. Whitehead, eds, *Transitions from Authoritarian
Rule*, Johns Hopkins University Press, Baltimore, 1986.
[132]   T. Karl, "Dilemmas of Democratization in Latin America," *Comparative Politics*,
vol. 23, 1990.

to warm endorsement for Gorbachov. He seemed the perfect technocrat, keen to admit that he had been impressed by Western standards of consumption and with a wife whose abilities in that area were not open to serious question. The attempt to reform received support from the leaders of the armed forces, and from the military-industrial complex. Why did such a conservative force contemplate reform? The Soviet Union was massively stretched by arms spending. If there is doubt about the claim that the United States was being hurt by defense spending in excess of that of many of its allies, the fact that Soviet expenditure took perhaps three times as large a proportion of national product – that is, at least a quarter of the total – unquestionably hurt the economy. This economic debilitation was beginning to have negative consequences for the military. Whilst skepticism may have been shown to the claims of Reagan's Star Wars initiative, the fears that American high technology would have military applications that could not be imitated were very real indeed. It was clear that Gorbachov's purpose was that of making the system work, but that pill was sugared by the promise of ever softer political rule. Further, the geriatric and worried elite had by the late 1970s lost their greatest virtue, that of considerable circumspection in foreign policy.[133] The fact that Gorbachov seemed prepared not just to leave Afghanistan but to let Eastern Europe go turned my endorsement into enthusiasm.

It must be said loudly and clearly that liberalization failed. For a short period it seemed as if round-table discussions leading to varied types of pacts, habitually creating electoral rules designed to reassure the elite, were part of the classical scenario for controlled liberalization. But this was merely a stage, and a very short one at that. What followed was an absolute and fundamental collapse. The round-table talks in Poland produced rules designed to keep the party in power, but these were invalidated utterly by the very first election. In general, what happened in Eastern Europe was that the removal of the Russian card meant that regimes simply crumbled. Once deprived of the capacity to repress their own people, party states fell apart – with the notable

---

[133]   J. Snyder, *Myths of Empire*, Cornell University Press, Ithaca, 1991.

exception of Rumania, where much blood was shed in the process of removing Ceauçescu.

Does this mean that we should accept the concept of civil society, that is, the view from below? As it happens, the notion is far from clear, with particularly striking differences being apparent between theorists in the West and in the East – the former hoping for new social movements to replace the proletariat, the latter often approving the spread of capitalism![134] Nonetheless, there is some truth to the view from below. If civil society was a much desired dream, the theory as a whole was not purely a matter of prescription. Bluntly, Solidarity provided the descriptive "beef" of the concept. This extraordinary movement, based on Christian mission and Polish destiny, changed the history of Eastern Europe as a whole. Solidarity undermined the socialist project by leading to martial law, thereby removing any pretence that socialism was popular. That military rule was imposed by Poles rather than by Russian tanks presumably reflects the Kremlin's calculation that the Poles would have been prepared to engage in armed struggle, whatever the cost. All in all, Eastern Europe owes its freedom in some part to the glorious Poles.[135] Further, it is almost certainly true that the introduction of bribery – that is, of clientelism, nepotism, and patronage in addition to sheer graft – did a great deal to discredit the party-states in their last decade.[136]

But if the view from below has some truth, its general direction misleads. Most obviously, Solidarity had been controlled by the mid-1980s, albeit at very great cost in terms of legitimacy, whilst no regime other than that of Poland was seriously threatened by

[134]   J. A. Hall, "In Search of Civil Society," in J. A. Hall, ed., *Civil Society*, Polity Press, Cambridge, 1995.

[135]   L. Kolakowski, "Amidst Moving Ruins," *Daedalus*, vol. 121, 1991.

[136]   G. Ekiert, "Democratisation Processes in East Central Europe," *British Journal of Political Science*, vol. 21, 1991 p. 304. An interesting argument along the same lines – that the brutal period of heroism engendered legitimacy whereas the corrupt period of stagnation undermined it – has recently been made by E. Gellner in "Homeland of the Unrevolution," *Daedalus*, vol. 122, 1992, especially pp. 146–7. I am not so sure, especially given that Yeltsin gained popularity precisely when he was attacked for being disloyal to the heroic demands of renewal – as noted by J. B. Dunlop, *The Rise of Russia and the Fall of the Soviet Empire*, Princeton University Press, Princeton, 1993. It may be that the demands of heroism are too great for most people to bear, at least over the longer term.

its civil society. Further, the lack of positive new initiatives should not be taken to mean that socialist regimes were bound to break down: a very long and messy period of "muddling through" would surely have been possible before unfavorable social trends gained real bite. It is important to recall that collapse was like that of a house of cards, with events in one place imitating – at ever greater speed – those in another; once the Russian card had been withdrawn, as it was when the Kremlin allowed Hungary to open its borders for East Germans wishing to go West, the regimes of 1945 began to crumble. In general, forces from below did not so much cause collapse, as occupy political space once it became available.

If none of the three theories identified works well, understanding can be enhanced by asking why liberalization failed in the crucial case of the Soviet Union. Whilst errors of judgement were certainly made, the fundamental reason why liberalization could not work in socialist society was that societal self-organization had been destroyed.[137] Let us see why this destruction took place, and then begin to note its consequences.

Authoritarian states throughout history have been nervous, as we have seen, about channels of communication which they can scarcely see. Accordingly, it has been very common to find that states ban horizontal linkages in civil society so as to privilege their own official means of communication and power networks. The spirit of such rule was neatly captured by Tocqueville:

> Any independent group, however small, which seemed desirous of taking action otherwise than under the aegis of the administration filled it with alarm, and the tiniest free association of citizens, however harmless its aims, was regarded as a nuisance. The only corporate bodies tolerated were those whose members had been hand-picked by the administration and which were under its control. Even big industrial concerns were frowned upon. In a word, our administration resented the idea of private citizens having any say in the control of their own enterprises, and preferred sterility to competition.[138]

[137]   R. Bova, "Political Dynamics of the Post-Communist Transition," *World Politics*, vol. 44, 1991.
[138]   A. de Tocqueville, *The Old Regime and the French Revolution*, Anchor Books, New York, 1955, p. 64.

To be fair, the modern atomization of society in Russia owes as much to autocracy as to totalitarianism.[139] Tsarism had been as suspicious of social forces, being utterly opposed to capitalism and the rule of law: what mattered was the possibility of isolated individuals being able to approach their Great Father. As is so often the case, a revolution merely intensified existing social patterns: secret police, government inspectors, atomization, boredom, and privatization were familiar to late nineteenth-century Russians, albeit in infinitely milder form. But whatever the exact genealogy, there can be no doubt of the sterility, together with the weakness it causes, that was characteristic of socialist society. Those who might have been reformers were turned into dissidents, with inner emigration depriving state socialism of still more energy.

The literature on transitions to democracy depends completely upon the striking of bargains, above all, of a reforming elite seeking to give a little, to receive in return a signal that this has been understood and accepted, so that more can be given without fear of any complete loss of position. It takes but a moment's thought to appreciate that what is involved here is a sort of partnership in which forces from below discipline themselves so as to reassure those at the top. But Eastern Europe is not Latin America. For all that the theory of totalitarianism exaggerated the powers of the state, it was right when stressing the destruction of society's capacity to organize itself. Liberalization was accordingly never really possible in the Soviet Union: the absence of partners in society made orderly decompression impossible. The key analytic point to be made about institutions is that they control as much as express social forces, thereby allowing the regulation of conflict by means of rational bargaining. A further interesting speculation has suggested that the absence of discipline at the bottom reflects more than the simple destruction of powerful social forces.[140] Had the forces at the top been organized and united, the threat of their return to power might have been so obvious as to create some discipline in society. But the elite was

<hr />

[139] T. McDaniel, *Autocracy, Capitalism and Revolution in Russia*, University of California Press, Berkeley, 1987, chs 2 and 3.
[140] Bova, "Political Dynamics of the Post-Communist Transition."

not at all like that. Very much to the contrary, party members –
at least, in *some* countries, most notably Hungary – had clearly
decided before 1989 that the most secure access to privilege had
come to be through the economy rather than through political
position.[141]

Three further points about the destruction of society's capacity
to organize itself must be noted. First, the manner of collapse, the
fact that it was so sudden, was very much the result of the absence
of intermediate structures – exactly as had been the case, in
Tocqueville's eyes, in the French Revolution: once the head was
removed, the absence of alternative organizing structures was
revealed. Secondly, the weakness of societal groupings helps
explain the paltriness of attempts to reimpose authoritarian rule:
beneath the surface gloss of power was emptiness as much as
organized interest. Finally, one cannot help but note how strange
has been the rule of both Gorbachov and Yeltsin: both seek to
create civil society from on top, by fiat and command. They are
right to appreciate that a strong civil society increases the capacity
of a state to rule, but this scarcely lessens the obvious self-
contradiction at the core of their program.

This brings us to a final point about liberalization and collapse.
Tocqueville long ago made us aware that liberalization is
extremely difficult, and his viewpoint has been expanded by
Przeworski who goes so far as to say that it is just about
impossible – at all times, rather than as argued here, in societies
that have suffered under totalitarianism.[142] Expectations tend to
increase, and to run ahead of the ability to meet them: the paradox
of the situation is that the new regime may fall even though it is
in fact more legitimate than the old one. Certainly, Gorbachov
felt these pressures. But he was by no means, as Western commentators imagined, the absolutely skillful politician, making the very
best of the small amount of room for maneuver available. The

[141]   E. Hankiss, *East European Alternatives*, Oxford University Press, Oxford, 1991. For
an analysis of the "political capitalism" that resulted, see J. Staniszkis, *The Dynamics of
the Breakthrough in Eastern Europe*, University of California Press, Berkeley, 1991.
[142]   A. Przeworski, "The Games of Transition," in S. Mainwaring, G. O'Donnell, and
S. Valenzuela, eds, *Issues in Democratic Consolidation*, University of Notre Dame Press,
Notre Dame, 1992.

worst possible conduct, during the liberalization process, as Tocqueville stressed when examining the policies of Louis XVI, is to dither: to raise expectations and then to dash them lends energized people virtually revolutionary feelings. What is necessary is consistency: a clear and absolute outlining of priorities, a listing of areas where change is permissible and of areas where it is not, and absolute determination not to retreat from announced reform when difficulties arise. It is necessary, in other words, to take the long view, to realize that an increase in liberalism will eventually diffuse conflict; in the politics of decompression, in other words, it is vital to do what one announces *and* to be sparing in what one announces.

It was particularly mad illogic on Gorbachov's part to offer much to the Baltic states, and then to threaten them. This is to say that some part of the nationalities problem – that is, the force which occupied that strange combination of vacuum and anarchy so as then finally to destroy the system – was created by Gorbachov. More generally, it is worth again recalling that nationalist secessionism flourishes in those circumstances of political exclusion which make exit an attractive option; loyalty results from the possession of voice. The legacy of distrust in the Russian socialist empire was, of course, extremely high, and any move to greater openness accordingly likely to be treated with skepticism. But the very difficulty of these circumstances meant that the only potential route for success lay through greater rather than lesser boldness. Early calling of union elections, which Gorbachov could not stomach, was vital.[143] To say this returns us, of course, to the question of democracy. Was not democratization rather than liberalization inevitable, if the nationalities question was to be solved? It is crucial at this point to make a distinction. There is all the difference in the world between democratization that follows collapse, that is, the chaotic vacuum whose prevalence in the region makes Hobbesian calls for a state comprehensible, and democratization willingly given so as to ensure the continuity of some structures which may thereby be shored up. Voluntary

[143]   J. Linz and A. Stepan, "Political Identities and Electoral Sequences," *Daedalus*, vol. 121, 1992.

renunciation of power enables more of it to be retained: differently
put, a firm, planned move towards elections could have been part
of a liberalization strategy. In a sense, the handling of the
nationalities question was the worst possible. There might have
been logic to letting the Baltics go and in being strict elsewhere:
what was disastrous was to pretend to be tough on the Baltics and
then to let them go, thereby giving occasion and precedent to
other regions whose nationalisms to that point had been very
weak. This situation gave Yeltsin the cards which he then used to
destroy his great rival.

One irony (amongst many) deserves underscoring. In one sense,
it was fortunate that proper sociological understanding was *not*
available. The key sociological discovery that totalitarianism had
so destroyed societal self-organization as to all but rule out any
careful decompression amounts to saying that it was nearly
inevitable that socialist leaders would lose control. Had this been
known in advance, it would have encouraged such bunker mentality that no change would have been attempted. Differently put,
Gorbachov destroyed state socialism perfectly because he was
blind. This loyal communist did everything that Tocqueville
warned against, thereby becoming the veritable angel of its
destruction.

CONCLUSION

The international order that came to an end in 1989/91 is still
familiar, and our present discontents make it tempting to look
back on it as an old friend. The cornerstone of the whole edifice
depended upon the workings of sophisticated realism: both the
United States and the Soviet Union were able – coherence being
possible in the former despite the tension caused by popular
participation and in the latter due to its status as a late, late
developer – to make clear if imperfect calculations of their
interests whilst nuclear weapons both lent their world a measure
of homogeneity denied in public utterances and ensured a measure
of prudence. In contrast to this simplicity, order within capitalist
society was maintained in a thoroughly novel manner: hegemonic

rule was distinctively present, as was a portion of international liberal solidarity and an ever-increasing measure of economic interdependence. Challenges from the Third World were, perhaps surprisingly, surmounted, with some developing countries making genuine progress in the 1980s.

Nostalgia should be resisted. Awareness of the appalling casualties within the postwar developing world must always make one question any moral glow around the notion of international order. Equally, recognition of the sheer number of deaths caused by socialism in power must make one welcome its collapse. The desire to have moral unity in a complex society involved such huge amounts of coercion that one is tempted to say: down with *polis* envy, forever!

But it would be equally madness to replace nostalgia with euphoria. The fact that a great tyranny has gone does not necessarily mean that any sort of international order will now come into place. The post-communist world may be unsettled by nationalism.[144] It may further be that the West will lose its sense of purpose, both at the domestic and international level, now that the discipline imposed by struggling against its great rival has been removed. Above all, the defeat of the challenge from the Third World may be both transitory – and unwise. Let us then turn from the sudden ending of a world to whose ways we had grown accustomed so as to attempt a chart of the new circumstances that face us and of the policies that should guide our actions within them.

[144]   E. Gellner, "Nationalism and Politics in Eastern Europe," *New Left Review*, no. 189, 1991.

5

Results of the Inquiry

This book opened by noting that President Bush's proclamation of a new world order came to be seen within a matter of months as both ridiculous and offensive. The concentration of attention and power that had so effectively dealt with Saddam Hussein's invasion of Kuwait was most certainly not replicated in the face of the brutalities of ethnic cleansing in the Balkans. The situation in some ways became worse than it was when hope was first questioned: the overrunning of the United Nations' "safe areas" in eastern Bosnia symbolized the bankruptcy of ill-considered policy. Despite this, repulsive though it is to say so, international order remained intact. For "trouble in the Balkans" remained localized, and not likely – although it was always possible – to spill over into generalized conflict between major powers.

I begin this chapter with an analytic summary both of the arguments made about different ideal types of international order and of the logic and descriptive force of the realism/liberalism mix. With that in mind, I then turn my attention to the nature of our current international order. This comprises a very special brew. The sudden collapse of the Soviet Union was not followed by any general peace treaty, thereby creating a legacy in which current rules curiously combine old institutions with new realities. In consequence, the initial characterization of our international order is followed by analysis both of forces of integration and disintegration and of differential levels of stability within it.

Finally, I propose certain ethical rules that follow from the inquiry as a whole. These normative points are meant to be based on a firm sense of social reality, the intent being to note possibilities rather than to replace analysis with hope.

Let me firmly state at the start that the sudden emergence of genuine world order, that is, of a world in which states would suddenly begin to welcome the universal stranger, is not here deemed to be likely. Above all, little sense resides in the popular notion that nation-states are losing their importance, above all in the eyes of those who lack the basic protections that they bring.[1] Such optimism as is offered thus concerns the creation of a more equitable and legitimate international order; this smaller move, for all that it sometimes seems surrounded by insuperable difficulties, thus concerns greater justice within a society of states.

ANALYTIC SUMMARY

Three of the ideal types of international order identified have provided only limited guidance when examining the periods of relative calm and extreme escalation that mark the historical record. The economism that lies at the heart of the theory of interdependence limited its cognitive power. In general, economic factors habitually reflect rather than cause geopolitical conditions, whilst war has often broken out between states involved in trade with each other – with clarity probably being lent to Soviet–American perceptions precisely by the absence of such links. Further, economic actors have been poor controllers of foreign policy: they often do not have geopolitical views and are anyway not often present in the key councils of their states. But perhaps this may now be beginning to change, given that direct investment is creating ever stronger domestic constituencies in favor of free trade rather than protection.

More mixed points can be made about international orders

---

[1] M. Mann, "Nation-States in Europe and Other Continents," *Daedalus*, vol. 122, 1993; J. A. Hall, *Coercion and Consent*, Polity Press, Cambridge, 1994, pp. 206–13.

created by a concert of great powers and those dominated by a hegemonic leader. The conditions that create the former have been unusual, notably in the years immediately after the Congress of Vienna and in the still shorter period of agreement between Moscow and Washington with regard to Saddam Hussein. This is not to say that a concert is without all effect: to the contrary, an increase in understanding can facilitate realist calculations. Nonetheless, it is noticeable that states do not for long submerge self-interest in a common cause, making this type of order exceedingly rare. International order provided by a liberal leader is still more unusual: the only such order has been that created by the United States for capitalism in the postwar era – and that order was also underwritten by additional components. The great interest of hegemonic stability theory is not, in other words, matched by the generalizations it makes about the historical record. Most notably, it has been demonstrated that the account offered by this theory of the Pax Britannica is clearly wrong, with occasional comments about Holland or Genoa as prior hegemons being well-nigh ridiculous.[2] A corollary of this point is that we may have less to fear, should the United States suddenly lose its power advantages, than this theory predicts: just as the nineteenth century was peaceful in the absence of a hegemon, so too may be our future. Further facets of hegemonic stability theory are equally question-begging. For one thing, there is little sense to versions of this theory which suggest that hegemonic war is economically necessary: Wilhelmine Germany certainly challenged a particular ordering of the world polity, but the explanatory variable for this behavior, certainly not necessary for material well-being, was found in the nature of its political regime. For another, skepticism needs to be directed, as we have seen, towards the implicitly favorable moral glow surrounding the idea of leadership: whilst this has occasionally been benign, it is important to remember that the United States always stood to gain from leadership, and that it now exercises that leadership in a petty, self-interested, and predatory manner.

---

[2]   I disagree here particularly with G. Arrighi, *The Long Twentieth Century*, Verso, London, 1994, despite learning much from its bold outlines.

What has mattered for many of the historical developments considered here has been sophisticated realism. Conflict has lost intensity within an homogeneous world populated by intelligent states, whilst escalations to the extremes have been occasioned by the absence of these factors. This amounts to being a first theoretical result of the inquiry.

But this position superimposes two variables upon each other. Many of the historical moments considered in this book have concerned the conjoined operation of these two variables: analysis has largely been of situations marked either by homogeneity in combination with intelligent states or by heterogeneity with states made incapable of calculation by fundamental lack of social coherence. It is by no means easy to discover historical moments when only one of the variables was present. Nonetheless, it was argued that the ability to calculate was of greater import than ideological homogeneity. The character of the Napoleonic regime rather than ideological division prevented an accord being reached by 1813; equally, the Soviet Union's conflict against capitalism – in fact by no means total, given shared stakes in nuclear weapons – did not lead to total war since the coherent state of a late, late developer had room within which calculation was possible.

A second set of theoretical results derives from refusal to take this finding as a mandate for a return to realism. The realism/ liberalism mix gained initial plausibility from the discovery that liberalism can help rational calculation on the part of states. Wilhelmine Germany lacked this ability to assign priorities, thereby so offending its neighbors that it created the encirclement from which it then tried to escape; in contrast, liberal states have benefited from institutions which provided a sociological base for the rational state calculation so properly stressed by sophisticated realism. If the provision of freedom within which to calculate mattered, still more important – for the rashness of Hitler must be set against the relative caution of the Soviet Union – were the checks that limited disastrous adventures. Extension of such checks matters enormously now given both the breakdown of late, late developing societies and the destructive power of modern weapons. If this is obvious, the burden of the argument as a whole can be highlighted by insisting that such extension should be understood as covering the United States: greater openness in foreign policy making would have prevented the second-rate James Bond machinations of Oliver North.

Reluctant scepticism needs to be shown to further parts of liberalism's view of international order. Some progress towards a Kantian liberal league can be seen in the insistence of the European Union that "membership must entail various liberal commitments, notably to democracy and to the protection of minority rights. Furthermore, the regimes of international society may be doing something, as Keohane suggested, to help international co-oper-ation.[3] But great validity remains to the view that such regimes remain the subjects of American power, for all that their presence sometimes masks the operations of that power.[4] Equally, claims made about the extensive reach of liberal norms must be handled with caution. For one thing, normative solidarities sometimes claimed as liberal are often no such thing, as was strikingly true of Anglo-Saxon solidarity a century ago. For another, those who share norms have tended to be a very particular social fraction, namely those leaders of states who genuinely inhabit an inter-national society. Most people are caged within their own countries, from which position their view of international affairs may well be limited. There are as yet only limited signs of transnational civil society, even within the European Union where self-identification remains national. Still, skepticism should not become cynicism, and membership within an international liberal society is slowly widening. And if the descriptive force of this statement is not especially great, the social construction of such an entity remains hugely desirable on prescriptive grounds: if such international solidarity would make the calculations of realism easier, it might equally mark the beginning of a world in which the shells of states were less necessary.

One final strand of the argument can usefully be drawn together at this point. I have stressed that the competition of states operating within the frame of a shared culture, that is, the pattern identified and endorsed by Edward Gibbon and by Hedley Bull, has moral advantages and disadvantages. On the one hand, this

[3]   R. Keohane, *After Hegemony*, Princeton University Press, Princeton, 1984.
[4]   S. Strange, "Cave! hic dragones," *International Organization*, vol. 36, 1982.

social portfolio encouraged economic development and pioneered political liberty; on the other hand, huge increases in power were used for a domination of the rest of the world that was far from liberal – with rivalry between these same "advanced" powers eventually causing wars which engulfed the whole world. As it happens, diversity still retains attractions when contrasted to any empire of the world. But recommendation of such diversity must depend, as will be seen, upon strengthening both states and international society by means of liberalism. Reserved commendation for the historical role of a particular social portfolio needs to be distinguished from enthusiastic advocacy of the extension of its better features.

SPECIAL BREW

The contemporary international order is a unique and quite extraordinary brew. Attention needs to be given both to the way in which it combines the various principles discussed and to the division of labor upon which it rests.

One striking element in the world polity results from the re-emergence of distinctive elements of multipolarity. Examples abound, and some should be cited. The United States did not uniformly determine everything that happened within its sphere of influence at the height of its power, with its role in NATO being, as argued, very much the result of an invitation.[5] Nonetheless, the sheer speed of Chancellor Kohl's drive for reunification paid no obeisance whatever to the United States. Equally, the European Union is now capable of articulating and sometimes of acting upon interests which are judged to go counter to those of the United States. Further, Japan is refusing to follow American orders to give aid to Russia unless and until it receives a satisfactory agreement about the Kurile Islands, and it has distinct resentments at the demands made by the United States for changes in its economic policies. Far more important, China looks set to

[5]   G. Lundestad, "Empire by Invitation?", *Journal of Peace Research*, vol. 23, 1986.

have an economic base such that its contribution to world affairs will need to be taken into account by all other powers. Size in combination with the possession of nuclear arms makes it certain that Russia will regain its status as a great power.

Multipolarity suggests realism, and that in turn raises the question as to whether some part of the current international order derives from traditional calculations about the balance of power. Calculation of this type is clearly present at the regional level. It is as important now for the French co-operatively to control the Germans as it was when they first helped create what has become the European Union. Of course, the means to achieve that end have changed: they now include, at one and the same time, co-operation with Germany in an armed brigade and a sudden appreciation of the benefits of American involvement in Europe. Many more examples of such regional calculations could be given, from South Korea's turn towards China to protect itself against Japan to the start of ideologically charged alliances in Central Europe. Such calculations can also be detected in the behavior of the great powers. The way in which China was called onto the world stage by Nixon to formally balance Russia classically showed the importance of this sort of behavior in modern circumstances. There are signs that balancing behavior may be on the increase. There are certainly pressures in Russia for a turn to the East, not least given the relatively cold shoulder shown to it by the West. Such autonomous behavior would probably increase attention and favor to Russia, just as China has improved its position by standing between East and West.

Balance of power behavior of this sort may have beneficial consequences. If the United States is confronted by autonomous actors, it may begin to respect them; efforts may be made to understand different societies, and attempts made to adjust its own behavior as a result. But realist calculations can go awry, not least as the control of foreign policy is still extremely limited, and it is only fair to point out that the dominant tone of some commentators noting renewed multipolarity has been pessimistic.[6] But a measure of optimism is justified because emerging multi-

---

[6]   J. Mearsheimer, "Back to the Future," *International Security*, vol. 14, 1990.

polarity takes place at the same time as obeisance is increasingly given to norms of interdependence and of liberalism. Let us consider each in turn.

One way of approaching interdependence is to note that the recognition given to nationalism as a principle of world politics has increased. There is a very positive side to this development which much recent commentary has ignored. Militarily, expansion no longer brings security: nuclear missiles ignore the size of empires and of buffer-zones possessed by leading states. That this generalization applied to the East European satellites was apparent to Gorbachov, almost certainly aware of the economics of the situation.[7] If possession of territory increased power and wealth in the agrarian era, it no longer has that role, for two reasons. Negatively, nationalist movements have the capacity to make the retention of imperial possessions prohibitively expensive. Positively, economic success seems ever more dependent on the creation of human capital capable of allowing one's economy to move up the product cycle; one way of helping such movement is participation in advanced markets rather than through trading with secure colonial markets – whose capacity to absorb one's product, given their poverty, was anyway often exaggerated. Europe was made to realize this largely within the two decades after 1945; as yet this lesson has been perhaps half-learnt inside Russia – or, perhaps better, learnt by some rather than others.[8] And it is worth noting that the disorder created by nationalist separatism is at least somewhat curtailed by the absence of any other empire ready to collapse.

Marx famously remarked that re-enacted historical events have an air of farce about them. This can indeed be so. But sometimes historical events catch up with theories which have preceded them, and there are good reasons for believing that this is true of the hope that interdependence would limit geopolitical conflict. One important change since 1945 has been the creation, for the first time, of a genuinely international division of labor. The demand for free trade now begins to have domestic political roots

[7] V. Bunce, "The Empire Strikes Back," *International Organization*, vol. 39, 1985.
[8] C. Kaysen, "Is War Obsolete?," *International Security*, vol. 14, 1990.

given that employment often depends upon companies whose very being depends upon world trade; both votes and campaign funds are now available to those who resist protectionism.[9] Some indication of what is involved can be gained by noting that perhaps a third of world trade is now intra-firm in character – something which makes nonsense of any simple view of national accounts. More important than this, however, is the fact that economic success depends upon participation in the market. The history of the world economy in recent years has seen that nations which protect their industries for any length of time after their initial nurturing condemn their societies to increasing poverty. If this is most spectacularly true of the former Soviet bloc, it applies quite as much elsewhere. Argentina is a prime example of the false trail of protectionism, but the Latin American practice of import-substitution industrialization makes the general point equally well, especially when compared to the export-led growth of the East Asian newly industrializing countries.[10] The basic underlying structural fact explaining this seems to be that the speed of technological change is now so fast that not to be involved in it invites inefficiency. All of this can be encapsulated in a single notion. In a loose sense, we are already in a third age of the history of industrialism, replacing statist planning which in turn had replaced the hidden hand of the first emergence of a new form of production. Human capital has always had importance for industrialism, but its role is now absolutely central: it is the mechanism that does most to create comparative advantage, encourage flexible specialization and allow for rapid adaptation.

Care has been taken in the choice of words used in this discussion of interdependence. No functionalist argument – presuming that the needs of late industrialism will automatically be met – is intended. The argument is rather that many political elites have realized and begun to act upon the connection posited. The

[9]   I. M. Destler and J. Odell, *Anti-Protection*, Institute for International Economics, Washington, 1987; H. Milner, "Resisting the Protectionist Temptation," *International Organization*, vol. 41, 1987.

[10]   C. Waisman, *Reversal of Development in Argentina*, Princeton University Press, Princeton, 1987; F. C. Deyo, ed., *The Political Economy of the New Asian Industrialism*, Cornell University Press, Ithaca, 1987; N. Mouzelis, *Politics and the Semi-Periphery*, Macmillan, London, 1986.

extent to which this has happened is, however, very considerable. The political elite in Mexico, for example, is risking its political base largely because it is convinced of these truths. The point at issue can be put usefully in a different manner: many political elites again inhabit international society. This is as true of President Clinton as it is of Prime Minister Klaus in the Czech Republic or of Prime Minister Rao in India, and certainly of the serried ranks of their economic and military advisers.

Membership in this larger society goes some way to explain the spread of liberal ideology. It is idle to hide the considerable tension that exists at this point. The liberalism that many of these international actors believe in is economic rather than political, and at least some of these figures openly argue for curtailing political freedom at transitional moments as a necessary price for economic reform. That is not a happy equation, nor is it a sensible one, given the record of economic and geopolitical disaster that it has occasioned in the twentieth century. Nonetheless, if Leszek Balcerowicz, the pioneer of Poland's shock therapy whose musings in this area became especially well known, contemplated the concentration of power in order to create capitalism from above, it was only in the belief that the development of capitalism eventually entails the growth of softer political rule. There is some evidence to support this secondary proposition. Societies which are heavily involved in world trade and which seek to move up the product cycle are ever more likely to generate pressures for liberalization. Economic success in these circumstances depends upon the willing participation of educated labor, that is, of people whose jobs depend upon freedom of movement and information.[11] If this goose is to lay a golden egg, it is imperative that rigidly authoritarian and ideocratic regimes loosen their hold. And if that hold is not loosened demands will be made, especially by students, for liberalization from below. The pressure generated by this segment may well prove to have more significance than that generated by European working classes at the end of the nineteenth century.[12] The analytic point being made in all this needs

---

[11] E. Gellner, "Plaidoyer pour une libéralisation manquée," *Government and Opposition*, vol. 14, 1979.
[12] J. A. Hall, "Classes and Elites, Wars and Social Evolution," *Sociology*, vol. 22, 1988.

to be highlighted and underscored. It has been seen that authoritarian regimes, especially when they are semi-mobilized, are prone to start wars. Every time pressure for liberalization is successful, the chances of war are reduced.

To this point in the discussion, less has been said about power than about the growth of transnational forces. But considerations of power are massively present in the special brew under consideration. A first way in which this is so is in the element of concert in the contemporary international order. One part of this concert stretches back a little time, albeit in very understated ways. Those powers which possess nuclear weapons have long been strikingly rational in wishing to prevent their spread, and the attempt to pre vent non-proliferation is quite properly seen as deriving from a very particular concert.[13] This non-proliferation regime has recently been boosted by the surprising renunciation of nuclear ambitions by some powers capable of the requisite technology.[14] Nonetheless, the possibility of a general concert of powers has really been ruled out since 1917, for the Soviet Union was rarely so isolated that the rest of the international community could establish a concert against its revolutionary principles. The confidence-building measures initiated by Gorbachov created a sufficient degree of unanimity amongst the great powers to establish an effective concert on key issues, notably during the Gulf War – one of whose dimensions was that of a war of the North against the South. This concert was in effect hidden, because it was channelled through the United Nations, whose new lease of life of course depended upon this novel background consensus, many of whose members were at once scared of the repulsive weapons of Saddam Hussein and exceedingly keen to support the norm of non-intervention on which their own sovereignty so often relied.

A second dimension of power is quite as important. The United States most distinctively has not lost pre-eminence. Further, if the power of the United States does diminish somewhat that may

[13]   R. Jervis, *The Meaning of the Nuclear Revolution*, Cornell University Press, Ithaca, 1989; M. Bundy, *Danger and Survival*, Random House, New York, 1988.
[14]   T. V. Paul, "Will the Systemic Basis of the Non-Proliferation Regime Persist beyond 1995?", unpublished paper, 1994.

matter far less than many pundits imagine. The period of its ascendancy was used to create a particular set of rules, that is, to codify the American view of the world, continued observation of which is one of the more striking features of the age.[15] More important still are the self-denying ordinances so characteristic of America's allied rivals. European countries are not particularly keen to create a complete multipolar system, in which each has its own nuclear weapons: at present only the French have a genuinely independent nuclear force, and their current policy has strikingly begun to join the European norm in wishing for an American presence in order to counterbalance and control Germany.[16] American leadership in the last years has, however, been exercised in a predatory rather than a benign manner, not least in order to supply its twin deficits with large amounts of cash. Remarkably, the Clinton administration began to make inroads on that problem; it remains to be seen whether this route is continued by a Republican Congress which, for all its deficit-cutting zeal, remains committed to cutting taxes. Nonetheless, the ability to use power is rarely given up, and it may well be worth considering aggression in the field of trade as further predation. For what does such aggression denote? Surely it is the ability of the most powerful player in the game to alter the rules, rather than to rationalize its own society, to its systematic advantage. This is not to deny that some of the changes that the United States desires, most obviously the recasting of Europe's Common Agricultural Policy, are entirely meritorious; but that does not apply to every policy, whilst it is hard not to object to the hypocrisy involved in the case cited, given the level of farm subsidies in the United States itself. Nonetheless, it remains unlikely that either Japan or Europe will do anything other than grin and bear American behavior, albeit with much hidden resentment.[17]

One way in which this list can be consolidated is in terms of a formula. An international order exists in which state leaders

[15]   S. Strange, *States and Markets*, Pinter, London, 1988, pp. 24–34.
[16]   This point is directed against the likelihood of multipolar nuclear situation envisaged in D. Calleo, *Beyond American Hegemony*, Basic Books, New York, 1987.
[17]   For a contrary view, see E. Helleiner, *States and the Reemergence of Global Finance*, Cornell University Press, Ithaca, 1994.

calculate that their best advantage lies in acting as traders within the world market, paying obeisance to social forces which are vital for their economies – and so for their legitimacy; but this order is based quite as much on a concert between leading great powers, whilst it is led and sometimes dominated by one power, whose varied strengths give it a command that many allied states in fact wish it to have. But there is a second way in which the points made can be consolidated, namely by means of a consideration of the highly idiosyncratic division of labor characteristic of this international order. The United States has power in every dimension conceivable, in military, economic, financial, and, perhaps increasingly, cultural affairs.[18] In contrast, Russia has a system of nuclear weapons capable of destroying the world, without any clear prospect, despite its resource base, of established affluence. That situation is neatly turned upside down by Japan and Europe: these key areas of advanced capitalism have considerable wealth but limited armed might. International relations for some years has had, as noted, a systemic element to it in that the United States has in effect taken some of the butter of such countries on the grounds that it provides the guns. The ending of the Cold War has suggested to many that such levies may come to an end, or at least that the system has become unbalanced. There is a certain logic to this position, but rich countries to the present point find the world sufficiently insecure to value American leadership – with all that this is likely to mean in terms of their own contributions to the underwriting of that hegemony. Military power may not yet have lost its relevance despite the increased attention given to economic competition.

All these features of our international order have nothing whatsoever to do with or to say about the vast majority of the countries of the world. One systematic feature of the new order may well be that its element of concert draws attention away from what was formerly called the Third World: if the world is no longer seen in Manichean terms, then local and regional dynamics will play themselves out without there being any feeling that they

---

[18]   J. Nye, *Bound to Lead*, Basic Books, New York, 1990; Strange, *States and Markets*, ch. 6.

concern the advanced world. Given some interventions that have taken place, one is immediately tempted to welcome this development: second thoughts will make the notion of such benign neglect rather less appealing.

PATTERNS OF INTEGRATION AND DISINTEGRATION

Many of the commentators who have sought to understand and characterize the shape of the world polity after the Cold War have made much of the co-presence of forces of integration and disintegration.[19] It makes sense to follow their lead here, for our current international order is idiosyncratic; indeed, one would certainly be tempted to predict its demise if anything remotely more plausible seemed present on the political horizon. Much that needs to be said is merely a restatement of the central tenets of Polanyi's *The Great Transformation*. What is noticeable about a more interdependent world is that it privileges some actors, trained in think tanks abroad, whilst disadvantaging those stuck at home: increasing tension in most societies is likely between these members of international society, and national citizens whose ways of life they seek to change rather than to protect.

Forces of integration have had their powers massively enhanced by recent social developments. A genuine revolution has taken place in communications systems. This underlies the extraordinary way in which the whole world has become a unified cultural supermarket, with the products of Anglo-American pop groups being as evident in East Asia as in Eastern Europe. Financial affairs have been similarly affected due to the speed with which money can now be transferred around the globe. Transactions of every country are now dwarfed by those of the market, and this has destroyed some traditional economic weapons of the state. Try supporting a currency today, when the market has no faith in its underlying strength!

[19]   The most powerful of such recent analyses is J. L. Gaddis, "Great Illusions, the Long Peace and the Future of the International System", in his *The United States and the End of the Cold War*, Oxford University Press, Oxford, 1992.

On the other side, however, stand forces of disintegration of equally great power.[20] Such forces are often seen through the lens provided by that currently influential social philosophy which asserts a need for communitarian involvement. This is yet another reiteration of the search for a unitary self, made especially dreadful now by lack both of any historical memory of the disasters to which this led and of evidence of much validity to support the key tenets of its position.Still, there is no gainsaying the influence of this position.[21] Thus the revival of nationalism is interpreted as a search for a sense of belonging ruled out of court by the febrile myths of liberal society. A more powerful force of disintegration can be noted by pointing again to the Islamic revolution in Iran and to the strength of fundamentalist Islam in much of its classical heartland. This force has no truck with a single world. Where most post-communist societies long to join a single world of consumerism and generally have great admiration for the United States, the Islamic heartland has a visceral hatred of the immorality of such a world. If our situation is that of an either/or opposition between, to use Barber's nice expression, McWorld and Jihad, there will of course be precious little room for liberalism and democracy.[22]

These forces are indeed potent, and they deserve consideration. This is not, it should be stressed, to accept the way in which they have been characterized. Islamic fundamentalism has little to do with traditional Muslim society. Nationalism is of course Janus-faced, taking on a more or less liberal character according to the political circumstances in which it finds itself. In general, it has much less to do with the search for roots than with the real services that a modern state can render a people. Differently put, the supposed alienation and anomie of those in the advanced West is far less general and less powerful than modern social philos-

---

[20]   R. D. Kaplan, "The Coming Anarchy," *Atlantic Monthly*, February 1994.
[21]   R. Bellah, R. Madsen, W. Sullivan, A.Swidler and S. Tipton, *Habits of the Heart*, University of California, Berkeley, 1985 can stand as exemplar of this position. Striking negative comments about this book were made by A. Greeley in his review in *Sociology and Social Research*, vol. 70, 1985, as was noticed by S. Lieberson, "Einstein, Renoir and Greeley," *American Sociological Review*, vol. 57, 1992. Cf. D. Phillips, *Looking Backwards*, Princeton University Press, Princeton, 1993.
[22]   B. Barber, "Jihad vs. McWorld," *Atlantic Monthly*, March, 1992.

ophers imagine, which is not, of course, to deny that they themselves suffer from it a great deal. More important still, there are good reasons to dissent from the view, put forward by its defenders quite as much by its opponents, that there is only a single slogan suited to McWorld – say, "Consumers of the World Unite" – and that this is scarcely likely to warm the blood like wine. As it happens, many do find that slogan very powerful, but the more important point is surely that other slogans are available. A social philosophy stressing individualism and political choice is not, at least for me, without coherence and attraction.[23] Beyond these detailed demurrals, however, stands the need to see how the forces in question play out in different regions of the world. For the greatest weakness of recent commentators has been to presume that social forces have or will have uniform consequences. This is not so, as can be seen in even the most cursory of examinations of the differential chances for the stability of international order within the contemporary world. My argument will be that while things are becoming quiet on the Western front, they are unsettled in the East, and potentially catastrophic in the South.

By and large, the forces of integration have the upper hand in the advanced societies of the West. In Europe, those forces have added a great deal to the power and salience of the European Union. This is now a supremely successful organization for furthering capitalist needs – which is to say that the regional and social policies of the Community pale into insignificance in comparison to regulations for industry and finance. Thankfully, the Union has insisted, as noted, upon democratization as a condition of membership, and it thereby has the capacity to exert massive influence over neighboring countries whose businessmen are often desperate to gain access to its markets. Less obvious than this is the way in which Western arrangements have undermined the principal force of disintegration, namely nationalism. Separatist nationalism within the advanced West deserves to be seen as a particular type of nationalism. Its most considerable theorists stress that it often seeks – or, in a different formulation, has as its best strategy – to protect rich areas from the taxing

23   J. A. Hall, *Liberalism*, Paladin, London, 1987.

powers of a central government keen to look after poorer areas.[24] It may well be that modern forces of integration make this strategy more efficacious. The classical opening chapters of Adam Smith's *The Wealth of Nations* argue that wealth is related to the size of the market. That this is so has done much to curtail separatist nationalism: the larger national state provided the greater market and so the greater wealth. But that may no longer be so. If Catalonia were to separate, it is extremely likely that it would continue to have the benefits of the European economic space, and it is certainly Quebec's hope – albeit, a hope which is by no means assured, given that the United States would be resistant to its Colbertist tradition of industrial policy – that it would be able to continue to operate within a North American Free Trade Area. But the fact that the costs of exit have been lessened should not, I think, lead to any generalized view that separatism will increase. Nationalism becomes political, as argued, when political interference forces a response from society; more particularly, there have been few examples of exit from democratic systems wherein voice is possible. In this matter demands for privileges should not be mistaken for a desire to separate: the strength of Scottish nationalism derives from the failure of the British state to devolve its powers. It is most likely that Catalonia and Quebec will stay within their political territories, albeit the relationships involved will always entail bargaining and conflict. It is, of course, more likely that tensions between Quebec and the rest of Canada will escalate, given that the asymmetrical federal bargain which contained Basque and Catalan nationalism seems ever harder to come by, both because of regional jealousy and the unwillingness of a multicultural society to recognize only francophone society as distinct. If separation does occur in any of these cases, it is unlikely, despite a good deal of localized pain, to disrupt international order: any new state looks set to stay within the rules of larger international society rather than, as between 1870 and 1945 when heroism was favored so much more than trading, being attracted to economic mercantilism and thereby to war.

---

[24]   T. Nairn, *The Break-up of Britain*, New Left Books, London, 1977; H. Meadwell, "The Politics of Nationalism in Quebec," *World Politics*, vol. 45, 1993.

All this may seem unduly sanguine. To begin with, does not the advanced West suffer from considerable economic problems likely to cause considerable discontent? Whilst capitalist society by its nature is one of movement and continual claim and counter-claim, there is a good deal to be said against the thesis implicit in the question, namely that the advanced West is currently facing a systemic crisis. To the contrary, what is most noticeable is that the great inflation has been defeated and economic growth restored on a sound footing – with the diminution of corporatist politics doing much to depoliticize economic life. Within such broad generalizations is hidden the fact that income differentials have increased with the position of the disadvantaged becoming noticeably worse not just in relative but also in absolute terms. I will provide prescriptive arguments against this repulsive development. But it must be said firmly that these developments, truly strong anyway, despite much rhetoric, only in Anglo-Saxon countries, do not look powerful enough to undermine social stability.[25] The radical right's repugnant politics are thankfully linked neither to genuine numbers nor to real effectiveness.

Equally importantly, is it not the case that the road to integration in Europe is now blocked, with the distinct possibility that backward steps may be taken? Whilst problems should not be ignored, their salience should not be exaggerated. In the United States discussion of European affairs is prone to swings of fashion of the most extraordinary kind, from a belief in a United States of Europe, to the notion of Eurosclerosis, to the rediscovery of integration, and on to despair at Europe's weaknesses. The European Union does face the major contradiction of a common economic space within which some states, notably Britain and Italy, can gain advantage from leaving the exchange mechanism by means of competitive devaluations. Still, the pattern of change within Europe has been that of "one steps backwards, two step forwards," and this may again prove to be true. The recession has made progress difficult, but a new atmosphere may again make change possible. It is worth digressing to say that progress is likely

---

[25] K. Bradley and A. Gelb, "The Radical Potential of Cash Nexus Breaks," *British Journal of Sociology*, vol. 31, 1980; M. Smith, *Power, Norms and Inflation*, Aldine de Gruyter, New York, 1992.

to be the more assured if it is of a particular type. The European design would likely do best if it gave the impression of being less bureaucratic at the moment when it is genuinely becoming so. This is to accommodate Denmark's concern with "subsidiarity" with the necessity (no less a word will do) to have economic policy taken out of the incompetent hands of the British elite. This is by no means impossible: Denmark tied its currency to the Deutschmark long ago and thereby lost control of crucial economic levers, whilst there is no need, and probably no intention, to destroy any other aspect of the nation-state in current plans. Further, there may be genuine demand for a "two plus or minus one language regime" which would replace the cumbersome proliferation of official languages. The adoption of English as the European language would appeal to bureaucrats and it might be generally acceptable given the lack of hegemony of Britain in the Union – especially since support for this change could well come from the provincial level, from the Catalans and Occitans, keen to downplay the homogenizing tendencies of the nation-states within which they live.[26] This would amount to the successful multinational organization that geopolitical commitments made impossible in Austro-Hungary – a comment that highlights the extent to which European development still depend on geopolitical peace brokered by the United States.

Any set of comments about advanced capitalist society which failed to end by considering the United States would be incomplete. Different policy options face America at this time, with debate being particularly lively on the vexed question as to whether the United States should seek to retain its hegemonic position as compared to becoming merely first amongst equals.[27] It is certainly the case that the United States is not used to the constraints of multipolarity, and so far there are few signs of adaptation to this condition. Thus the attempt to force open

---

[26]   These speculations are those of D. Laitin, "The Cultural Identities of a European State," unpublished paper.

[27]   For representative views, see K. Waltz, "The Emerging Structure of International Politics," *International Security*, vol. 18, 1993, R. Steel, *Temptations of a Superpower*, Harvard University Press, Cambridge, 1994, T. Smith, *America's Mission*, Princeton University Press, Princeton, 1994, and S. Hoffmann et al., "What Should American Foreign Policy Be?," *Dissent*, Fall, 1994.

markets habitually shows hegemonic muscle rather than the commitment to liberal regimes. It is intensely ironic to see these politics of "strategic reciprocity" being disowned by the economist most associated with their creation, essentially on the grounds that the American state lacks the capacity to improve upon the market![28] Still, the resentment caused by such policies is unlikely to disrupt international order, given unwillingness to challenge the United States. What may matter more is that the American political elite has yet to regain that unity and sense of purpose which was destroyed by involvement in Vietnam. The way in which it deals with its own wounds will do most to determine the future stability of advanced capitalism.

Analysis of what was once the second world can begin by looking at the extent to which the fates of Central Europe and Russia may remain entwined. Let us start with general issues before turning to particular countries. The tone of the argument will be mildly pessimistic on the grounds that the breakdown of communism throughout the region is unlikely to be followed by equally generalized consolidation of democracy.

The extent to which the collapse of communism in Eastern Europe has been total has already been stressed. There is a sense in which this has created the peculiar phenomenon of a social vacuum. The consequent retreat into private life is seen in the very low turn-out at recent elections in both Poland and Hungary, and in the generalized uncertainty, given the weakness of social organization, as to what one's interests *are* let alone how to *represent* them. If this is one legacy of Leninism, another is deep distrust between different groups – caused in part by the way in which divide-and-rule policies of the regime set groups apart from each other. The words used by Tocqueville to describe the consequences of such policies in France apply nearly perfectly to post-communism:

> It was no easy task bringing together fellow citizens who had lived for many centuries aloof from, or even hostile to, each other and teaching them to co-operate in the management of their own

---

[28]   P. Krugman, *Peddling Prosperity*, W. W. Norton, New York, 1994 and "Competitiveness," *Foreign Affairs*, vol. 73, 1994.

affairs. It had been far easier to estrange them than it now was to reunite them, and in so doing France gave the world a memorable example. Yet, when sixty years ago the various classes which under the old order had been isolated units in the social system came once again in touch, it was on their sore spots that they made contact and their first gesture was to fly at each other's throats. Indeed, even today, though class distinctions are no more, the jealousies and antipathies they caused have not died out.[29]

The reservation in my last sentence is occasioned by the need to make a consideration of nations rather than the classes of civil society our most immediate task. For nations have been able to organize far more effectively than have other interest groups in society.

The emergence of nationalism in Eastern Europe was inevitable. In retrospect, it has become obvious that the Bolsheviks carried on the legacy of the Russian empire, with Stalin adding to it in the years immediately after 1945. Differently put, the end of the First World War saw the destruction of the Ottoman and Habsburg empires, but the remarkable restoration of Russian power by military means. States such as Georgia and the Ukraine quickly lost the independence that they had gained because of revolutionary turmoil, and they were thereafter reintegrated into the empire. That this was supposedly a union of socialist republics misled many, with some of the analyses declaring the impossibility of nationalism under socialism being published astonishingly late.[30] The Soviet state did, of course, seek to control nationalism by traditional means, that is, by the stick of brutality (including a licentious use of deportations) and the carrot of metropolitan subsidies. But, it remained the case that the empire was run for and by Russians: the local elite was always likely to stake its claim when the opportunity arose, not least since the Soviet state had linked "titular" nationalities to particular territories.[31]

If much that is taking place in Eastern Europe is inevitable and

[29]   A. de Tocqueville, *The Old Regime and the French Revolution*, Anchor Books, New York, 1955, p. 107.

[30]   A. Motyl, *Will the Non-Russians Rebel?*, Cornell University Press, Ithaca, 1987.

[31]   R. Brubaker, "Nationhood and the National Question in the Soviet Union and Post-Soviet Eurasia," *Theory and Society*, vol. 23, 1994; I. Bremmer and R. Taras, eds, *Nations and Politics in the Soviet Successor States*, Cambridge University Press, Cambridge, 1993.

necessary, it should not be forgotten that the power of liberal democracy to dilute nationalism retains considerable force. Had Gorbachov chosen national elections early on, the presentation of voice might have diminished the amount of exit.[32] Equally, the fact that Yeltsin does hold out the promise of varied accommodations means that the nationalities question in the former Soviet Union has largely been conducted in an orderly manner: for it is the established republics which have sought independence, with relatively little movement from the nationalities inside Russia – whose actions, were they scared by the reimposition of autocracy, could lead to endless nationalist demands, along the lines of *Matrioshka* dolls.[33] This factor helps highlight the extent to which nationalist demands result from the manipulation of those members of the old nomenklatura who, being incapable of retaining advantage by means of capitalism, played a very different card to avoid downward social mobility. Milošević best represents this position. All the same, there is a good deal of local understanding of the dangers represented by nationalism, and some of the nationalist noises made by politicians should not be taken as a guide to their actual conduct. Consider the dangers that seemed attendant even on the "velvet divorce" between Czechs and Slovaks – a divorce, it should be noted, that resulted from a deal between politicians rather than from a referendum, which might well have failed to endorse the split. If the Slovaks had begun to treat their Hungarian minority harshly, it was likely that the appeal of an irredentist radical nationalist party in Hungary would have increased, with consequential escalations on both sides being all too easy to imagine. But none of this actually took place: to the contrary, the irridentist nationalist party of Hungary did exceedingly badly in the elections of 1994. Still, the absolutely crucial factor for the whole region will surely be that of the future evolution of Russia. We have seen that nationalism in Western Europe can lose its bite in circumstances in which international society expands whilst the geopolitical functions of the state decline. If international *insecurity* increases in the East, the powers

---

[32] J. Linz and A. Stepan, "Political Identities and Electoral Sequences," *Daedalus*, vol. 121, 1992.
[33] I comment later on the Chechen situation.

of the state – and hence of nationalities denied voice – will
certainly increase.

Let us turn from nationalism to the reform of the economy. The
fact that the transition in post-communist societies is a double
and simultaneous one, to the market as well as to democracy, had
led some scholars to suggest that the region faces a vicious trap
from which it is unlikely to escape.[34] On the one hand, democracy
seems a prior condition to market reform. But the people will not
accept any reforms which cause a devastating fall in their standard
of living whilst a few are enriched. But this may be exactly what
reform entails. If this rejection becomes full-blooded, disaster will
surely follow. For the legitimacy of the new regime can only be
secured by some measure of economic success, and this will never
come about unless the principle of the market is embraced. This
suggests an alternative view, that democracy depends upon a prior
introduction of economic reforms by authoritarian means. The
logic of this position is much reinforced by banal considerations
of the political benefits of economic growth. On the one hand,
money-making may serve as an avenue of advancement sufficient
to distract former power-holders; on the other hand, adjustments
will be made by larger sections of the populace through bribery,
that is, social peace will be purchased by the provision of
Danegeld. The early liberalization of British and American politics
was certainly much aided by the surrounding presence of prosper-
ous capitalist relations.

This picture does describe difficulties, but its starkness is
nonetheless overdone. For one thing, reformers still have plenty
of room to maneuver, given the shell-shocked vacuum that
characterizes groups not mobilized by nationalism. More importantly, loyalty to democratic norms may undermine politicization
by class in post communism just as it does elsewhere. Ellen
Comisso makes the point nicely:

> ... it also follows that it is entirely possible to have pluralism and
> a wide variety of small groups competing for influence without

---

[34]   The most sustained analysis is that of A. Przeworski, *Democracy and the Market*,
Cambridge University Press, Cambridge, 1991. But see too J. Elster, "When Communism
Dissolves," *London Review of Books*, 24 January 1990 and C. Offe, "Capitalism by
Democratic Design?," *Social Research*, vol. 58, 1991.

ever pulling large numbers of people into political life . . . if states remain strictly liberal and do not grant organizational advantages to large groups, it may well be possible to maintain pluralism without extensive mass movements. If, for example, workers are free not to join unions, many will simply not join.[35]

Liberalism before democracy may be best, especially if it is part of a package which includes a successful economy, but liberalism by itself may depoliticize – and so continue that vacuum of post-communism which leaves the state sufficient autonomy to press through economic reforms. There is some evidence that this is beginning to happen. One recent strike in the Fiat works in southern Poland was not broken by the state but by workers prepared to accept the company's offer; and there is evidence that varied negotiations are beginning to take place between capitalists and workers, without benefit of state involvement.

Depoliticization is far from being enough. Post-communist societies need something altogether more positive, namely a much stronger state. This formulation is designed to shock, but the point at which I am getting is entirely straightforward. The socialist state was despotically powerful, but in the last analysis rather limited in its infrastructural reach: power in the last analysis depended upon destroying societal self-organization, and upon blocking horizontal linkages which the state could not control. This type of state was imposed upon, and perhaps suited, a pattern of historical development which anyway gave Eastern and Central Europe unwieldy, despotic, overmanned, and infrastructurally weak states. Such states had been colonized by landed elites opposed to commerce; late industrialization added to this by making state service an avenue of social mobility for new middle-class segments.[36] In principle social revolution was supposed to have changed all this, but severe limits to basic legitimacy meant that socialist states remained cumbersome and essentially weak – as was so dramatically proved by the manner of their demise. Not

[35] E. Comisso, "Property Rights, Liberalism and the Transition from 'Actually Existing Socialism'," *East European Politics and Society*, vol. 5, 1991.
[36] A. Janos, "The Politics of Backwardness in Continental Europe, 1780–1945," *World Politics*, vol. 41, 1981.

much has yet changed. At present, states have few interlocutors.[37] The Solidarity movement was a great crusade, based on an extraordinary national tradition of romanticism, nationalism, and Christian salvationism, representing a move of society against the state. But organization against the state is not the same thing as the self-organization of society – and of co-operation with a constitutional polity. Civil society in the full sense in which it has been understood in this book has not yet been born. The state may have some autonomy, but this scarcely makes up in power terms for the limited capacities consequent on the absence of linkages with society. In the long run a democratic deficit is a problem, not a solution. Settled social groups and political parties lead to regularity and predictability because they control their members. But this is only one way of looking at the matter, and it is not perhaps the most important. The ultimate justification for democracy lies in its capacity to produce better political rule than that provided by other systems. Wise men can no more be relied upon to produce economic success than social harmony; only democracy has the capacity to correct mistakes that arise, to provide the input of information necessary for rational policy making. The key problem can be highlighted by noting that it is mistaken to say that old nomenklatura members have the choice of becoming either nationalists or capitalists. There is a third option: such actors can benefit from privatization whilst retaining linkages with the state. It may be that the greater the destruction of the communist party, the greater the chances for security as well as for social transformation.[38] Privatization without market-ization is extremely dangerous. Such political capitalists may not be efficient, whilst their skimming-off of profitable sectors will subject the state to an intolerable fiscal crisis if greater subsidies are required to support remaining industry; both processes may well give capitalism a bad name, and thereby encourage cynicism, apathy, and rage. There are dangers here for foreign policy. Just as Germany after Bismarck lost coherence, so too may late, late industrializing states once they begin to democratize – with semi-

[37] W. Wesolowski, "The Nature of Social Ties and the Future of Postcommunist Society," in J. A. Hall, ed., *Civil Society*, Polity Press, Cambridge, 1995.
[38] I am indebted at this point to Anatoly Khazanov.

mobilized part-authoritarian regimes being the most prone to geopolitical adventure.[39]

Let us leave generalities so as to spell out some hunches about particular countries that are implicit in what has been said. Only a few states are likely to make a full transition to recognizably Western politics. The Visegrad countries, that is, Hungary, Poland, the Czech Republic and Slovakia, are obviously best favored: they have some memory of oppositional politics from Austro-Hungary, suffer least from symbolic politics, broke clearly with communism, are beginning to gain stable political parties, are likely to draw most investment, and may gain access to the European Community. Success is of course not guaranteed: nationalist sentiments may still cost Hungary dearly, albeit they have probably ensured Czech success – at the cost of Slovak backwardness; the European Community may seek to deepen rather than to broaden; and reversion to the inter-war situation of a set of geopolitically non-viable states threatened on both sides is a real possibility. Slovenia may draw close to Austria, and the Baltic states to Scandinavia, thereby ensuring a successful transition. It is difficult not to be more and more pessimistic, in contrast, the further east one looks. It is hard to see the role of the state diminishing in Bulgaria and Rumania. It is almost impossible to exaggerate the extent to which the fate of hopes for social transformation in all countries depend upon the situation in Russia. It is at least encouraging to note that greater sympathy is now being shown by the West to Russia's problems. But help from the outside will not determine events. Capital grants and debt remission do not come close to matching the capital currently being exported from Russia – as was the case with Latin America throughout the debt crisis. One has to be awed by the size of the problems, but cheered by the presence of some sort of background consensus that now thankfully seems to make it hard – and this is a genuine historical novelty – for any section of the Russian elite ruthlessly to eliminate its rivals.

The contrast between these scenarios and that of China is so

[39]   J. Snyder, "Averting Anarchy in the New Europe," *International Security*, vol. 14, 1990.

190 RESULTS OF THE INQUIRY

obvious and stark that little time needs to be devoted to it. China's experience of central planning has been much shorter than that of Russia, and it seems to have maintained entrepreneurial and peasant talents across the divide, as is true of some of Russia's former satellite countries.[40] This has meant that the re-introduction of the market has been, as noted, relatively easy and by the early 1990s hugely successful. The state now has its hands on less than 50 percent of economic transactions, which is to say that the basis for social organization apart from the state is being laid. This factor combines with the fact that *perestroika* has come before *glasnost* so as to make it possible that liberalization from above may yet have a success within socialism.

Let me turn finally to the less developed parts of the world. Any consideration of the economic situation now facing the developing world engenders further pessimism. The debt crisis in Latin America led, as noted, to large sections of the population having their living standards cut for the last several years so that capital could be exported to the advanced world. Equally, the development of most East Asian newly industrializing countries required highly idiosyncratic gifts – most notably traditions of bureaucracy, high levels of literacy, and land reform pushed through by the Japanese – which do not look replicable elsewhere. Particularly important in this regard were the large capital grants given to such countries for geopolitical reasons, that is, because they formed the perimeter of defense against communism. The end of the Cold War looks set to diminish such free-floating aid. There may be no more – or at least few more – newly industrializing countries.[41] There may instead be an increasing number of failed states, in which authoritarian elites use Western monies to sit on top of varied social groups without attempting much modernization.

All that has been said to this point accentuates the misery under which the many live. This is offensive to liberal values, but at first sight it does not matter in terms of traditional *Realpolitik*. Are these countries not weak and helpless? Is it not the case that most of them scarcely matter economically, as is so clearly shown by

40   I. Szelenyi, *Socialist Entrepreneurs*, University of Wisconsin Press, Madison, 1988.
41   R. Broad and J. Cavanagh, "No More NICs," *Foreign Policy*, no. 72, 1988.

trade and investment figures? Such a position seems to me as blind as it is cruel. I have always feared that nuclear weapons may fall into the hands of leaders of mobilized and ideocratic societies who feel, justly or unjustly, aggrieved at the advanced world. Several such societies have considerable funds as the result of oil wealth, and are accordingly in a position to purchase much advanced technology. The behavior of Saddam Hussein, already possessor of terrifying chemical weapons and reputedly close to the nuclear threshold, has turned private nightmare into public horror. A great deal more political intelligence needs to be shown by both elites and peoples of the advanced world if the world is to survive, let alone to make the most of developmental trends that otherwise promise so much.

KNOWLEDGE, MORALITY, AND ACTION

The moral to be drawn from the discussion of the ways in which forces of integration and disintegration affect different parts of the modern world polity is straightforward: some social developments may encourage greater equity in world affairs, even though this must be set in the context of events in Rwanda, Bosnia and Chechnya. Open discussion of ethical matters will make it clear, however, that these elements are the result of luck rather than of design – as well as making apparent the gap between what is taking place and what could and should be happening. The ethical principles to be advocated here follow closely on the argument as a whole. Whilst a background sympathy exists for the intelligent states and international understanding necessary for sophisticated realism, normative advocacy is for the liberalism/realism mix. In practical terms, this means that endorsement will be given to policies designed to strengthen states and to ensure wide membership within a liberal international society. But before spelling out these considerations in more detail, it is as well to draw attention to a new context within which any principles of international relations must now work. That context is the potential replacement of the norm of sovereignty with a new norm favoring liberal interventionism.

Even though the norm of sovereignty and non-intervention can be traced back to 1648, it is fair to say that it attained canonical importance in the world polity only after 1945. The respect that was given to this norm derived in part from nuclear weapons having placed some limit on adventures by the superpowers, but the stability engendered by the norm was felt to be quite as much in their self-interest. As important was the fact that Third World leaders embraced this norm wholeheartedly, going so far as a result as to condemn Julius Nyerere for toppling the tyranny of Idi Amin.[42] Observation of this norm certainly curtailed territorial change, and it probably limited inter-state wars. But the quasi-states which survived were, as argued, not things of great beauty. These states were distinctively the preserve of the few, and they very often used international recognition to ensconce themselves in power, not least by using the monies following from it to buy arms. The leaders of the West far too often had little concern with the domestic records of such states so long as they proved to be firm allies in the Cold War; to that end, the leaders of such quasi-states defined popular oppositional movements as communist so as to ensure American support, which arrived time after time with all too little questioning. If this was unpleasant and vicious, matters have become perhaps worse: many of these states are failing, making them unreliable members of the international community. This is as true of Algeria and Ethiopia as of Zaire or Nigeria, that is, of states previously members of communist as well as of Western spheres of influences. Hence for reasons at once practical and moral, it is now suggested that the respect previously given to sovereignty be replaced with active interventionism in order to further liberal goals. This new norm has been implemented in Iraq since the end of the Gulf War: a "no-fly zone" has trumped the notion of national air space, whilst effective protection of a national minority in the north of that country, in the form of a safe haven for the Kurds, completely undermines traditional notions of sovereignty. If this is unprecedented in the postwar period, responses to events in Rwanda and Bosnia suggest that it may be merely the beginning. Is this the direction in which international morality ought to go?

[42] C. Thomas, *New States, Sovereignty and Intervention*, Gower, Aldershot, 1985.

I will argue that any casual move from respect for sovereignty to liberal interventionism is likely to be a mistake. Two preliminary points about complexity should be made before proceeding to substance. It may be helpful, to begin with, to remember Sartre's quip that not taking a decision amounts to a decision in any case. Something like this is true of intervention. If one extreme is that of absolute isolation and another that of takeover by force, many intermediate positions are far more complex. It was sometimes suggested, for example, that allowing trade with South Africa would do more to help liberalize that country than an absolute boycott, and this case is regularly made in connection with American trade with post-Tiananmen Square communist China. It is certainly possible to be suspicious of full-scale armed intervention whilst favoring alternative means by which states can be cajoled and persuaded to move closer to universalist norms. Any discussion of morality in politics, secondly, can only benefit from remembering the distinction drawn by Max Weber between the politics of responsibility and the politics of ultimate ends.[43] Although Weber's position is riddled with ambiguities, it does suggest the need in politics for consequentialist thought, that is, of thinking through practicalities rather than being wholly dominated by moral absolutes.[44] One difficult example concerns policy towards the former Yugoslavia. Absolute ethics would suggest sending the requisite numbers of soldiers, perhaps half a million for a very extended period, so as to impose a liberal solution. It is a fact that we do not live in a situation in which this is politically possible.[45] The United States effectively disengaged from Somalia as soon as television viewers saw a dead American soldier being dragged through the streets of Mogadishu, and it has long been apparent that the sole remaining superpower is not prepared to allow its citizens to die in the Balkans. Policy choices should take

[43] M. Weber, "Politics as a Vocation," in H. H. Gerth and C. W. Mills, eds, *From Max Weber*, Oxford University Press, Oxford, 1946. Weber's greatest disciple in this matter was, of course, Raymond Aron – whose concern with consequentialist calculations was discussed in the opening chapter.

[44] P. Anderson, "Science, Politics, Enchantment," in J. A. Hall and I. C. Jarvie, eds, *Transition to Modernity*, Cambridge University Press, Cambridge, 1991.

[45] J. Dunn, "The Dilemma of Humanitarian Intervention," *Government and Opposition*, vol. 29, 1994.

available means into account if they are not to mislead by promising what will not then be delivered.

This leads into the first of two reasons for wariness towards the view that interventionism can extend liberalism by force of arms. The vexed issue of military intervention in the former Yugoslavia makes it clear that Weber's distinction can be treacherous: to accept every political reality just as it is may not just be lazy but positively criminal. Still, it is one of the greatest of all illusions, in life as well as in foreign affairs (and perhaps above all in liberalism), to imagine that everything is within our grasp, to accept responsibility for every action of other people. Liberalism most certainly did "come out of the barrel of a gun" in the cases of Germany and Japan, but this was so because there were local elites willing and able to work with occupying forces. Equivalent action in Iraq would not have been possible even had an unconditional surrender been secured, nor is it possible to do everything all at the same time. All this, it should be noted, is expressed with some moderation, given the endless occasions on which imperial proconsuls have pontificated about and sought to re-engineer human cultures of which they knew nothing. A second reason concerns moral psychology. On the one hand, the means of power tend in the long run to defeat the most responsible of aims. On the other hand, liberal principles cannot anyway be given by means of some political hypodermic syringe. John Stuart Mill realized this when arguing – whilst knowing full well that authoritarianism prevented popular voice – that it is only the struggle to be free that creates free human beings.[46] Perhaps human beings only ever become adult because they are treated as adults.

The reader ought to know that this bias against intervention may result from membership in a generation opposed to involvement in Vietnam. But the bias is not absolute: against it stands an intellectual realization that the resort to arms can be necessary and the failure to appreciate this disastrous. The bombing of bridges between Serbia and Bosnia at the very start of the recent Balkan war would have been wise, in large part because this might

---

[46] J. S. Mill, "A Few Words on Non-Intervention," in J. S. Mill, *Essays on Politics and Culture*, ed. G. Himmelfarb, Peter Smith, Gloucester, MA, 1973, pp. 381–3.

have had an effect then that could only now be matched by committing large ground forces – which, rightly or wrongly, will not happen.[47] More generally, the difficulty of organizing coercion underlines the need for preventive measures. In this important and revealing case, the international community made a fundamental mistake. Yugoslavia jumbled together ethnic and religious identities in such a manner that homogenizing state practices were sure, as should have been apparent from reflection on the inter-war history of Central Europe, to lead to disaster. Given this, it was a terrible mistake – and sheer madness for Europeans given that the Badinter Report noted coercive pressures being placed on Croatian Serbs – to recognize Croatia, the move from which more general conflagration followed, without a prior commitment by the new state to respect its minorities.[48] Milošević was given his opportunity by this turn of events, and controlled policy has not again proved possible.

The minor moral to be drawn from this is that the power given by the desire for recognition should not be wasted. But the major moral is slightly different, and it concerns the best way in which to strengthen divided states. Nationalist separatism flourishes when voice is denied, making it all the more important – especially, as noted, in modern circumstances – to extend civil rights. The Chechens would very probably have been satisfied with the rights given to the Volga Tatars, and military intervention against them is a disaster since it makes many loyal groups wonder if exit is after all the most rational course to pursue.[49] If the empirical finding that voice limits exit allows us to be clear as to the nature of proper policy, its advocacy on the liberal machiavellian ground that state power will be strengthened by

[47]   These lines, written in June 1995, might seem wrong given the sudden interest of the United States in achieving a political settlement in the Balkans. But the chances for a settlement were created by Croat success in Krajina, and not by the actions of the United States or its allies.

[48]   R. Brubaker, "National Minorities, Nationalising States, and External National Homelands in the New Europe," *Daedalus*, vol. 124, 1995. The best account of the process of recognition, and in particular of German pressure for that move, is B. Crawford, "Germany's Unilateral Recognition of Croatia and Slovenia," unpublished paper.

[49]   A. Khazanov, *After the USSR Collapsed*, University of Wisconsin Press, Madison, 1996, especially ch. 8; "How Many Other Chechnyas?," *The Economist*, January 14, 1995.

this route may give it some chance of adoption – not least in South Africa where federal and consociational arrangements are desperately needed. But it would be silly to be too optimistic. On the one hand, minority rights rather than multinational civil nationalism may be the best that can be hoped for when one ethnic group is dominant.[50] On the other hand, a stable solution akin to the "three plus or minus one languages regime" of India described by David Laitin may not be available or possible, in which case the advice from the international community must be to allow for territorial change.[51] The paradox of the matter remains that the easier it is to leave, the less likely it will be that this actually happens. But if demands for separation continue, there is everything to be said for a controlled process of divorce: secession might well be deemed legitimate, for example, only after two votes so as to ensure reflection (and in particular to limit the appeal of demagogues thriving on sudden hatreds) and only ever when guarantees for minorities are in place.[52]

As there are perhaps 8,000 languages and only about 200 states in the world today, policies designed to ensure fundamental territorial continuity are hugely important.[53] But of course, the basic ethic at work here can be generalized. Social movements direct themselves against states in a revolutionary manner when they are deprived of the chance of acting through normal political channels, there being nothing about socio-economic circumstances that inevitably, for example, entails revolution even in the developing world. Opening the political system will eventually bring stability as liberalism diffuses conflict throughout society, and the policy of the international community ought to be to underwrite something which happily is both morally desirable and likely to make the conduct of foreign policy easier by making states stronger. Unfortunately, a great deal hangs on the word "eventually" in the last sentence. Tocqueville's great fear, that the legacy

[50]   R. Brubaker, "Nationalising States in the Old 'New Europe' – and the New," *Ethnic and Racial Studies*, vol. 19, 1995.
[51]   D. Laitin, *Language repertoires and state construction in Africa*, Cambridge University Press, Cambridge, 1992.
[52]   A. Buchanan, *Secession*, Westview Press, Boulder, 1991.
[53]   E. Gellner, *Nations and Nationalism*, Blackwell, Oxford, 1983, pp. 43–50.

of hatreds left by divide-and-rule politics would make co-operation difficult, has proven to be prescient. If a destination is clear,
the means to get there is far from being so. We still know far too
little about methods by which social trust can be restored and co-
operation made possible.

If the first general injunction that follows from the argument of
the book is that of the desirability of strengthening states, the
second concerns the importance of creating a genuinely liberal
international society. At the institutional level, an immediate and
obvious step towards this end is the simple one of making sure
that international regimes cease to be a facet of American
hegemony: it would be wise for the United States for example, to
give Japan and Germany central roles in the liberal regimes over
whose future it has the deciding voice. Further, regimes which go
beyond economic towards political liberalism are overdue: the
free movement of human beings, and the provision of monies to
help make this possible, remains particularly desirable. But
beyond these points, what matters most of all is probably political
skill. The most difficult balancing act of all in life is that of
creating an atmosphere in which criticism can be accepted because
awareness of continuing respect remains in the background. In
international affairs, it is vital to condemn practices of inhumanity
whilst making it utterly clear that their extirpation will ensure
eventual membership.

Three points can be made in conclusion. First, the policies
recommended amount to banning for the contemporary world the
style of nation- and state-building that characterized the history
of the West. There is an awful air of hypocrisy about advice given
from a safe point, that is, after key social transitions have been
made. Whilst there is everything to be said here for openness on
this point, and for humility about it, the insistence on the need
and desirability of making key transitions in a more co-operative
manner retains all its validity. A second point follows from this.
It occasionally seems as if Western social thought has lost its
nerve, most obviously when it is trapped in a miasma of postmod-
ern relativism. But any attempt to deal with the horrors that
international relations can bring depends upon the possession and
reaffirmation of the values of universal liberalism. It should of
course be remembered here that liberalism is an idiosyncratic

ideology in that it values difference, albeit always within a common frame of respect for persons. Given that liberalism has sometimes been arrogant as well as supine, there is an urgent need for liberal states to listen and learn within a diverse society of communities, many of which have much to offer humanity.

The final point moves us still further from the *de haut en bas* flavor of this section, since it places pressures for change squarely in the court of the most advanced part of the world. Although heroic military acts may still be necessary, the principal task of the West should now be that of sticking to the market. A concert directed against the South is scarcely likely to last, and it is anyway not a policy with long-term promise. Development in the South – and in the East! – depends upon their having access to Western markets, something which very often, especially in regard to agricultural products, has not been allowed, with protectionism in the West often being adopted in the face of market failure.[54] Greater openness of this sort requires belief in two elements of liberalism, namely the right of all peoples to develop together with the awareness that abandoning labor-intensive industry so as to move up the product cycle allows economic life to proceed on a positive-sum basis.[55] For all that a good deal of social life in the West proceeds in a non-politicized form, it is unlikely in the long run that such a policy can be achieved behind the backs of the citizens likely to be affected by it. Acceptance and endorsement will accordingly depend, in the long run, upon domestic policies designed to make it possible for modern citizens to succeed within capitalism. National social policies are needed precisely because the principles of Adam Smith rule externally.[56]

[54] This is a minimal proposal, given that some countries in the South have almost nothing to export.
[55] Adam Smith's arguments at this point have not been bettered. For those arguments and their social context, see I. Hont, "The 'rich country-poor country' debate in Scottish classical political economy," in I. Hont and M. Ignatieff, eds, *Wealth and Virtue*, Cambridge University Press, Cambridge, 1983.
[56] This formulation is that of James Mayall, as reported by R. Gilpin, *The Political Economy of International Relations*, Princeton University Press, Princeton, 1987, p. 355.

Index